THE EYE OF ILLUSION

THE EYE OF ILLUSION

Eli Ginzberg

Transaction Publishers
New Brunswick (U.S.A.) and London (U.K.)

HB
119
G56
A3
1993

Library of Congress Catalog Number: 92-15675
ISBN: 1-56000-072-4
Printed in the United States of America

Library of Congress Cataloging-in-Publication Data

Ginzberg, Eli, 1911–
The eye of illusion / Eli Ginzberg.
    p. cm.
Includes index.
  ISBN 1-56000-072-4
  1. Ginzberg, Eli, 1911- 2. Economists—United States—Biography. I. Title
HB119.G50A3   1992
330'.092—dc20
[B]

                                         92-15675
                                         CIP

For Ruth
Many waters cannot quench love,
neither can the floods drown it . . .

Contents

Preface

There are a few things that the reader may like to know up front, such as the origin of the title and where this volume stands in the line of my many books.

As to the title: In the summer of 1927, just before I entered Columbia College as a freshman, my family were at the Crescent Country Club, Milton, Vermont. Moss Hart was the club's social director and one way that he sought to keep the guests entertained was to stage periodic debates on current issues, in which he elicited my participation. At the end of the summer he gave me a copy of Chekhov's *Notebooks* with the following inscription: "To Eli: who can spit in the eye of illusion without getting his bowels in an uproar."

The present work is clearly autobiographical in the sense that I tell a story based on personal exposures and experiences. But I am primarily interested in sharing with the reader my evaluation of the events, much more than my role in them.

Twice before I resorted to a similar approach. In *The Skeptical Economist* (1987), I reported on my training as an economist, how I developed my specialization as a researcher in human resources, and my criteria for assessing economic policy.

In *My Brother's Keeper* (1989), I dealt at length with the Jewish dimension of my life and thought, in particular my changing views of American Jewry and my assessments of the state of Israel.

Neither my relation to my discipline nor to my ethnicity is dealt with more than tangentially in the present book. That does not mean that I have ignored or disregarded them, only that I have sought to avoid repeating myself.

Acknowledgments

This autobiographical story dealing with ideas, events, and people was written on Martha's Vineyard during the summers of 1989 and 1990 and rewritten in 1991. Never having kept a diary, with limited files that were not readily available, I had to rely on my memory, which I have reason to believe served me well, but not well enough to have remembered all of the details correctly. Hence I owe an overwhelming debt of gratitude to my long-term associate and coworker, Anna Dutka, who took on the arduous task of checking all of the facts, figures, names, and dates. An error or two may remain, but surely not more than a very few. And that is her accomplishment, for which I am greatly in her debt.

She in turn has asked me to acknowledge the help that she received in checking the manuscript, particularly from Karl Cocke, historian, U.S. Army Center of Military History; Sar A. Levitan, director, Center for Social Policy Studies, the George Washington University; Andrea Taylor, deputy director, Office of Communications, Ford Foundation; and Sara Vos, Office of the President, Columbia University.

As has been true for more than half a century, I inflicted a draft of the first manuscript on my friend, Professor Moses Abramovitz of Stanford University, and received some early incisive feedback that helped to guide my revisions.

For a second time, I was greatly aided by the incisiveness of a more recent friend (and publisher), Professor Irving Louis Horowitz of Rutgers University, who, as in the case of my earlier effort at autobiography, *My Brother's Keeper*, forced me to confront challenges that I had avoided the first time around. To both of these friends, I owe a special debt of gratitude for telling it to me straight.

My wife, who some years earlier had been released from editing my manuscripts, was willing to return to that arduous task, for which author and reader are deeply in her debt.

Finally, I want to thank Sylvia Leef, who has struggled successfully and good naturedly once again with reading my bad hand; and Shoshana Vasheetz, who oversaw the successive versions of this manuscript through our word processing system.

PART I

The World of Academe

1

New York, New York

It is up to an author to decide whether to deal first or second with the community in which he grew up. He may decide to focus first on his immediate family and the influence of parents, siblings, relatives, and friends in the shaping of his development and value system. I have opted to deal with the familial forces second, since they provide the most direct clue to my selection of economics and to the policy-research career that I have pursued.

"New York, New York" is a popular song, which is sung in foreign countries to immediate applause. Here, it is something of a misnomer. It is true that New York has been my home for all but a few of my eighty years. I spent two semesters as a college sophomore enrolled at Heidelberg University in Germany. During my postdoctorate year, I used my Cutting Traveling Fellowship from Columbia not to broaden and deepen my cultural sophistication by living in Western Europe, which was the pattern that most of the Fellows followed, but to visit various corporate headquarters throughout the United States. I hoped to understand why American management a few years earlier had believed that it had entered the New Era (free of economic depressions) when it had in fact just survived the most devastating three-year depression in the nation's history. And I spent the four war years in Washington (1942–46) working for the Army Services Forces, first as a consultant on manpower and personnel to the commanding general, Brehan B. Somervell, and then as director of the Resources Analysis Division of the Surgeon General's Office.

New York has been my home for all but six of my eighty years. And now the qualifications: not so much New York as Manhattan; not so much Manhattan as the West Side; not so much the West Side as Washington Heights during my youth and Morningside Heights during most of my adulthood. As this chapter tells, I have also had an opportunity to become

3

acquainted with a few other sections of the city, but Brooklyn, Queens, and Staten Island to this day remain terra incognita to me.

In 1922 and again in 1928 the family loaded baggage and itself into a large taxi and undertook the long drive through Manhattan and much of Brooklyn to the pier where the North German Lloyd steamers left for Bremen. It was not until 1934, when I had made friends with Moses Abramovitz at Columbia and he drove me to his home in Brooklyn to have dinner and spend the night, that I understood that Brooklyn was more than a way station to Europe.

It is not easy to capture the essential qualities of a major metropolis such as New York. The challenge is greater if we seek to assess changes over the larger part of a century, even if we restrict the focus to a few dominant trends such as the demographic characteristics of the population, economic opportunity, public services (especially the effectiveness of the public educational system), crime and safety on the streets, and a few other dominant qualities of urban life, such as housing, transportation, and cultural activities.

The conventional wisdom is that New York has been in a decline that some would date from the end of the New Era (1929) and others would correlate with the large influxes of blacks and Hispanics after World War II. The doomsayers back up their pessimistic appraisals by pointing to the litany of what has gone wrong: daily and nightly murders, many of innocent bystanders; large numbers of homeless persons; block after block in each of the boroughs of apartments boarded up or burnt out; hundreds of thousands of people, mostly single mothers and their children, on the welfare rolls; many schools that fail to prepare their pupils for jobs; and on and on. No informed person would minimize the evidence pointing to urban turmoil, even if they might hesitate to define the difficult circumstances as proof positive of urban decline and decay.

The fact that New York City came within a few hours of having to declare itself bankrupt during the 1975 financial crisis, and two years later started to reverse its seven years of decline and was able in the succeeding decade to add about a half-million new jobs, should serve as a potent reminder, if only the most recent, that major cities have great resilience.

Frederick Rose, the New York builder, has reminded me on several occasions of the acrimonious discussion that Roger Starr and he had with me in 1977 about the bleak future facing New York City and the abysmal outlook for the construction industry. I took the view that the real estate market was just about ready for a turnaround, a judgment that they found ludicrous. Rose regrets that he failed to act on this forecast, for indeed that is what happened. I never pretended then, or later, to have any special knowledge of New York real estate, but I was carrying out a study at the time for the Rockefeller Brothers Fund that had alerted me to the fact that New York was nearing the end of its transition from a manufacturing to a service center. About 600,000 factory jobs had been lost since the end of World War II, but there were mounting signs of a burgeoning demand for commercial space to meet the needs of the expanding business-services sector. Although the expansion of the late 1970s and the 1980s has now come to an end, only an unreconstructed pessimist would conclude that New York, the premier city in North America since the late eighteenth century, has entered a period of permanent decline.

There are several difficulties in the way of getting a proper fix on New York. The first is to overlook the extent to which New York, like all major cities in advanced countries, has been affected by untoward trends, especially the increase in street crime. I recall over a decade ago visiting the home of a senior official of the U.S. embassy in Paris who lived in one of the most affluent sections of the city. When I was ready to leave in the late afternoon to return to my hotel, my host inquired how I planned to get there, and I replied that I planned to use my private form of transportation—walking. He warned me not to do so since the area was unsafe. In recent years, I have been advised by the doorman of the London hotel that I stop at in Mayfair to be alert walking around after dark.

Even with a record of about six homicides every twenty-four hours, New York is nowhere near the top of the list of the most lawless cities in the United States. It ranks relatively far down the list. A New Yorker, like myself, who knows his way around, tends to avoid being on the streets, especially after dark, in areas of the city where the pedestrian flow is light. I was caught in such a predicament only once—after I lectured to the Board of Directors of the 92nd Street Y on Lexington Avenue. No taxis were coming that night, and I had to walk four blocks to pick up the 96th Street crosstown bus. It was a few blocks' walk that I did not enjoy, but I fortunately was able to negotiate them without trouble. It is the one and only time in recent years that I have been apprehensive.

To turn the clock back many years: My friend Clarence and I, at age ten or so, took a long subway ride from 145th Street and Broadway to the Brooklyn Navy Yard in the hope of visiting a battleship that was moored there. We had no sooner come out of the kiosk than we were spotted by the local gang and chased back in. We never even got a look at the battleship!

My last two years of high school were spent in the main building of DeWitt Clinton, which was located at that time in an area of the city known as Hell's Kitchen, at 59th Street and 10th Avenue close to the Hudson River. Most of the seven thousand students on its rolls arrived via the subway, which had an entrance at 59th Street and Columbus Circle. Between 8:30 and 9:00 A.M. and again between 3:00 and 3:30 P.M., New York's finest patrolled the two long streets to be sure that the local Irish toughs did not beat us up. At lunchtime, all seven thousand of us were confined to the school as a safety precaution.

During the fourteen years during which my family lived on 149th Street and Broadway (1914-1928), the locale was home for middle- and working-class families, a basically secure neighborhood. But not completely so. Our gang used to play stickball on the side streets, but once or twice a year a warning shout would go up that "the toughs are coming," which alerted us to the imminent invasion by the Harlem River Irish, who dealt roughly, if not brutally, with any of us whom they could trap. Furthermore, the father of my sister Sophie's friend, the owner of the local jewelry shop, was shot to death by robbers; at about the same time, a junior colleague of my father, carrying a new briefcase, was returning home in Queens when he was hit over the head with a lead pipe and killed.

I am able to report that in all of the subsequent years—the more than six decades during which I have been on the Columbia campus—I know personally of only one murder victim, my colleague from the Law School, Wolfgang Friedmann, who was robbed, fought back, and was killed on Amsterdam Avenue, close to Teachers College.

Morningside Park, the eastern boundary of Columbia University, has undergone the most striking change with regard to areal security in my lifetime. In the late 1930s, when I lived across the street from the campus on 119th Street and Amsterdam Avenue, I garaged the family car at 8th Avenue and 121st Street, where I subleased space from the mechanic for five dollars per month. I did not have a moment's hesitation in walking through the park in daylight and along 123rd Street, the northern boundary of the park, at night. But only a total innocent would dream of doing so since shortly after the end of World War II. The park has become out of bounds for any and everybody who seeks to avoid trouble.

While I was attending DeWitt Clinton I developed warts on my forehead, and my cousin, who was interning at Beth Israel, had met a newly arrived European physician who had brought with him an advanced piece of radiological equipment that my cousin thought might do the trick of burning off my warts.

The Chamber Street bus was the best way to reach Beth Israel, which was still located at that time in the midst of the Jewish ghetto, close to Madison Street. I recall that I ran the two blocks with a handkerchief over my nose, so overwhelming were the stench and odors from the refuse that was piled up in the streets. In all of my later travels in Europe and to Third-World countries, I never came face to face with anything worse, except the slums of Naples, which I approached but did not enter in 1929. Drugs and all, the lower East Side is surely less degenerate in the early 1990s than it was in the mid-1920s!

New York neighborhoods have frequently undergone radical transformations within relatively short periods of time, often from a low-income to a high-income area; for example, the Tudor City development once the nearby slaughter houses were relocated; or the Lincoln Center neighborhood after many older tenements were torn down to make way for the new opera house and Avery Fisher Hall, the new home of the New York Philharmonic. But the reverse process can also be readily identified—Bedford Stuyvesant in Brooklyn, the Grand Concourse in the Bronx, and the area around the Columbia-Presbyterian Medical Center at 168th Street and Broadway. The last was once home to multiethnic middle- and working-class families, who moved away and were replaced by large numbers of Hispanic immigrants, primarily Dominicans. The deterioration of the area has had serious adverse effects on both recruiting university and hospital staff and attracting patients. I recall running into my friend Dan Tosteson, the dean of the Harvard Medical School, at the Martha's Vineyard airport one summer almost a decade ago, and his asking me whether I had heard of the double murder at the Columbia Medical Center. I had simply assumed that he was referring to a neighborhood struggle in which people had died, something that happened from time to time. But in pursuing the matter, I learned that he was referring to an academic upheaval that had just taken place and that resulted in both the vice-president for medical affairs and the dean of the Medical School being peremptorily removed from their posts.

So much for the changes in the physical environment of the city and safety on the streets. These examples were intended to point out that much that has happened for the worse relates to all large American centers—and European urban areas as well—and is not distinctive to New York. Moreover, it is just plain wrong to assume that the city before World War II was a center of peace and civility. It was anything but that. And third, difficult as the environment has become, most of the middle- and upper-class families face few added risks by continuing to live in the city. New York was never an attractive environment for the timid.

I was born in 1911, close to the pre–World War I peak immigration that brought more than a million newcomers to the United States every year. I must quickly add that most of these newcomers came from Italy, primarily from Sicily, and from Eastern Europe. Included in the latter stream were large numbers of Yiddish-speaking Jews, many of them with an urban background. The influx was vastly reduced with the outbreak of the war in Europe and was further reduced when new, restrictive, legislation was passed in 1924. In fact, large-scale immigration did not return until after the new immigration act of 1965, when most of the newcomers came from Latin America and Asia.

But New York City's demographic profile underwent a major change during and particularly after World War II with the relocation north of large numbers of southern blacks, followed within a decade by large numbers of Puerto Ricans. There had been an occasional black student in my high school and college classes, but the emphasis is on the term *occasional*. In 1939, when I was structuring a sample of the long-term unemployed men whom we planned to interview for a research project on long-term unemployment, I was unable to locate a relatively concen- trated group of black families that met our screening criteria. The nonwhite, largely black population of New York City according to the 1940 census numbered 478,000 out of a citywide total population of 7.5 million, or about 6 percent.

In the quarter-century after World War II, approximately two million whites who had lived in New York City moved out to the neighboring suburbs or beyond, and two million newcomers, mostly blacks and Puerto Ricans, moved in, an unparalleled exchange in populations within such a short period of time. The out-migration of the whites opened up much of the housing and many of the jobs that the newcomers needed to establish themselves in their new surroundings. When one considers the depth and pervasiveness of prejudice against people of color, it is less surprising that many newcomers failed to make a satisfactory relocation than that the majority became self-supporting in their new environment.

In 1956, when my book *The Negro Potential* was published, I planned a luncheon at the Columbia University Club at 43rd Street off 5th Avenue that was to be addressed by U.S. Secretary of Labor James P. Mitchell. But when the club's administrator learned that the luncheon guests included some of the city's leading blacks, I was asked to please find another locale. I am not vindictive, but I found some poetic justice in the fact that a few years later the club, having fallen on less-affluent days, had to sell its property to the Moonies.

As late as the early 1970s, when I gave a lecture to one of the leading downtown investment-banking firms, I was taken on a tour of their premises, and my guide pointed out to me with much pride that they had several persons of color among their back-office staff. It would be not only foolish but preposterous to deny that the post–World War II changing population profile of New York, from an overwhelmingly white community to a community in which nonwhites have now become the majority, is the principal source of many stresses and strains among the body politic and underlies much of the pessimism about the city's future. But the parallel point which needs to be assessed, is that a population upheaval of four million persons in a quarter century—two million established white persons moving out and two million newcomers of color moving in—was a critical event. The amazing fact is not that there were stresses and strains but that after 1977 the city enjoyed a decade of substantial growth and well-being, although many of the newcomers did not participate in the expansion.

The 1980 census reported that slightly more than one-quarter of the city's population was foreign-born (which, it must be noted, does not include Puerto Ricans, who are U.S. citizens by birth). There are forecasts that 55 percent of New York's population will be foreign-born by the year 2000, up from the mid-20-percent range only two decades earlier. But these forecasts must be looked at critically because of the unsatisfactory state of the 1990 census. If this forecast proves to be right even within a wide margin, it will represent another unparalleled upheaval in the composition of the city's population within a period of only two decades.

What needs to be emphasized and understood is that such large-scale compositional changes are without parallel in the history of any other large city. It tells us a lot about the underlying vitality and flexibility of New York.

It is only within the last five years that I first heard the expression "new-Jews" applied to the increasing numbers of Asiatic students on the Columbia campus. Since then, I have learned that whites now account for only a minority of the undergraduate students on the Berkeley campus. In recent years I have played a game with myself, making a rough estimate of the number of Asiatics among any group of campus students that come into my vision and estimating their proportion. Each time I play this game the rate seems to have gone up, from 25 to 33 to 40 percent and on occasion to over 50 percent. One thing is sure: the principal coastal cities of the United States, from San Francisco down to San Diego, across to Miami, and up to New York, are being transformed at a rapid rate by immigrants. On a recent trip to Houston, the bellboy told me he had come from Lagos, the taxi driver from Addis Ababa.

There is one more critical comparison between New York then—when I was growing up—and now, one that looks at the condition of the public schools and compares how they performed then and are performing now. To put matters bluntly: I enjoyed only two years of my ten years of public school instruction (I have no recollection about my years in kindergarten). I was bored stiff most of the time and found it easy to escape by doing errands for the assistant principal of my school—P.S. 186 at 145th Street off Broadway—and by not showing up, with permission, because of severe headaches during the early years when I was getting appropriate glasses fitted to cope with my farsightedness.

Although my parents took me out of school at the beginning of June and returned me to class, not at the beginning of September, but at the beginning of October after we returned from vacationing on the Jersey Coast, determined by my father's teaching schedule at the Jewish Theological Seminary, I still found sitting in class a bloody bore.

But the situation improved at the beginning of seventh grade, when I was selected to attend an accelerated junior high school course (three years in two) at Speyer Junior High School, which was operated for the Board of Education by Teachers College of Columbia. The attendees were selected from among the three top male students of each Manhattan public school. Freedom rather than regulation was the rule. The students were in charge of discipline. We had to read and report on at least one book per week. When the Fire Department condemned the top story of the school's ancient building on 126th Street close to Amsterdam, our French class was canceled and instead we played stickball at the trolley depot across the street.

I have one deeply etched recollection of those two years beyond my positive recollections of the entire educational experience. My social science teacher, Ms. P., suggested that when riding in a crowded subway we close our eyes and draw an imaginary circle around ourselves that would give us the space we needed. I have used this technique on occasion, found it helpful, and occasionally had my pocket picked because of my absorption!

The important point that I want to convey about the school system of those bygone days is that the effectiveness of the instructional process was indifferent; the schools were not, as so many romantics assume, doing an excellent job preparing their students for college and a life of socioeconomic mobility. There may have been some high schools in Brooklyn that fitted this image, but DeWitt Clinton, the largest of the Manhattan schools, did not. Most of my classmates dropped out at the end of the second or third year largely from boredom and because they, and their parents, saw more point to their getting a job and adding to the family's income. I doubt that more than 30 percent or at most 40 percent went on to graduate, divided between those who were college-bound and those who aimed for a civil service or higher clerical position that required a high school diploma.

DeWitt Clinton had some gifted teachers on its faculty, and over the four semesters that I attended classes at the main building I had the good fortune to be assigned to three or four where the instructor had a flair for the subject and an interest in his or her students. But for the rest, students came to class largely to watch the clock. When the Jewish holidays rolled around, I was looked to as the expert who was expected to alert my Irish and Italian classmates that a religious holiday was approaching so that they too could get an extra day or two off.

I was able to advance in that part of my education that depended on reading, but in subjects where classroom instruction was important, if not the key to progress, as in the case of mathematics, science, and foreign languages, I limped along. I can still recall being at the board in my last term in high school and getting stuck translating some phrase from

French. My teacher snapped out, "What do you plan to do if we let you out of here?" and I replied, "Go to Columbia," which led her into mild hysterics.

The fact that I got into Columbia without special difficulty, despite its severe restrictions on Jewish students from the New York area, was a function of two facts. First, I had read a great deal and had a good memory, so I was able to remember much of what I had read when I sat for the entrance examination. But equally important was the extra margin in my examination-taking skills, which reflected the two years of experience that I had accumulated as a volunteer subject in Professor E. L. Thorndike's testing laboratory at Teachers College. I had taken a great many different types of tests during this two-year period and had learned most of the tricks, such as when to guess and when not, when to pursue optimal speed and when to take a little longer to get the right answer.

The Columbia College administration and the Admissions Office closely linked to it placed great, probably a disproportionate, weight on applicants who did well on the entrance examination. For the reasons just noted, I not only did well but went off the curve, which not only assured my admission but also, later on, elicited favorable responses from Dean Hawkes whenever I asked for some special consideration in the selection of my college courses. I have a vague recollection that my score on one of the Thorndike achievement tests placed me at the mean level of the second-year class at the Yale Law School. Even at that early date I had mastered the intricacies of test-taking!

The point I want to emphasize, in bringing the theme of public education and this chapter to a close, is the basic difference between the educational preparation and work that existed in the 1920s from that which prevails today.

Although education was critically important in the 1920s for the minority who were heading for a professional career in medicine, law, engineering, or even teaching, their combined numbers represented a much smaller proportion of the future workforce than is true of the U.S. economy of the 1990s. Even more important has been the substantial upward shift in educational requirements for the mass of nonprofessional, nonmanagerial, nontechnical positions. A young man in 1992 cannot hope to get an entry-level position that holds much promise of advancement unless he applies for a job with at least a community college degree under his belt, preferably with a BA or BS degree. In the mid-1920s basic literacy, defined as two years of high school, sufficed as a way into any of the literally millions of jobs in the goods or service sectors of the New York economy. The testing ground for advancement was the world of work, not the preparatory setting of the educational system. But in the 1990s those who falter in the educational environment are not likely to have a chance to compete in the world of work. Therein lies a major difference, one that has skewed the rewards very much in favor of those who come from backgrounds where book-learning is valued, where doing well in school comes naturally.

What lies at the heart of my unending love affair with New York? Clearly both the city and I have undergone a great many changes over the past eight decades, but though many of the bonds that bound us, even some early bonds, have loosened and have even been broken, others have been forged and tightened. New York remains my favorite city.

Despite the fact that both my parents were immigrants and that they were Sabbath observers, I never had any sense of being a deviant in New York. As a born New Yorker, it was my city as much as it was the city of my Irish, Italian, and American schoolmates. I felt totally at home on its streets and subways and in its schools. Early on, I came to recognize that New York was very much a European city on the North American continent, a conclusion that I reached as a consequence of the steady stream of Europeans who visited my parents' home. Many of them turned out to be interesting and lively guests, and I enjoyed their table conversation, at least that part of the discussions that fell within my cognizance.

Washington Heights, where the family lived during my youth and adolescence, still provided us with side streets where we could play stickball without being unduly disturbed by what were still predominately horse-drawn delivery wagons. And there were city tennis courts within a fifteen-minute walk, just over the Harlem River at 155th Street.

Starting in the seventh grade and continuing through my first year at Columbia College, I had to rely on public transportation, but with the exception of the one year that I attended the annex of DeWitt Clinton on East 77th Street, which required a long ride on the bus, getting to and from school was no more than a twenty-minute subway ride.

And the same subway took one quickly and safely to the downtown area, where one had access to theater, music, movies, and other entertainment at modest prices for balcony seats. And the city streets, especially south of 59th Street, were always fun places to walk and window shop.

In 1929, after my father returned from his one sabbatical, a year during which I had attended Heidelberg University, the family moved into an apartment on 114th Street, directly opposite John Jay Hall, the newest and largest of the Columbia dormitories. For the next four years, while I finished my undergraduate studies and pursued my doctorate, I lived at home, but home was cheek by jowl to the campus. Nothing could have been more convenient.

When I completed my field studies (in 1933–34) of U.S. corporations under my Cutting Traveling Fellowship, I found a small apartment at another corner of the campus, at 119th Street and Amsterdam Avenue, where I remained for the next eight years, until I relocated to Washington early in World War II. During this eight-year stretch I came to appreciate another of New York's great assets—anonymity. As a bachelor I had no desire to have my neighbors become knowledgeable about the persons with whom I was keeping company, and to the best of my recollection my personal life remained strictly personal during these years. Looking back, it is hard for me to account for the fact that, although I had luncheon dates twice weekly through most of this period in the Terrace Restaurant at Butler Hall with the same female companion, we never encountered anybody there, on 119th street, or in my apartment house who knew both of us.

When I returned to the campus in the fall of 1946, Columbia found us (I had married that summer) a small apartment at Butler Hall, where we remained for several years, until we were expecting our first-born. Although Columbia owned a great many apartments on Riverside Drive and Claremont Avenue, we never sought to move into one of them because I resisted the idea of having the university dominate my life to that extent. One of the great virtues of New York is that it enables individuals to select their own circle of friends, and I early recognized that I did not want to be that closely associated with my colleagues, at work and at leisure. This explains why we have always lived within walking distance of the university, but not in a Columbia apartment.

From the time of my post–World War II return to the campus until Ronald Reagan asked for the resignation of all the members of the National Commission for Employment Policy in December 1981, I was heavily involved in consulting with the federal government, which required my presence in the capital every week, surely every other week, over the thirty-five year span. The shuttle alone made it possible for me to pursue my academic career alongside my active involvement with policy assignments. I had two friends, Lee Du Bridge, the president of Cal Tech in Pasadena, and Ralph Tyler, the director of the Center of Behavioral Sciences in Palo Alto, both of whom were deeply and continuously involved in Washington assignments; but I never was able to figure out how they managed to work successfully on both coasts. New York appeared to me to be the preferred location for such an effort.

Great cities are great by virtue of their ability to attract and retain persons of talent. There is no question that I have found New York a particularly satisfying place to live because of the great variety of interesting and talented people who make it their home or, in the case of great artists, visit it regularly. Even though my wife and I have followed a restricted rather than an open-ended social calendar, we have enjoyed the opportunities to tap into the large pools of exciting and interesting people who live, work, or visit New York.

One of the reasons that great cities such as New York, London, or Paris do not die is that they undergo a continuing exchange of populations between those who move in and those who move out. I belong to the small band of native New Yorkers who has no intention of ever living anywhere else. I never anticipated living anywhere but in New York, for I recognized early on that what I wanted to do and was able to do required the stimulation and reinforcement that I receive from living in New York. I was born in New York, and I expect to die in New York.

2

An Unusual Family

This chapter sets out the influence and impact of each of my parents' personality and values on the formation of my own ways of thought and styles of behavior. I can state unequivocally that they differed greatly in vitality, their approach to others, their concern for things of the mind, their involvement in social change—in fact, over the entire matrix of activities. The difficulty of my task is not to be underestimated. Had they been more alike it would be much easier for me to find the sources of my own thinking and behavior, but the striking differences between my father and my mother suggest that much of my own development was rooted in finding a middle way by synthesizing what I had abstracted from each of them into a life-style that I found congenial. Difficult or not, I will make the attempt, for otherwise all that is recounted in the chapters that follow would be suspended in mid-air without a foundation.

Since I have written a longer memoir of my father—*Louis Ginzberg: Keeper of the Law* (1966)—there is no need for me to recount his eighty years either in detail or selectively. What I need to do is to call attention to those aspects of his life and work that in retrospect I believe provided many of the building blocks for my own life.

By the time I was born in 1911, my father, then thirty-eight, had achieved a position of preeminence among Jewish scholars in the United States and ranked with the top cadre the world over. He was not a vain man, but he was fond of quoting Goethe's phrase—"Ich bin mein eigine wert bewusst"—I am conscious of my own worth. On occasion he would make the same point slightly differently: "There are many subjects about which I know nothing; some about which I know a little; and a few about which I know more than anybody else."

I came to take it for granted that a person, particularly a man, could scale the peak of accomplishment if he were well endowed, worked hard, and did not dissipate his energies. My father followed such a regimen.

17

He was in his study at eight thirty in the morning, where he remained till lunchtime when he emerged to eat and rest; he was back at his desk by two or so, and reemerged in time for dinner. Such was his schedule except for two mornings a week, when he left home to lecture at the seminary, and on Saturdays when he walked to the seminary synagogue for services. The seminary was somewhat over a mile from our home, and Saturday mornings until my adolescence I usually accompanied him to services.

I have tried to recall the nature of our conversations during this weekly exercise, but I have drawn a blank. My preadolescent years were centered around a consuming interest in baseball, which I played every day, and in following the fortunes of the Yankees, whom I had the good fortune to be able to watch often by using the season pass of a neighbor-friend who was on the *New York Times.* My father had surely heard of Babe Ruth, but he didn't know the difference between a batter and a fielder, a shortstop and a catcher. I suspect that my father's lack of knowledge of baseball, as well as his ignorance of all other sports, the movies, and much else in the popular culture, goes far to explain why, since I was eleven, I have drifted away from much if not all of the sport and entertainment world.

But it was the positive elements in my father's life and work, not the negative, that left their deepest impressions on me. I early came to recognize that my father enjoyed the hours that he worked in his study, even though for a long time I had no understanding of what he did during the long hours that he was at his desk. Over the years, I came to recognize that his work did not always progress on an even keel and that he encountered periods when his energies slackened and his progress slowed. But I suspected that these periods of difficulty and blockage were linked to periods when his generally indifferent health—insomnia, stomach trouble, low energy (in contemporary nomenclature, mild depression)—was the cause of his trouble.

The lesson that I absorbed unconsciously but firmly was that my father had found a way of relating to his work that provided him with great satisfaction that involved nothing more, but also nothing less, than control over his time and how to use it.

Having mentioned time, let me elaborate at least briefly on that crucial dimension of a scholar's life. While my father was always generous in making time for persons who wanted to consult him about their work, he avoided getting involved in a whole range of activities, from Zionist politics to meetings of the Oriental Club, because he had concluded that on balance he could have little or no effect on the outcomes of the former and that the enjoyment and intellectual stimulation from the latter were not worth the time and effort they involved.

As hundreds of his former students came to occupy the more important conservative pulpits around the country, my father, had he wanted to, could surely have spent some part of each year on a lecture circuit. But in fact, except for the very rare academic invitation, I recall no external commitments.

Part of the explanation was his disdain for the overwhelming majority of the Jewish lay leadership, which in his opinion was, with very few exceptions, as uneducated in Judaica as they were insensitive to the importance of Jewish scholarship and scholars. There was nothing in the two earlier cultures to which he had been exposed, Eastern European and German, that had prepared him for the uncouth nature of American laity-scholar relationships. Convinced that the successful stockholders, real estate investors, and merchants knew too little about Jewish history to be trusted with policy, and recognizing that he could do nothing to challenge their communal leadership, he withdrew to his study, not because he wanted to but because he saw no practical alternative. He was an aristocrat living in a democracy where worldly power, not scholarship, was respected. He had little difficulty with and considerable admiration for the democratic process that shaped this nation and its future. His concern, anguish, and bitterness related only to matters affecting the vulnerable Jewish minority, which he believed was at serious risk by being led by the uninformed.

As noted earlier, our family relocated early June to the New Jersey coast and returned to the city in late September or early October, a pattern congruent with my father's teaching schedule at the seminary. I grew up taking more or less for granted that a four months' relocation out of the city was par for the course. Clearly my father took his work with him. And that is the same pattern that I have followed throughout the whole of my academic life. In fact, the last true vacation that I took was in 1938, when, after finishing *The Illusion of Economic Stability*, which was four years in the making, I went mountain climbing in Norway and then spent a month in Paris in the company of my artist cousin, Herzl Rome.

The role that money played or didn't play in our household is worth some brief consideration. My father received a salary all the years that he was in the seminary that approximated that of a full professor at Columbia University, amounting to about $7,500 a year at the end of the New Era (1929). He was understandably worried about money matters because his distinguished physician-friend, Solomon Solis Cohen of Philadelphia, had once told him that he was unlikely to live beyond fifty or fifty-five, which meant that my mother might be left a widow with two minor children at home and with no assured pension (at the time the seminary trustees handled each case as it arose). Small wonder that my father carried a large amount of life insurance!

Despite this anxiety about an early death and the burden of heavy life insurance, our family gave next to no consideration to matters of money. We always knew how much we had. My mother was an excellent manager. There were no major emergencies. And after his wealthy bachelor brother, Asher, died in South Africa in the early 1930s, my father inherited two-seventeenth of his brother's estate, which removed whatever prior concerns there might have been about family finances.

Except for the very wealthy, it was not easy to grow up in the twentieth-century United States uninterested in and inattentive to matters of income and wealth, but such in fact was the environment in which I grew up and which left its mark on me. The only occasion that I recall that my father had an opportunity to make some additional money was after his opinion for the U.S. Treasury (1920) in which he determined that nonfermented wine could be used for sacramental purposes. One of the large grape juice companies asked him to go public and recommend their product; they offered a sizable fee for this endorsement, a proposition that he turned down out-of-hand.

My father was a true intellectual, with interests that stretched far beyond the domains of his own work. He had attended the lectures of many of the major contemporary German thinkers, including Virchow, Mommsen, and Kuno Fischer. Late in life he was able to engage Einstein in a discussion of the influence of Poincaré's equations on Planck's physics. With his paternal family living in Amsterdam, he became interested in and knowledgeable about painting. He had read most of the masters of literature often in their own tongue, and he himself wrote in eight languages. Only music was beyond his ken. I don't recall that he ever attended a concert, and even if my memory is faulty he did not manifest any real interest in music.

Although he often referred to his basic training as a philologist, he never saw himself as a member of that or any other technical craft. He had a deep respect for scholarship but a deep disdain for pedants. As an expert in the postbiblical period, circa 500 B.C. to A.D. 1000, he worked as a legal and social historian to shed new light and understanding on the economic developments that shaped Pharisiac Judaism, but he was equally interested in the interrelations between the Jewish world and the world outside.

I have not the slightest doubt that the raison d'être of his life and work was to contribute to the pool of knowledge of Jewish experience in Palestine and in the Diaspora in the belief and conviction that the Jews, a small, vulnerable minority, had succeeded in surviving against the most horrendous hate and oppression only through its core commitments to God, law, and land. But if Jews were going to continue to survive, they had to tighten their bonds to their past through new knowledge and understanding, even while they faced the tremendously difficult tasks of meeting the new challenges they were encountering, both from the oppressors who continued to persecute them and from the democratic nations of the West that had begun to moderate their hostility and see them as people, not as children of the anti-Christ.

My father succeeded in mediating among the three distinctive cultures to which he had been exposed by maintaining close ties to his roots, although these were surely loosened with the passage of time. He once told me that he could not have published his life's work—*A Commentary to the Jerusalem Talmud*—during the lifetime of his father, who would have found his interpretations beyond the ken of a believing Jew. His emotional bonds to his father were far deeper than the linkages between the two of us.

Although the bonds between us were considerably looser, they were sufficiently tight to leave me with a powerful residue of understanding. No Jew could come to peace with himself (or herself) without straightening out his relations with his fellow Jews, not only with those in his immediate environs but also with those throughout the Diaspora and, since 1948, particularly with the growing remnant that was involved in establishing the Third Commonwealth in Israel. In addition to acknowledging and responding to these bonds and obligations toward all Jews in all locations, there was a vertical axis of equal importance—the linkages to the Jewish heritage of earlier centuries and millennia and a concern for the history that is still to unfold in the centuries that are still hidden from view.

My father would have wished that I had become an observant Jew, one who like himself followed traditional practices. But that was not his criterion of the essence of Judaism, much as he valued and respected tradition. His test of integrity was not in the realm of belief, nor even in the realm of ritual, but rather in behavior that demonstrated ongoing commitment to the past, the present, and the future of the Jewish people.

George Pegram, the dean of the Faculty of Political Science, Philosophy, and Pure Science at Columbia during the late 1930s and the 1940s (with whom I was well acquainted despite the fact that his discipline, physics, was completely beyond my ken), remarked to several of my mentors that he thought I was excessively sensitive to and aware of my father, a relationship which he presumably considered deleterious to my development. But I think it will soon become clear that Pegram, sensitive and sophisticated as he was, did not know of my mother, Adele Katzenstein Ginzberg, whose influence was sufficiently strong to moderate and modify whatever excesses Pegram ascribed to my father's influence.

My first recollection of my mother goes back to my third year, when the lifeguard at Bradley Beach told her not to swim far out because of the undertow, and she proceeded forthwith to do so, leaving me terror-struck on the beach. She was an accomplished swimmer, and it made no sense to her to follow the lifeguard's warning. Reference to her skillful swimming reminds me of a slip of the tongue that she made while swimming many decades later at Martha's Vineyard: She said, "Not bad—for a seventy-eight-year-old," when in fact she had passed her eighty-eighth birthday.

The first and most dominant of my mother's characteristics was her lack of respect for authority, convention, or conformity. She couldn't stand being told *not* to do something. In fact I long considered it one of my great achievements that, despite repeated requests, I kept her from visiting my class at Columbia. I had heard that when my father had gone beyond his allotted time in one of his seminary lectures, she had taken off her watch and chain and had begun whirling them around to catch his attention.

During our family's first postwar visit to Europe in 1922 my mother wore knickers, which attracted the attention (and implied criticism) of everybody in Wildbad in the Black Forest, where we had settled for a prolonged stay. She had never worn knickers at home, but she had no intention of not wearing them just because every German man, woman, and child whom she encountered found them outlandish.

Another early recollection, from the summer of 1917 or 1918: When we were on the Jersey coast, my mother would walk through the streets singing German lieder for no reason other than to show her disdain for the xenophobic climate that our entrance into World War I had generated, which proscribed all things German, even German songs. Although my mother was a German by birth, coming from a family that had been rooted in Germany for centuries, she really didn't like her *Landsleutter* very much and had been nicknamed *Amerikannerin* when she was growing up in Berlin, which was testimony to her independence and nonconformity.

Her mother had died when she was eight, and her father married the governess, who was a petty tyrant. My mother promised herself, according to her oft-repeated account, that if she had children she would bring them up in exactly the opposite manner, allowing them as much liberty as possible. There is no question that she kept that promise to herself in my case, her firstborn. But I seriously question whether my sister was the beneficiary of a similar hands-off policy of parenting.

There were two additional incidents on the 1922 European trip that reveal a lot about my mother's personality.

She had taken my sister and me down the Rhine to spend the night in Cologne and to join my father the next day on the Frankfurt-Amsterdam express. We intended to spend time with my father's relatives in Amsterdam. Having been alerted by some passengers on shipboard that Cologne was crowded to the gills because French troops had recently moved into the city, my mother decided that we would disembark at Bonn, spend the night there, and leave the next morning to meet my father's train around noontime.

But it turned out that hotel rooms in Bonn were also scarce, in fact nonavailable. After a half-hour's fruitless search, the cab passed an impressive public building, and my mother asked the cab driver to stop and identify the building. It turned out to be a former castle of the emperor, now a museum. My mother asked the cab to wait; she then went in and made an arrangement with the custodian couple, and we spent the night in one of the guest rooms. My mother simply explained to the caretaker that she had no lodgings, that she had two young children in tow, and that she would make it worth their while. All very simple. My mother hated complications, especially unnecessary complications.

My father's train arrived on time, we joined him, and after a short while we all had to descend for customs control at the German-Dutch border. Many foreigners had bought lots of German merchandise with depreciated marks, only to have the goods confiscated by the customs officials because they lacked proper export licenses. My mother, sensitive to the plight of the Germans, had, on a matter of principle, avoided taking advantage of the falling value of the mark. At the end of the inspection, men were asked to go through one gate, women through another. After my father and I were back in our compartment for ten minutes or more, we realized that my mother and sister were still not aboard. After another ten minutes we saw a large commotion at the end of the platform, with my mother in the middle of a group of officials. When she rejoined us we learned that her customs official in the final checking had wanted to confiscate her Zeiss binoculars, a gift from her brother-in-law, which she contended she had brought into the country. She refused to give them up. So strenuous were her objections that the customs officials called on the border commander to determine what should be done. He asked a Solomonesque question: Did my mother wear the binoculars openly, or did she try to hide them? On being told that she wore them openly, he permitted her to keep them and the train left twenty-five minutes late. My mother never questioned that she had the right to lie—after all, she had gone out of her way not to take advantage of the falling mark.

My mother had had only a finishing-school education in Berlin and had worked briefly in her father's real estate office. Although she had acquired all the skills necessary to run a household effectively and economically, she didn't get any special pleasure out of using her domestic skills, other than enjoying the large number of guests, expected and frequently unexpected, that my father would invite.

She was definitely not an intellectual, and reading books was a minor part of her life. She had little or no background for understanding the scholarly problems that engaged my father. She simply accepted the fact that he was preeminent in his field. But she knew that there were a great many things that she could do well, especially after she won a prize for collecting the most money for postwar Jewish refugees in Eastern Europe.

She called on a great number of businessmen, some of whom she knew well, others whom she knew only slightly or not at all. But they welcomed her, enjoyed talking with her, and were pleased to be dunned for a charitable gift. Once having learned that she had this talent, she used it to the hilt all the years of her long life. She was active in all sorts of eleemosynary undertakings, mostly within the Jewish community but also for nonsectarian causes such as the Girl Scouts, who nominated her one year as New York State's mother of the year.

When I began to write books and would present her with an inscribed copy, she would often raise the same question: Would the book be of any use or help to those who needed to be helped? By implication—and sometimes by direct phrasing—she would ask why anybody would spend the time and effort required to write a book unless it could do somebody some good. Clearly this is not a question that she would put bluntly to my father because she had too much love and respect for him, but in point of fact she found occasions when she could get her oar in.

My father considered, how seriously I don't know, calling a Sanhedrin in Paris of the most learned rabbis in Europe at the end of World War I in the hope of finding a modus vivendi to ease the burden of the "deserted wife," who could not remarry without definite proof of her husband's death. My father recognized, probably sooner rather than later, that he would not be able to find a point of accommodation with those of strictly Orthodox persuasion, and his plan was early aborted. But my mother was deeply troubled that he had retreated without ever having tried to do something for the tens of thousands of women whose husbands' deaths had not been substantiated; their condition cried out for help and remedy.

When, at the end of his sabbatical in Palestine (where he had spent the year of 1928–29 inaugurating the chair of Talmud at the Hebrew University), pressure was brought on my father to remain permanently, my mother was definitely open to the idea but my father vetoed it. She found the committed settlers a congenial group of people and would gladly have joined them, but my father, deciding that he was too set in his ways and dependent on a few creature comforts to which he had greater access at home, declined with regret. His decision was also rooted in the fact that he could see no constructive role for himself in moderating between the old-fashioned Orthodox rabbis on the Right, such as Chief Rabbi Abraham Kook, and his Western-trained friends and himself.

To return to my mother: she was very much an enfant terrible; she enjoyed having fun without worrying about the consequences—knowing ahead of time that the consequences were likely to be unimportant or nonexistent. At the time of the Harvard Tercentenary, when my father received an honorary degree, I ran into her one day walking behind a stooped old man, with a bookbag slung over his shoulder, who was making his way across the yard at a slow gait. A few paces back was my mother, mimicking his walk. After a short time, the gentleman turned and doffed his hat. It was the president-emeritus, the venerable A. Lawrence Lowell!

After my father's death in 1953 (shortly before his eightieth birthday; my mother, like the rest of us, accepted his death as a merciful release, since he had suffered acutely for five years from the sequela of a severe attack of herpes zoster (shingles)), my mother decided to close her large apartment and move into Morningside Gardens, a new cooperative a few blocks to the north of the Columbia and seminary campuses. She was sixty-seven at the time and decided to buy all new furniture. But she insisted on a twenty-five-year guarantee. This amused us all, but she had the last laugh, since it turned out that she still had twenty-seven years of life left in her, $26\frac{1}{2}$ years of which she lived alone in her Morningside Gardens apartment pursuing an active life that included many trips to the West Coast, Europe, Israel, and even to the U.S.S.R.

After she returned from a multi-week trip through the U.S.S.R., during which she had visited several of its principal cities—from Leningrad to Kiev—she called the Russian consulate in New York City to give them a summary appraisal of what she liked and what she didn't like about what she had encountered during her trip. I asked her what she hoped to accomplish by her telephone call to the consulate, and she replied, "I thought they should know how I felt about my experiences there so that they could start correcting some of the things that needed fixing." She always acted on the belief that everybody, even the Soviet government, could benefit from her advice!

It was difficult to see any evidence of her advancing age, either in her features—her face remained uncreased—or in her daily routine, which continued at an active pace. Once a year she made the rounds of the large number of physician friends that she had accumulated over the years, primarily to inquire how they were faring as they were aging. My mother's health was extraordinary. In the twenty-two years that I lived at home, I have no recollection of her spending a day in bed. Thereafter, she was hospitalized once in her forties, when her gallbladder was removed, and she was depressed for a short time at the onset of her menopause, but she snapped out of it without psychotherapy. When she was in her early eighties, her New York physician wanted an angiogram taken. Since I had been a friend of Michael DeBakey since World War II, I took her to Methodist Hospital in Houston, where DeBakey performed the angiogram. The two of them hit it off, and my mother sought to persuade DeBakey to operate on her to improve the circulation in her legs. I vetoed the idea, however, under pressure from our friend Stanley Robbins, a Boston pathologist, who was devoted to my mother (and in fact, he called her "mother").

When friends used the expression "You should remain well to 120 years," my mother challenged them and asked why only to 120! More revealing about her attitudes toward life and death was the discussion that she had with me, not once but several times, along the following lines: It is true that everybody who was ever born up to this point in the world's history has died. But it does not follow that all who are alive (like herself) need necessarily die, since science may find a way to achieve eternal life in the years ahead.

This was more than just idle speculation. She really entertained, at least for a while in her seventies, the prospect of remaining around indefinitely. She decided to go on a safari when she was eighty-seven; it was a long safari, involving four East African countries, and required a month or more of field trips. When she returned and we asked her how it was, she replied "Just wonderful—but a little too strenuous for older people"—a category to which she clearly did not see herself belonging.

Even in her early nineties, when I dropped in during the late afternoon to say hello, and asked, "How are you doing, old lady?," she would jump up from her chair and look me straight in the eye and say, "Who do you think you are addressing as 'old lady'!"

But I was the firstborn, an only son, who could do no wrong. At one point my bride complained that my mother's daily telephone calls (early in the morning, lasting for twenty to thirty minutes) were more than she welcomed. I only had to drop a hint to my mother to put an end to the unwelcome practice. The same went for expected appearances at her dinner table on Friday evenings: Ruth found that too much of an obligation. Again, a word to my mother was sufficient. Ruth has told me, not once but many times, that she could not have asked for a more non-interfering mother-in-law, recognizing full well that the noninterference was the direct outcome of my mother's desire to keep her relationships with me as easy and uncomplicated as possible.

But I cannot conclude even this brief chapter on our unusual family without calling attention to the fourth member, my sibling Sophie, about three years my junior. Hers was not nearly as relaxed a childhood as mine, partly because I wanted no competition and never failed to impress upon her that I was the firstborn male offspring, and partly because my mother found it more difficult to rear a girl than a boy. She gave me much more freedom. And as time went on, all sorts of competition developed between mother and daughter, competition that continued throughout my mother's long life. She died only a few years before the sudden and totally unexpected death of my sister. Fortunately, my sister had been able to establish a significant life of her own in the Boston area with her husband, an MIT professor of microbiology, Bernard Gould (who had been her teacher), and with her three attractive sons. Sophie had the unenviable task of making her way early in life in a household of three rugged individualists. The fact that she survived and was able to shape a satisfactory life for herself and her family is no small testimony to her resourcefulness.

But however one reconstructs what went on in the Ginzberg home, it surely was an unusual family. I did not realize it at the time, but that is how it appears in retrospect.

3

Columbia University—A Long View

When I entered Columbia College as a freshman in the fall of 1927, Columbia was generally recognized at home and abroad as one of America's three leading universities, sharing the position of preeminence with Harvard and the University of Chicago.

In the fall of 1990 Columbia University entered upon a fund-raising effort whereby it hopes to raise $1.15 billion. This effort is heavily focused on the establishment of new named professorships and expanded student aid. Columbia continues to have considerable strengths in various faculties, schools, departments, and research institutes, but it has surely slipped from its premier position of the late 1920s.

The question that we want to explore is what forces, external and internal, played leading roles in affecting Columbia's ranking among the top U.S. universities.

A revealing piece of evidence of Columbia's pre-World War II position is the fact that at the Harvard Tercentenary, held in 1936, when sixty-two scholars from the entire world were honored for their outstanding contributions, Columbia had three among the galaxy of stars—Franz Boas in Anthropology, Robert M. MacIver in Sociology, and Wesley Clair Mitchell in Economics. The fact that I had been a student of all three and considered the first two my mentors—and as well as the fact that my father was also among the honorees—made my participation in the Harvard conference that preceded the ceremonies one of the highpoints of my early academic career.

Since the end of World War II, Harvard, the clear leader today, and the other Ivy League colleges and universities, including Yale and Princeton, have faced increasing competition from institutions in the South, the Southwest, and, particularly, the West, from the University of California in San Diego to the University of Washington in Seattle. The University of Texas in Austin was able to attract a Nobel Laureate from Harvard, the University of Texas in Dallas one from Columbia. The dean of the Faculty of Arts and Sciences at Harvard has recently relocated to Stanford. Over the years, two Nobelists in Economics left Harvard—Kenneth Arrow returned to Stanford, and Wassily Leontief joined the faculty at New York University.

Since the end of World War II, all universities, and especially the East Coast universities, have been facing a more competitive environment in attracting and retaining world-class scholars and scientists. As far as external forces are concerned, special attention must be focused on the changing urban environment within which the university is located. It is well to recall that Columbia's full name is Columbia University in the City of New York, a name that suggests a special relationship to the city.

The New Era came to an end in 1929, and New York City, as did the rest of the country, moved into an ever-deepening depression that had brought the economy to a halt by the time of President Franklin Roosevelt's inauguration in the spring of 1933. As the New Deal took hold, the city experienced a modest improvement, but the rest of the 1930s were characterized by stresses and strains, with the large numbers of unemployed persons creating a pall over both the city's activities and its mood and aspirations. However, depressed as the city's and the nation's economy remained during FDR's first two administrations, public security and personal safety—important environmental factors affecting all urban universities—remained adequate.

In 1927 and up to World War II, Columbia University was a WASP oasis bounded on three sides (the Hudson River was the fourth) by black, Jewish, and other minorities including large numbers of Irish Catholics. To the best of my recollection, the support staff at the university included no blacks. The housekeeping and security staffs were primarily Irish; the secretarial and library staffs, primarily WASPs.

The war and the immediate postwar years saw a major change in the external environment of the university. New York City was attracting large numbers of blacks from the rural South and there were the beginnings of a large influx of Puerto Ricans. Both streams of newcomers sought and found living quarters north of 120th Street and south of 114th Street—the university's north and south boundaries—as many lower-income non-Hispanic whites relocated to the suburbs. The Columbia neighborhood also became the site of a number of SROs (Single Room

Occupancy). Their many marginally adjusted tenants spent much of their time out of doors, contributing to the area's increasingly seedy look.

The Rockefeller family, with heavy investments in two of Columbia's northern neighbors—Union Theological Seminary and International House—invited Wilbur C. Munnecke (vice-president of the University of Chicago, which had had an early exposure to neighborhood deterioration) to undertake an assessment of the Columbia area and to propose a plan for remedial action. Munnecke and I had been close friends since our service in the Pentagon during the war, and my recollection is that when he asked to meet with the Columbia trustees, his request was turned down—a refusal that grew out of the trustees' limited understanding of the emerging problems and their unease with the Rockefeller family's initiative.

Nicholas Murray Butler had not included the Rockefellers among the coterie of millionaires whom he had asked to provide much of the funding for Columbia's expansion during the first quarter-century of his incumbency as president. The longer-term relationship between Columbia and the Rockefeller family was complicated by the fact that Columbia was the owner of the land on which Rockefeller Center was erected; this was a relationship in which each of the two principals was suspicious that the other was seeking unfair advantage. At long last, in 1985, Columbia sold 11.7 acres of land to the Rockefellers for a price ($400 million in cash) that appeared to be agreeable to both buyer and seller.

The most dramatic and portentous environmental conflict that beset Columbia in the post-World War II era, which contributed to the campus explosion of 1968 and had other adverse consequences, arose from the university's determination to go ahead with the building of a gymnasium in Morningside Park. This project provided the neighboring black population and its leadership with a target on which to focus its long-simmering antagonisms to the colossus on the hill.

I had served as a messenger from a friendly black leader some months prior to the explosion in April 1968 to convey to the Columbia authorities that the climate had changed since the state legislature—with local black support—had first approved the project. The civil rights movement had in the interim eroded such local support for the gymnasium, despite the fact that the Columbia trustees had agreed that the neighborhood residents could share in the use of the new facility.

I was told by the vice-president of the university to whom I delivered the warning message that he doubted that President Kirk would be able to dissuade the trustees from moving ahead with the project, so committed were those who had spearheaded the fund-raising effort.

The lack of sensitivity and awareness of the Columbia officialdom about what was happening in the Harlem community is reflected in the following episode, which occurred a few days before the campus erupted. A group of French rectors from urban universities was visiting the United States to explore university-city relations and were being hosted by the president of Columbia and his senior staff. I had been invited to attend, presumably because some of my research had focused on the problems of the black minority and its search for jobs and income in urban America.

As the morning's discussion drew to a close, one of the Columbia vice-presidents suggested that the rectors might like to visit Harlem in the afternoon, a suggestion that I had trouble getting him to withdraw. I had read in the morning's newspaper that Harlem planned a protest march to the campus that same afternoon, but our suburban-based vice-president was not cognizant about what was about to happen.

In fairness, I must note an earlier conversation that I had had with the then vice-president for academic affairs about the desirability of Columbia's opening one or more adult educational facilities in Harlem, partly because of the contribution that they might make to the local community, but also because of the desirability of Columbia's building up a little credit with its disgruntled neighbors. Neither of us believed, however, that an exploratory discussion would go anywhere, since there was little interest and less concern on the part of the power structure at Columbia or for that matter in Harlem, to pursue such an approach.

In 1966 Columbia received a $10 million grant from the Ford Foundation to fund a group of social improvement projects for Harlem that would be locally initiated and implemented. Although I was not privy to the thinking of the Ford Foundation's staff and trustees in making this grant, a reasonable assumption is that they thought it might be beneficial to all three parties—the Ford Foundation, Columbia, and Harlem.

President Kirk appointed a five-person committee that included Dean Clarence Walton of General Studies as chairman; President John Fischer of Teachers College; Professor Wallace Sayre, Columbia's great expert on the government of the city; Samuel Lubell, the well-known pollster, of the Journalism School; and myself; a distinguished black educator, Dr. Franklin Williams, served as executive director.

Never has a group of such well-intentioned and well-informed persons botched their assignment as badly as we botched ours, for a number of reasons, none of which was clear to me at the time nor since. My best long-distance guess is that, with the initiative in the hands of the community, the university was forced to follow, not lead. But if the truth be told, the university was not competent to lead.

A short time after the Morningside Park episode which led to the student riots of April, 1968, Mayor Lindsay and his senior staff arrived for an early morning meeting with the Columbia administrators and a few specially invited professors to review the university's changing relationships to its immediate neighbors, primarily south of the campus. The mayor emphasized his unhappiness with the plans that Columbia had on file with the City Planning Commission, which stipulated that Columbia retained the right to ask for condemnation proceedings against the owners of and tenants in apartment houses that might stand in the way of the university's future expansion to the south.

The mayor noted, not once but several times, that such plans were outdated and irrelevant and that there was no prospect whatever that the state legislature would agree to the eviction of large numbers of tenants to make room for Columbia to expand. He urged the Columbia administration to get its plans up to date. The replies of the Columbia administration underscored how far it still had to go to understand the changes taking place in its environment.

Courtney C. Brown, the long-time dean of the Graduate School of Business, looked to the north as the preferred area for the university to expand, since there were no tenants to displace and relatively few businesses to relocate. Over a number of years he had explored with local leaders in Harlem a large redevelopment project between Broadway and the Hudson River between 125th Street and 135th Street, which would include a mixed housing development for Columbia and for the residents of Harlem, as well as new space for university research and other uses. But the scale of the project and the softness of the commitments and financing both in Harlem and at Columbia doomed it.

Despite its slow and hesitant responses to neighborhood trends, after World War II Columbia had acquired a large amount of residential property in its immediate vicinity to meet its growing needs for housing for faculty, students, and staff. When I headed a special university committee to review the management of these rental properties in 1983, the university owned approximately six thousand apartments, from the Gold Coast units on Claremont Avenue and Riverside Drive between 116th Street and 125th Street to a large number of marginal apartments for students in the side streets, especially east of Broadway between 116th Street and 122nd Street.

The important point to note is that these sizable real estate holdings came nowhere near meeting the needs of the university as it sought to attract young professors with growing families to Columbia. With property values in the inner suburbs increasing steadily and steeply, most newcomers to the Columbia faculty had to locate in communities that were an hour or more commuting time from the campus. To make matters worse, even if the university found them a place to live close to the campus, they still had to contend with the steep costs of private education for their school-aged children, who would be ill-served by the local public schools.

The reversal of New York City's downward spiral after 1977 contributed considerably to improving the ambience of the Columbia neighborhood. Most of the local SROs were closed, and the buildings were converted for alternative use, largely by the Columbia administration. The continuing upswing of New York City's economy, especially in the early and mid-1980s, helped the university to recruit two-income faculty families, since a growing number of younger academics were willing to tolerate the metropolis's negatives so they could enjoy the growing cultural vibrancy of the city.

Important as the changing external environment was on making Columbia viable in the post-World War II era, of much greater importance was the leadership vacuum at the top of the university, which began at the onset of the Great Depression in 1930 and which continued without interruption to 1969; and, with regard to aggressive fund-raising efforts until 1980, when Michael Sovern was inaugurated as Columbia's seventeenth president.

By 1929 Nicholas Murray Butler had succeeded in transforming Columbia into an institution of international distinction, with the highest average salaries for professors in the United States—$7,500. A university such as Columbia is a loose confederation of some eighteen or so major departments under the control of the tenured professors, organized into faculties and schools, with varying amounts of influence and initiative residing in the deans. All march to a single drummer, the president, who must set directions, add to the institution's revenues, and make allocations among the competing divisions.

In such a loose organization, an assessment of a university's strength and well-being can never be more—nor should it be less—than an on-balance reading. In the heyday of Butler's presidency—in the late 1920s—there were evidences of weaknesses. For example: there were major resignations from the Law School faculty as a consequence of Butler's appointment of Young B. Smith as dean; in the view of the several leading jurists who resigned, he was unfit to hold that position. Or, for example: Earlier, at the end of World War I when Columbia was already in full stride, three of the most distinguished members of the Political Science faculty resigned—Charles A. Beard, Wesley Clair Mitchell, and James Harvey Robinson. Each did so for his own reasons, but restiveness with the top administration played a role.

In the late 1930s and early 1940s, Charles Beard was invited back to serve as a visiting professor, and at that time I had the opportunity for an extended talk with him. Beard told me in no uncertain terms that, looking back, he felt he had made a mistake in resigning. "There are some people who belong at a university, and it is better for them to put up with minor inconveniences than to bolt and seek a career elsewhere," he said.

A related observation: Unlike the other Ivy League institutions, the college has played a lesser role in the evolution of Columbia than at Harvard, Yale, or Princeton. Butler had singled out the graduate faculties of Philosophy, Political Science, and Pure Science for major attention and growth, together with strong central administrative support for selected professional schools, in particular medicine and law but not business. Although Butler, under pressure from both inside and outside forces, eventually agreed to establish a School of Business (1916) he never gave it its head. Columbia, located in the nation's greatest business center, should have been able to develop a business school second to none, but that was clearly not Butler's desire.

In 1929 Butler appointed a prestigious committee of five leading businessmen, including then president of AT&T, Walter Gifford and Bernard Baruch, to prepare a financial plan that would provide a solid foundation for the continuing long-term growth of the university. But the stock market crashed in October 1929, and by the following year the

United States was falling ever more deeply into a depression that undermined not only the economy, but all nonprofit institutions that depended on a continuing flow of philanthropic funds.

One of the serious consequences of the long period of strained resources—that is, from 1929 to 1941—was the substantial, though not total, freeze on new appointments. The dean of the School of Business, Roswell McCrea, who pieced together an assistantship and a lecturer's position for me in 1935—sat on the university's top budget committee. As the years of the money shortage lengthened, McCrea kept pushing Butler to speed up the retirements of the high-salaried senior professors, but Butler refused, taking the position that those who had served faithfully in earlier years were not to be thrown overboard.

It would have made good sense for Butler to have retired in 1932 at the time of his seventieth birthday, but despite his failing health he gave no evidence of such an intention, and the trustees, all his handpicked men, failed to rise to their responsibility and to request it. Butler hung on till 1945; by then he was blind and could barely hear. In the last decade of his incumbency, his inability to lead went far to undermine the great institution that his imagination and his energy had earlier fashioned.

McCrea, having pressed the issue of early retirements and having lost the battle, felt obliged to resign in 1941 from his position as dean of the School of Business. He was succeeded by Robert Calkins from the University of California, Berkeley. Calkins, a man of quality and energy, did not take very long to appreciate that, with Butler holding on tenaciously to the presidency, there was little that he could do on his own as dean of the School of Business. He decided that he would not wait around for a crack at the presidency and took himself off expeditiously, first to the General Education Board (Rockefeller) and later to assume the presidency of the Brookings Institution, which he revived and transformed into a major policy think tank.

The end of World War II found Columbia with an acting president, Frank Frankenthal, the long-time dedicated secretary of the university, who knew more than anybody else where the bodies were buried. However, although the trustees and the senior faculty looked on him as an able administrator, he was not perceived to be a person capable of redirecting a major university that had suffered from fifteen years of neglect.

Trustee and faculty committees went looking separately for Butler's successor. Since I did not return from Washington to the university on a full-time basis until the fall of 1946, the faculty committee asked me in the spring of 1946 to interview Senator William Fulbright, the recent president of the University of Arkansas, to determine his availability. I had a pleasant tea with the senator, who told me that he was flattered by the inquiry but that it came either too late (he had only recently been elected to the Senate) or too early (before he had had his fill of political life). I reported accordingly, and one more name was scratched from the faculty committee's list of possible candidates.

Some months later, rumors began to circulate that General Eisenhower, chief of staff of the U.S. Army, would be Butler's successor. Major General Howard Snyder, the former assistant inspector general (medical), with whom I had worked closely during the war, arranged that I have lunch with Eisenhower to talk about Columbia as well as about a research project on military manpower in World War II that Eisenhower believed should be initiated.

During the course of that luncheon, Eisenhower told me that the trustees assured him that he would not be heavily involved in fund-raising for the university. I commented that the trustees were either badly informed or misinforming him or both, because Columbia was in bad financial straits and needed lots of new money and probably could profit from downsizing. It was attempting to do too much with too few resources.

Eisenhower arrived on the campus in time for the fall semester of 1948 and left to head SHAPE (Supreme Headquarters Allied Powers Europe) in December 1950, a tenure of about thirty-eight months, including the breaks when he was designated by President Truman to serve as the temporary chairman of the Joint Chiefs of Staff (after Secretary Forrestal's illness and premature death), and for an extended convalescence in the South, which General Snyder insisted upon after Eisenhower suffered a bout of illness.

Eisenhower's first provost was Albert Jacobs, a professor at the Law School who resigned in 1949 to become chancellor of the University of Denver and who moved, a few years later, to become president of Trinity College. Jacobs had concluded that Eisenhower would remain for an extended time at Columbia and that he had better move on. Eisenhower selected Grayson Kirk, a professor of political science, with whom he had developed an acquaintance at meetings of the Council on Foreign Relations. Many on campus were surprised at Kirk's selection, and in time Eisenhower questioned his own impetuous choice. When Eisenhower went to SHAPE he did not resign, but took a leave of absence. In fact, he resigned just prior to entering the White House. At that point Kirk, who had been in charge during the intervening years, got the nod from the trustees and became president of Columbia.

Once again, the School of Business, because of weakness in the central administration, was an innocent victim. It had chosen an outsider, Philip Young, as dean in 1948, and Young was moving the school steadily ahead. But Young had concluded that he could not work effectively with Kirk and resigned to go to Washington as personnel chief for Eisenhower.

With students crowding the campus in record numbers, with the GI bill providing a large inflow of new funds, with the U.S. economy heading up, with new large-scale federal funding for research, many of Columbia's serious financial problems were eased and others were papered over. Departments added large numbers of newcomers to their staffs to make up for the lost momentum in the 1930s and the war years and to help them cope with the large influx of new students. For instance, the Graduate Department of Economics added David Landis, Albert Hirshman, and Abram Bergson, but within a few years all three had relocated to Harvard. These were strong appointments even if they left after a few years. But in many departments, including the School of Business, although additional teaching staff was added to cope with the influx of students, appointments standards slipped.

A striking illustration of the type of mistakes made by the central administration was the case of George Stigler, who was chairman of a special committee that had advised the president's office on how to handle competitive bids for strong faculty members that Columbia wanted to keep. In 1958 Stigler got an offer from Chicago, and Columbia's counteroffer was below the figure that Stigler's committee had earlier recommended for the retention of top faculty. He left, and some years later was awarded the Nobel Prize in Economics. No one will ever know how much slippage occurred because of weak administration at the top.

In the nineteen years that Kirk was in the president's office, first as provost, then as acting president, and finally for sixteen years as president, Columbia continued to function with uneven success and distinction. The Business School under Courtney Brown got its act together, and in 1964 moved into a new building of its own, which could have been more effectively designed but which was a sizable improvement over its old quarters. The Medical School and the Law School, long centers of major strength, continued to rank high among their leading competitors. The college continued to be well led and continued to attract good students, although Columbia's drawing power was becoming more regional than national. But the critical faculties of Philosophy, Political Science, and Pure Science began to show a number of serious fissures.

The most serious slippage was in the social science departments— economics, sociology, history, anthropology. Outstanding strength in the immediate post-World War II years in mathematical statistics was dissipated within a relatively short span of years. The remarkable point is that a large number of departments—including geology, English, art history, East Asian studies, and others—were able to maintain strong faculty and high productivity. But there was simply not enough revenue flowing into the university to enable it simultaneously to expand the scale of capital improvements, to improve the overall quality of faculty, and to maintain student aid, which slipped far behind Columbia's major competitors. The central administration was forced to increase the levy on schools and departments that were big tuition earners in order to help finance the weaker departments. There was little effort to reassess the university as a whole with an eye to cutting back on the range if not the depth of its commitments.

I recall a conversation with Kirk in which I suggested that Columbia and New York University (NYU) act conjointly to persuade Governor Rockefeller that the best way for New York State to expand opportunities for graduate education in New York City was to use its two largest and strongest institutions. Failure to act defensively meant that CUNY (the City University of New York) would get into the field of graduate studies and would provide new competition for both Columbia and NYU. Kirk's reply was that he had no intention of approaching the state government, because Columbia was a private institution. A simple analysis of the flow of revenues into Columbia would have contradicted his simplistic conclusion.

Shortly before the campus explosion of 1968—which in all fairness could have occurred even with a strong president—I suggested in a conversation with Kirk that we were making such slow progress in adding blacks to the faculty that he should consider seeking special foundation funds to facilitate the appointment of fifteen to twenty black professors—one for each of the departments—outside of the budget, on the ground that only thus would the departments add minority members. But Kirk saw no merit in this suggestion, and it was not resurrected until twenty years later.

The crisis of April 1968 grew out of the counterculture of the 1960s, reinforced by the growing civil rights agitation, and the threat of cancellation of deferments for military service for college and university students. The police's entering the campus to evict the students who had occupied various buildings brought the university to a standstill. To add to the confusion, the faculty, even the tenured faculty, had no role to play in policy formulation. The only machinery that existed was a council of deans, whose discussions were largely advisory.

As the tension mounted, there were impromptu meetings of faculty on the main campus, but some days into the trouble the administration reluctantly agreed that it would meet with the faculty and arranged to do so in the chapel, the only meeting place of adequate size. The dean of the Law School was selected to preside; Michael Sovern, a law professor, served as parliamentarian; and President Kirk was scheduled to speak. At a prearranged signal from a member of the Law School faculty, the chairman was to call for a vote to adjourn. He missed the signal and recognized instead the proposer of a motion that stated that there should be established an Executive Committee of the Faculty, made up of ten distinguished professors (he named five), to help mediate the disturbance. His motion was quickly amended, with ten specific names placed in nomination, and immediately passed. The new committee was divided among five liberals from the college, three conservatives, and Sovern and myself in the middle. For a brief period it had cochairs Alan Westin and Sovern, but we persuaded one of the liberal college group to switch and elected Sovern as sole chair.

Since William Peterson, the recently elected chairman of the Board of Trustees, was a graduate of the School of Business, I got the assignment of liaison with the trustees, which included arranging for an emergency meeting the very next evening. The trustees met first at dinner with Kirk and his second-in-command, David Truman, and then sat down with the Executive Committee members for a session that broke up at 2:30 A.M., but only after a trustee subcommittee had been appointed as our counterpart. As the meeting drew to a close, several trustees remarked that they had learned more about Columbia at this one meeting than from all of their prior service on the board.

By the time summer rolled around, it was clear that Kirk had lost the support of the faculty and many of the trustees and that he would have to leave. The Executive Committee of the Faculty, after an extended discussion with Truman, decided somewhat reluctantly that he too could not lead the divided university. The trustees insisted on appointing an experienced administrator as acting president, and chose Andrew Cordier, recently of the U.N., and accepted the Executive Committee's nominee, the Nobel-Laureate physicist, Polykarp Kusch, as provost. Cordier proved himself to be a leader-pacifier of great skill, and the campus quickly returned to a condition approaching normal.

A major contributor to speeding the campus's return to normalcy was Frank Hogan, vice-chairman of the Columbia Board of Trustees, who, at the outbreak of the trouble, had withdrawn from active participation on the ground that it might conflict with his responsibilities as district attorney for the County of New York. Hogan, my Martha's Vineyard neighbor that summer, agreed under promise of anonymity to advise me as to the actions that the trustees could take so that the student leaders, who faced possible jail sentences, would not go to trial. With Hogan's guidance I put various suggestions before the trustees, some of whom were resistant to letting the student leaders off the hook. But I finally persuaded them that squashing the indictments was a sine qua non if classes were to resume in September.

The spring explosion of 1968 had serious long-term costs. Columbia had received a lot of bad press, which alienated many of its faithful out-of-town alumni as well as others in the metropolitan area. Faculty relations had become strained, and some able members decided to relocate. IBM took the first hint of being an intruder on the campus and closed down its prestigious Watson Laboratory. Many promising students thought again about applying to a university that had just been through such a serious crisis. And the succession to the presidency remained open for another year, during which the leading candidate was derailed at the last minute in favor of William McGill, the former chairman of the Columbia psychology department, who had made his mark as chancellor at the university of California in San Diego.

Cordier, recognizing Sovern's unique role in helping to restore the campus to normal by negotiating successfully with agitated faculty and excited students, and having been the beneficiary of Sovern's excellent advice during the period of the fall reconstruction, appointed him dean of the Law School. This led later to his selection as provost and eventually, in 1980, to the presidency as successor to McGill.

McGill broke the mold of Columbia presidents. He was the first Catholic to be appointed, a native New Yorker and a graduate of Fordham University. His primary assignment was to bring the seriously unbalanced university budget under control and to shore up the much-weakened administrative structure that had demonstrated serious limitations during the crisis and its aftermath.

Early on, McGill had bad luck with the appointment of a new dean to the Graduate School of Business. Uncertain about the faculty committee's choice, McGill spent a weekend checking out the candidate on his own campus, and was misled because of the local administrators' eagerness to unload the candidate. When truth and expediency come into conflict, truth is frequently, even in an academic community, the victim. One is reminded of the inscription on Columbia's chapel: The truth will make you free.

Faced with the embarrassment of having to unload a dean whom he had only recently recommended to the trustees, McGill insisted that the Business School faculty unite behind a single internal candidate who would be acceptable to him. By insisting on this quid pro quo, McGill salvaged as much as he could from a costly error that was largely the faculty's doing.

Although McGill made some efforts at external fund-raising, this was not an area of his strength. As a result, when he decided to retire at the end of a decade, Columbia had been without a successful fund-raiser for a half-century, that is, from the onset of Butler's decline in 1930. In the face of this untoward experience, it was amazing that Columbia could still boast of so many strong departments and schools, although it had slipped in many areas.

Sovern, having moved from the deanship of the Law School to the office of provost near the end of McGill's term, was in a preferred position to succeed him. Arthur Krim, then chairman of the board of trustees, wrote to many seeking nominations. In my answer I suggested that he measure all candidates against Sovern and that if a stronger candidate emerged the trustees should go ahead with the appointment; otherwise Sovern should be their choice.

The Sovern era will come to an end in June 1993, so it would be premature to attempt a definitive assessment, but a few observations can be ventured. As McGill was the first Catholic to hold the office of president, Sovern was the first Jew. Unlike McGill, Sovern was pure Columbia, except for a single year that he had spent teaching at the University of Minnesota's Law School.

Sovern decided initially on a three-headed provostship—arts and sciences, graduate faculties, and medicine—but Fritz Stern quickly returned to the teaching faculty, and Peter Likens became president of Lehigh University, which left Robert Goldberger, M.D., a former senior administrator of the National Institutes of Health, as the ranking academic official. As the years went on, Goldberger encountered more and more difficulties with various faculties, starting with the Medical School and ending with the resignation of the dean of the Graduate School of Business and the entire Committee on Instruction over his recommended reversal of an ad hoc committee's recommendation for a tenured appointment.

In my first decade at Columbia, the senior academic officials had been Frederick Woodbridge, Howard Lee MacBain, and George Pegram, chosen respectively from the faculties of philosophy, political science, and pure science, each a person of stature and strength.

While the post-World War II period saw able people for longer or shorter periods in the offices of dean of the Graduate Faculties, vice-president for academic affairs, or provost, their leadership and effectiveness were not of the same order. Of course the university had become a much more complex institution to shape and direct.

Sovern, recognizing that Columbia could not possibly be reinvigorated, reformed, and reconstructed without large amounts of new money, set himself the task of doing what had last been done well by Butler in the 1920s! In the five-year period between 1982 and 1987, Columbia's capital campaign netted $602 million. And, as noted at the beginning of this chapter, in October 1990 Columbia announced another five-year capital campaign with a new goal of $1.15 billion.

Sovern has spearheaded this extraordinary fund-raising effort, the more remarkable when one recalls that since the days of Butler, Columbia had deliberately avoided seeking funds from wealthy New York Jews, and after the 1968 crisis, many of its WASP alumni became disenchanted with the institution.

To complicate Columbia's fund-raising activities, New York University had recognized several decades earlier the potential of attracting large sums from affluent New York Jews and had succeeded in establishing many successful relationships. These handicapping conditions make the Sovern efforts that much more impressive.

There is no certainty that the second Sovern-led campaign will be as successful as the first, particularly since the United States economy may face a period of slow growth and low profitability. Nor is it certain that, if the second fund-raising campaign is successful, it will assure that Columbia will regain its former luster. But the prospects for a significant turnaround are bright, and in the history of universities a period of partial decline, even of fifty years' duration, may turn out to have been only a minor hiatus in the institution's life, which is measured in centuries, not decades.

4

The Conservation of Human Resources

I have been asked many times whether the title of our research group is center, institute, program, department, or school, when in point of fact it long carried the designation "project." But it was awkward to use the term "project" for an ongoing research activity that has been underway for forty years, and, if its predecessor's activities are added, for half a century. On the university's books, the Conservation of Human Resources (CHR) has long been designated as an "ancillary department," which differentiated it from full-blown departments with faculty members, students, curriculum offerings, and degree- recommending powers. CHR is exclusively devoted to research. It has gone afield only in having accepted for a few years some research trainees recommended and paid for by the U.S. Department of Labor, and it has provided a temporary base for some visiting scholars.

In the late summer of 1990, in anticipation of the university's celebration of the centennial of General Eisenhower's birth, President Sovern recommended to the Board of Trustees that the Conservation of Human Resources Project be renamed the Eisenhower Center for the Conservation of Human Resources, an action that they enthusiastically approved. The day before the university's centennial celebration, the U.S. Senate, in a special resolution introduced by Senator Moynihan and cosponsored by senators Dole and D'Amato, commended the Columbia trustees for their action and stated that the Conservation of Human Resources has the "full and enthusiastic support of the U.S. Senate."

As noted earlier, this long-term effort in human resources research began in the late 1930s in response to two quite different stimuli. My mentor, Professor Wesley Clair Mitchell, strongly encouraged me to initiate empirical research into the borderline between economics and psychology, since he recognized that I was thoroughly disenchanted—as he was—with the psychological propositions of classical, neoclassical, and Marxian economics.

At that time, my cousin Sol W. Ginsburg, a psychiatrist-psychoanalyst with an interest in the world of work, offered to donate a significant block of his time without remuneration if we could design a collaborative investigation in an area that could encompass our mutual interests.

The first grant that I received from the Columbia University Council for the Social Sciences in the spring of 1939 turned that potential collaboration into a reality. The key investigation focused on the long-term unemployed in New York City. In addition to the two of us, the initial staff consisted of three experienced psychiatric social workers, one of whom was Sol Ginsburg's wife, Ethel. A second was the wife of a Columbia colleague at whose wedding I had served as best man. But tension soon developed between this member of the staff, who considered herself a full-fledged professional entitled to autonomy, and the other members. My conviction was that as the director of the project I had the responsibility to shape and direct it.

The situation deteriorated rapidly, and, after consulting with Dr. Sol and my dean, I informed the secretary of the council that I had to dismiss the noncooperating staff member. Fortunately, the secretary had the reputation of being a misogynist and he offered no opposition to my intended move. But two months into my first research project I became the center of a campus brouhaha. The discharged worker voiced many complaints against me, and since our social life moved in the same academic circles, many awkward situations arose. I early decided to hold my tongue, to say nothing and explain nothing. The charges leveled against me became increasingly shrill and irrational, and my tactic of total silence eventually paid off. Even those who enjoyed taking me down a peg or two got tired of listening to her recriminations. I came away from the episode with one important lesson learned: If one can get and keep his priorities straight—and in my case it was carrying the project to a successful conclusion—all the troubles along the way would eventually fade into insignificance. And I never had any difficulty knowing where my work stood in my value hierarchy.

The establishment of an interdisciplinary team was one of our early tasks. The selection of a representative sample of unemployed families to include in our study was a second challenge. We focused our inquiry on three religious-ethnic groups: Protestant families; Irish Catholic families; and Jewish families. We sought to discover whether they responded in the same way or differently to the traumatic experience of the long-term unemployment of the male head of household. The answer was that their responses were the same except for special tensions about birth control in Catholic families. A second question was whether there were important differences between families on home relief (welfare) and those where the unemployed man was assigned to WPA or PWA. The answer: WPA or PWA were much better than welfare, since a man was able to work for the money the government gave him. Still another question related to the impact of the man's unemployment on his wife and children. The answer: They were among the major victims. The fourth important question related to the future employability of these long-term unemployed men, many of whom had been without a regular job for five to seven years. Through good fortune, a graduate student in the New York School of Social Work was able to undertake a follow-up study once the job situation had turned around in response to the nation's mobilization. The answer was that all of the unemployed, even those with chronic illnesses, except the severe alcoholics, were back at work by 1942.

The Unemployed, which was published during World War II, never made much of a splash. However, General William C. Menninger, the Chief Psychiatrist of the Army, based his congressional testimony in favor of the Full-Employment Act (1945) on it. One thing is certain: The study went far to focus the long-term interests of CHR on the role of work in contemporary society. And it also confirmed our conviction that interdisciplinary research focused on human subjects promised to add to the pool of knowledge about the relationships between psychology and economics.

The Columbia Council renewed its grant in 1940, and in 1941 we received our first external funding from the Rockefeller Foundation, which we used to initiate an inquiry into the processes of occupational choice, with a specific focus on the career choices of young men who had been drafted and who were scheduled to be released after twelve months of military service. The results were published in an article in the *American Journal of Sociology*: "The Occupational Adjustments of 1,000 Selectees."

We initiated several additional exploratory studies in and around the themes of the nation's potential manpower supply. Before we had made much progress, however, the United States entered the war, and shortly thereafter our research activities were suspended for the duration. In addition to *The Unemployed,* our original Columbia Council grant included support for a study of labor mobility in South Wales, the results of which were published during the war: *Grass on the Slag Heaps: The Story of the Welsh Miners* (republished in 1991 as *World without Work,* with a new foreword); *The Labor Leader*—the third exploratory investigation—was completed and published in 1948.

An amusing sequel to the last: The United States Information Service had the book translated into German for distribution to interested groups, but within a relatively few months it had to withdraw it from circulation because of the leader of the German trade union confederation decided that it showed him in an unfavorable light. In point of fact, the labor leaders we studied were all members of the executive boards of ten leading unions belonging to the American Federation of Labor!

Upon my return to Columbia from my four-year stint in the Pentagon, I reconstituted our research team, but with important changes. The social workers were gone, and in their place I had found John L. Herma, a Viennese student of Charlotte Bühler and later an assistant of Jean Piaget. Herma became a major contributor to our work in the late 1940s, and continued to contribute until his premature death in 1967. Sidney Axelrad, a sociologist with Freudian training, was the fourth member. As a team we set about studying occupational choice systematically in the late 1940s with support from the Columbia Council.

Our modest funding was hard to come by, because Paul Lazarsfeld, a sociologist and a key member of the council, who justifiably considered himself a sophisticated methodologist, sought to persuade us that we should plan a large-scale statistical study. Our decided preferences were for a modest exploratory effort aimed at working our way into what was clearly a complex area. Lazarsfeld, together with his first wife, Maria Yahoda, had collaborated many years earlier on a pioneering investigation of the *Arbeitslosen von Marienthal* (The unemployed of Marienthal). In the early 1930s, Lazarsfeld had mastered both the literature and the methodologies suitable to studying occupational choice, work, and the unemployed. Since he had been over the terrain and had made up his mind about the best way to proceed, he was not an easy man to convince.

Fortunately a compromise was reached: I was to talk with Professor Abraham Wald, the distinguished mathematical statistician, who after hearing me out came down on our side, in favor of a modest exploratory undertaking. And modesty paid off. *Occupational Choice: An Approach to a General Theory*, published in 1951, is generally recognized as the breakthrough publication in providing a theoretical structure for the messy and confused field of vocational guidance that had long been mired in empirical research uninformed by an adequate conceptual framework.

Our key contribution was to recognize that occupational choice is a process stretching over many years; at around the age of eleven individuals first build on their interests and then come to understand, as they mature, that they also have to take account of their capacities and their values, and eventually have to reach a compromise between these personal strengths and preferences and the objective realities that they face, such as the number of years that they can afford, or are willing, to remain in the educational system.

General Eisenhower accepted the presidency of Columbia University in the spring of 1947 and arrived on the campus in the spring of 1948 to assume his office. Since CHR is as much (or more) Eisenhower's creation as it is mine, with a significant assist from Philip Young, the dean of Columbia's Business School who helped in the fund-raising, the story must shift gears and set forth how Eisenhower became involved.

As noted earlier, at the long luncheon that General Snyder had arranged for me to have with General Eisenhower when he was considering the Columbia offer, General Eisenhower elaborated at length on his interest in having the military manpower lessons of World War II assessed in depth and the lessons extracted for management and the nation. He indicated that this interest was an important factor that might lead him to accept the offer from the Columbia Trustees to become president of the university. General Snyder had briefed Eisenhower about my manpower analyses for the War Department, as well as about our earlier research efforts at Columbia, which had focused on human resources. I assured General Eisenhower of our interest in working with him if and when he moved ahead with his proposal to study the manpower lessons of World War II.

A few months after Eisenhower had settled in at Low Library, he called me in for an extended discussion about how best to proceed with his World War II project. By that time, Eisenhower had come to appreciate that the only prospect for launching an ambitious human resources inquiry into World War II would require outside funding. The university's budget was much too tight to provide the necessary support. Accordingly, the general developed the following plan: I was to draft an explanatory letter for his signature, which he would review and modify; I would work with his personal staff assistant, Kevan McCann, to develop a list of about fifty of the nation's leaders to whom the proposal would be sent for comment and criticism; and in his letter Eisenhower would inform the corporate, philanthropic, and other leaders that if their replies were affirmative, he would be back to them to request funding for an initial five-year period.

Contrary to popular belief, Eisenhower was a good stylist, and I have in my files his many emendations and corrections to my successive drafts. While most of the individuals on the list were corporate CEOs, Cardinal Spellman and a few other figures of national prominence were also included. Eisenhower noticed that the tentative list of recipients failed to include any labor leaders, and I quickly added four or five, including Walter Reuther. It was Reuther's objection to the use of the term "adjustment to work," which was the project's original title, that led to my finding a new name. Reuther had pointed out that the word "adjustment" had a manipulative connotation when applied to human beings and recommended that we find a better title.

At the time, I was reading a book about Theodore Roosevelt and discovered that while he was a great advocate of conserving the nation's natural resources, his original formulation encompassed both human and natural resources. Accordingly I suggested to Eisenhower that we use Roosevelt's term, the Conservation of Human Resources, which he accepted.

When the replies came in, they were bucked to me from the president's office for tabulation and analysis. A reasonable number were highly complimentary and offered financial support without waiting to be asked; the majority were cautiously positive, leaving the matter of later sponsorship open; only a few were negative; and perhaps five of the fifty respondents failed to reply. I reviewed my analysis with General Snyder, who spent each working week at 60 Morningside Drive, the president's residence, as well as with Dean Young. We decided that the responses were sufficiently positive to proceed with the effort. We had a meeting with Eisenhower, where this decision was confirmed.

Over the succeeding months, the list of sponsors took shape: Coca Cola, Dupont, General Electric, General Foods, Cities Service, Cluett Peabody, Standard Oil of New Jersey.

At about this time, the Ford Foundation was speeding up its grant-disbursing activities and gave a number of large universities a check of $100,000 each, to be distributed by the president for social science research. Eisenhower gave half of the Ford check to the recently constituted CHR project, to the chagrin of the foundation's staff, who felt that he had misunderstood the terms of the grant and who quickly sent the university a second check of equal amount so that the university could be more responsive to the foundation's nebulous objectives.

That was only the first of several sources of tension between the Ford Foundation and Columbia University in which CHR was directly or peripherally involved. Rowan Gaither, who had undertaken the key planning exercise that predated the foundation's accelerating its disbursements at the beginning of the 1950s, had talked with Philip Young about possible projects at Columbia, and they had reached a tentative understanding that CHR would be a large-scale recipient of Ford funding. But before this decision was implemented, the Ford Foundation decided that it was more interested in supporting studies in manpower policy than in basic research in human resources; they asked the university whether it would sponsor and direct a National Manpower Council, with a distinguished national membership, that would study priority manpower problems and report to the public on how they could best be resolved.

I was disappointed with this shift in the foundation's focus, but agreed with Dean Young that we should move ahead with the formation of the council, and I agreed to direct it alongside our expanding CHR project. But I attached one condition: I needed more support from Henry David, a labor historian who was working part-time with CHR. It was agreed that he would be offered a tenured position in the School of Business, which would enable him to reduce the heavy teaching load that he had been carrying at Queens College.

The council's leadership and membership were both strong: James D. Zellerbach was the first chairman and served for several years until his appointment as ambassador to Italy; he was succeeded by Erwin Canham, the editor of the *Christian Science Monitor*. From the outset, the ten members always included a woman, labor leaders sat alongside the

CEOs of some of the nation's largest companies, and there was strong representation from academe.

I directed the council during its first studies (1951–1955) on Universal Military Training, Scientific and Professional Manpower, and Skilled Manpower and Womanpower, and at that point Henry David took over as director, an appropriate shift in view of the outstanding work that he had performed in molding the council into an effective deliberative body by visiting sequentially with each of the members and refining each member's positions, working toward a council consensus before the infrequently scheduled meetings.

But this unique mode of operating the council, which was highly pleasing to the members and which contributed to the council's high productivity—four major policy reports in four years—did not protect the council or its staff from the Ford Foundation staff's negative evaluation. This was precipitated largely by complaints from the engineering societies that the council had failed to understand the importance of expanding the nation's supply of scientific and engineering manpower. It looked for a time as if the foundation might abruptly end its support of the council, but that was before Chairman Zellerbach talked to Henry Ford II. This conversation put an end to criticism from the foundation's staff, and shortly thereafter it led to the relocation of one of the foundation's vice-presidents. The lesson that I carried away from this episode is that foundation bureaucrats should avoid conflicts with the personal friends of the foundation's most powerful trustee, especially if they lack a watertight case.

A related lesson: The Ford Foundation had selected a former member of the CIA to undertake the interim assessment of the council's work. In my opinion, he was much more impressed with the complaints from the professional societies' staffs, who were beating the drums for an expansion of the engineering supply, than he was with the counterarguments that David and I, two academicians, offered in defense of the council's position. In later years I got to know our former appraiser quite well, and found that he held reasonable views on most subjects. But in the case at hand, I am afraid that his judgment was warped by the fact that he considered the engineering groups to be sound and practical, while he felt that the council was too far out in uncharted territory.

Since Dean Young was strongly supportive of both CHR and the National Manpower Council—and with General Eisenhower directly involved in both—the fitting of these new organizations into the university's structure proceeded smoothly, almost without notice. At one point I was about to recommend to Eisenhower that he appoint a five-person advisory group to oversee CHR, but at the last moment I scrapped the plan, realizing that even if I packed the group with leading professors with whom I was close friends, a board at some point down the road was likely to cause me trouble that I didn't need.

But trouble came nonetheless, from two sources: from Courtney C. Brown, who succeeded Young as dean of the Business School, and from Grayson Kirk, who succeeded Eisenhower.

When Brown approached various large corporations for contributions to the School of Business, they informed him that they were already providing such support via their annual contributions to CHR. Since their average gift to CHR amounted to $5,000, the dean had no reason to give much weight to their replies except that they reinforced his opposition to having two independent operations, over which he had no direct control, located in his school. Moreover there was bad blood between Brown and David because the latter had not masked his critical views of the dean's policies.

Fortunately John A. Krout, the provost of the university, decided to intervene and assumed administrative responsibility for both projects. Brown became the sole master of his domain. On the rare occasions when the university had to report to the Ford Foundation or request a new allocation for the council, Kirk demonstrated minimal interest and enthusiasm. His preference would have been to cut the council loose, but uncertainty about the foundation's interpretation of such an initiative held him back.

Because of Eisenhower's unique role in establishing CHR and my deep roots at Columbia I never considered, and certainly did not explore, the possibility of setting CHR up as a nonprofit entity outside of the university. The early staffing pattern of CHR also militated against such a move. In the 1950s and the 1960s I added to the CHR staff a growing number of my Business School colleagues, particularly Dale Hiestand, Ivar Berg, James Kuhn, Boris Yavitz, David Lewin, and Raymond Horton. The university rules permitted me to work out an arrangement whereby I could supplement their basic professorial salaries, in the amount of 50 to 55 percent per annum, for one day's research a week during their teaching terms and two months full-time research in their nonteaching terms.

A second source of staff members, mostly on less than a full-time basis, were members of the instructional staff of academic institutions located in the New York region, particularly New York University, and in one or another of the CUNY institutions. Among the most important long-term staff associates were Thomas Stanback, Jr., Matthew Drennan, Harry Greenfield, Stanley Friedlander.

Women predominated among the full-time members of the staff. I had early discovered that the pool of able, well-trained married women interested in joining a research group far exceeded the pool of qualified men, since many women were returning to the labor force after having raised their families and were not competing for tenured teaching positions. Moreover, I was able to trade flexibility in work time for higher salaries. All the women were married to professionals, and when the opportunity offered they wanted to be able to travel with their husbands. Three key women members of the staff, for more than two decades, were Beatrice Reubens, Marcia Freedman, and Alice Yohalem. Two have continued for an even longer period and are still active today: Miriam Ostow and Anna Dutka.

Among the men who had extended full-time staff appointments were James K. Anderson, Douglas Bray, Alfred Eichner, Charles Brecher, Richard Knight, Dean Morse, and Michael Millman. And in the last decade Thierry Noyelle (deputy director) and Thomas Bailey have joined us. Respectively, they head two of our three research programs—technology and the changing global economy, and labor markets and employment. Miriam Ostow has responsibility for the third area of health policy.

In 1979 the Conservation Project published its *Fortieth Anniversary Report*, which used 1939 as the starting date for our investigations into human resources although the renaming of the project occurred a decade later. In 1979 we were at or close to our all-time high in the number of senior and total staff. The anniversary report lists eleven senior research associates, ten research associates, eleven researchers, and eight research assistants, or a total of forty, with another six persons in administrative and support services.

Long before 1979 I had reconciled myself to the fact that it was not necessary or even desirable that I be directly involved in all of the research that was being carried on in CHR, since my senior colleagues had demonstrated that they were able to take charge of their own work, both in planning and execution. I saw my responsibility, at that late date, as one of making sure that the Conservation Project continued to have a sharp focus on the new opportunities for significant research in human resources and manpower, and to assist staff members who sought my counsel. I took care, however, not to let the staff continue to expand, and if the truth be told, I was not fully aware that we had approached a total of fifty until I counted up the names in our anniversary brochure.

I started CHR because I recognized that I could not pursue interdisciplinary research in human resources without the active collaboration of specialists from disciplines other than economics. Further, my primary interest was to be a productive researcher and not a research director. Therefore in the early years—that is, for the first quarter-century—I was the principal though not the sole author of almost all of the books that we published. It was only in the second quarter-century that other members of the senior staff began to dominate the publication list.

The best proof that the term "interdisciplinary" was accurate is revealed by the discipline designations printed next to the staff names in the fortieth anniversary report: economics, political science, education, business administration, psychology, sociology, law, urban affairs, industrial administration, medicine, mathematics, labor economics, city and regional planning, international affairs, computer science, history, anthropology, statistics. While economists and political scientists dominated, accounting for more than half of the forty professionals, an additional sixteen disciplines were represented on the CHR staff.

The ability to attract and retain staff depends on the research group's ability to attract funding. Fortunately, in our multisectored society and economy the sources of such funding are many and varied. We have noted in passing that CHR was started with two grants from the Columbia Council for Research in the Social Sciences and that it received support in 1941 and 1942 from the Rockefeller Foundation; immediately after World War II it obtained another modest multiyear grant from the Columbia Council.

Eisenhower had decided in 1949–50 to seek initial corporate support for the Conservation Project for a period of five years. But very early on the financing of the Conservation Project almost took a radically different turn. General Eisenhower had set up an appointment for me to talk with Secretary of Defense James V. Forrestal about our research plans and the type of help that we would need, particularly in gaining access to the military records of World War II.

My meeting with the secretary proceeded on two planes. Much of the secretary's energies and much of my attention were focused on his continually tightening his belt (which reached a point that must have been exceedingly painful for him), an aberrant behavior that was inexplicable until the news came of his suicide a fortnight or so later. Despite this erratic belt-tightening activity, Forrestal waxed enthusiastic about our research plans, so much so that he inquired whether we wanted the Department of Defense (DOD) to provide the funding. I thanked him for his offer and said I would relay it to General Eisenhower. But I emphasized that in any event we needed the wholehearted cooperation of DOD in gaining access to and using the records, and he assured me that such cooperation would be forthcoming.

Before I reviewed Forrestal's offer of financial assistance with General Eisenhower, I gave the matter considerable thought. It would save lots of time and effort for Dean Young and me if the Defense Department provided the financing. But I concluded that the risks were not worth it. I feared that the Pentagon might object to some or even many of our findings, and DOD might interfere with the eventual publication of our findings and recommendations. Furthermore, I thought it was unwise for General Eisenhower to accept money from DOD for a Columbia project in which he had a strong personal interest. It might result in unfavorable criticism down the road, and I wanted no part, however small, of embarrassing him. Eisenhower was convinced by my arguments and thanked Forrestal for his offer of financial assistance but added that the university would handle the funding.

The corporate support that Eisenhower elicited carried on beyond the initial five-year period that he had requested. In fact the principal publication of the military manpower studies did not appear until 1959, a good eight years after the inquiry had been initiated. But as the decade drew to a close most of the sponsors felt that they had done their part and wanted out. The next few years represented a major threat to the continuing viability of CHR, for without new money the staff would be forced to seek alternative employment. Fortunately the Carnegie Corporation, among others, came to the rescue. John Gardner, the president of Carnegie, took the initiative by telephoning and inviting me downtown to talk to him about my current and future research interests. I asked for and received a respectable grant of over $100,000 for a study of talent and performance.

The study dealt exclusively with career patterns of talented men. We found that since an identification of talent was determined by the field in which the men had sought and received fellowship support at graduate-school level, it was not surprising that many pursued what we designated as a "straight pattern." They remained in the same discipline that they had chosen for graduate study. Another large group had used their graduate-study base as a point of departure but demonstrated a "broad pattern," moving from narrow disciplinary areas to fields of endeavor that, while related to their subject matter, often led them into management, government, or entrepreneurship. The third group we designated as having a "variable pattern" because there was little in their later careers that could be related to their graduate studies or even to earlier positions that had they held, often with distinction.

When the study of talented men was completed, we sought additional funding from Carnegie for a parallel study of talented women but we were not successful, in part because there had been a change in the foundation staff, in part because the outside consultant who reviewed our manuscript had damned it with faint praise. Fortunately, the Rockefeller Brothers Fund came to the rescue. These two foundation grants helped to keep us alive and afloat during the late 1950s and early 1960s. By 1963 the federal financing of manpower research was initiated as a result of new authority embedded in the Manpower Development and Training Act of 1962, which authorized the Department of Labor to fund external research.

My original request to the department was for annual funding of about $55,000, but the request sat on the desk of one of the senior Manpower Administration officials, Seymour Wolfbein. I later learned that his principal adviser on research grants, Howard Rosen, had raised a number of questions about our work, but Wolfbein decided to act even while these questions awaited an answer. For the remainder of the 1960s, all of the 1970s, and into the early 1980s, the Department of Labor was the single largest funder of CHR, with a peak annual contribution of more than $400,000.

Rosen early learned that we delivered, on time, what we promised; that we were willing to take on an occasional extra project for which the department was looking for a sponsor; and that we were interested and

concerned with policy issues, not with methodology. As a consequence
he dealt with CHR in an exemplary fashion. Once a year a senior member
of his staff, Joseph Epstein, would spend a day at Columbia being briefed
about the projects that were nearing completion and about our plans for
the coming year. He carried back to Washington a detailed understanding
about the status of our current research and our future plans. The budget
that we had negotiated during his visit became the basis for next year's
funding. One day's focused discussion about several hundred thousand
dollars of annual governmental funding was surely a record of administrative efficiency.

But in the mid-1970s, this splendid arrangement almost came apart.
Under a reorganization of the Department of Labor, the Office of the
Assistant Secretary for Research and Evaluation gained the right to sign
off on grants approved by the Manpower Administration (under a different assistant secretary). The young Turks in the former office decided
that CHR had been supported long enough and, moreover, that Columbia
was not at the cutting edge of research since we were not making much,
if any, use of econometric analysis. The conflict landed on the desk of
Secretary John T. Dunlop. His decision was quickly forthcoming. Our
budgetary request would be cut by 10 percent, a decision that caused us
only minor inconvenience but that satisfied each of his feuding bureaucratic factions. My long-time admiration for Dunlop's good sense and
good judgment, as well as for his great skills as a negotiator, were further
enhanced by this decision.

The *Fortieth Anniversary Report* noted that the current budget of CHR
was in the $1.5 million range, and that our support was quite diversified.
In addition to sizable funding from the U.S. Department of Labor, we
also had grants or contracts from the Department of Commerce, HUD,
and HEW, as well as from the Port Authority of New York and New Jersey
and the City of New York (Human Resources Administration). In addition, we acknowledged funding from eleven foundations, among which
several provided substantial amounts of support: the General Electric
Foundation, the Ford Foundation, Robert Wood Johnson Foundation,
Charles H. Revson Foundation, Rockefeller Brothers Fund, and the
Rockefeller Foundation.

The election of Ronald Reagan in 1980 cast a shadow on all employment and training programs as well as on future funding for social science
research, including research in human resources and manpower. While

Congress did not go all the way to meet the president's preferences, which were to end all federal involvement in employment and training programs, it cut the budgetary appropriations of the Department of Labor for employment and training by about two-thirds. As a consequence, after eighteen years of substantial support, CHR found itself without ongoing funding from the Department of Labor.

Fortunately this untoward development coincided with the approaching retirement of several members of the senior CHR staff. The sizeable reduction in funding accelerated the resignations, and CHR was able to develop a new equilibrium at a much-reduced level, about one-half of its former expenditure level. This new equilibrium was achieved in part because of new and expanded financial support from several health foundations, in part because the two new program directors, Thierry Noyelle and Thomas Bailey, succeeded in opening up new sources of support, including funds from the OECD (Organization for Economic Co-operation and Development) and from the U.S. Department of Education, via research consortia including Rand, the University of California at Berkeley, and Teachers College at Columbia, with which we had developed effective ties. Later, CHR was also able to reestablish funding linkages with the U.S. Department of Labor, though at a level far below that of former days.

In 1988, I came to appreciate more clearly that CHR was at a crossroad. I had to decide between assisting in its reconstruction and renewed growth or planning to shut it down. It could no longer operate effectively at a suboptimal level, with only five senior researchers. My first move was to appoint Thierry Noyelle as associate director, and the second was to initiate staff discussions aimed at transforming CHR from a benign dictatorship, in which for decades I had exercised sole responsibility and raised all the required funding, into the early stages of a partnership in which the senior members would have to share power and responsibility.

The timing of this reorganization and the fiftieth anniversary of the start of our research in human resources, and the fortieth anniversary of the Conservation Project, made 1990 an appropriate time for restructuring and refinancing, including the search for longer-term support to supplement primary reliance on short- and medium-term research grants. This effort will not be easy, but we are reasonably optimistic that we will succeed.

The fortieth/fiftieth anniversaries of our research effort at CHR provide a basis for some retrospective evaluations of the strengths and weaknesses of carrying out interdisciplinary research into human resources, at least in the environment that dominated the United States in the decades after World War II.

Academe is not a friendly environment within which to pursue interdisciplinary research, since academic advancement and rewards are so heavily discipline-based. But the availability of large-scale federal financing after World War II for all types of research, including research in the social sciences, created enlarged opportunities even for interdisciplinary work to obtain funding, and for two decades, the 1960s and the 1970s, CHR was able to expand and prosper in what turned out to be a highly supportive environment, in which the federal government was the key provider of funds.

Further, additional nongovernmental sources of funding were available and could be tapped. A number of large new foundations were established with strong interests in contemporary social and health policy, in particular the Ford and Robert Wood Johnson foundations; and several of the long-established foundations, such as Rockefeller and Carnegie, continued to fund individuals and programs in the social science arena.

Note must also be taken of a new (post-World War II) source of support from corporate foundations or from corporations directly, many of which made occasional grants for social science research. And other sources of new funding included state and local governments and international bodies, which came to appreciate that their policy initiatives could be more effective if they increased their understanding of the problem areas that they sought to affect.

This emphasis on the sources of potential support for social science research is not misplaced. I have not sought to reconstruct with any degree of care the total grants and contract funds, primarily the former, that CHR received over the past half-century, but rough calculations suggest that without any adjustment for inflation (simply adding up the annual grants received in the successive decades), the total would approximate and possibly exceed $30 million. During this extended time period, CHR has published more than 250 books, monographs, and reports.

At today's prices, a modest project—consisting of one senior researcher, one associate, and support staff, including fringe benefits, travel and other costs, and modest university overhead—requires a budget of about $150,000 to $175,000 a year.

The greatest assets of CHR without question were the initial support that I received from Professor Mitchell; the active participation of General Eisenhower in expanding the scale and scope of our research goals; the excellent administrative support from Dean Young of the School of Business; the major cooperation of the Department of Defense, the Veterans Administration, and the Selective Service System in providing access to the records of men in World War II; the long-time financial support from the U.S. Department of Labor under Dr. Howard Rosen; significant foundation and corporate support; and the degrees of freedom that Columbia University allowed me to chart CHR's course over the successive decades without interference, subject only to our conforming to the university's basic financial systems over which the Office of Project and Grants has jurisdiction.

In the final analysis, all of the above relate to the preconditions for a successful, long-term research effort. The success of the effort depends first and foremost on the quality of the researchers as reflected in their ability to identify significant intellectually stimulating and policy-relevant issues and to research them so that at the end of their investigations they are able to add to the extant pool of knowledge and point out new directions for public policy. The extent to which the CHR staff were able to meet these crucial challenges is set out in the following chapter.

5

The Changing Human Resources Agenda

I cannot easily review a research program that has stretched over five decades and involved about fifty senior researchers, and whose work has led to the publication of over 250 books, monographs, and reports. As noted earlier, in the early days of the Conservation Project the researchers worked on projects that were largely of my design, and in which I had primary responsibility for determining the approaches and assumed most or all of the responsibility for writing up the results. But it was not long before I moved to a more equal sharing of the burden, often with a single collaborator. And later on, I further reduced my role by limiting myself to providing advice at the outset and at the end of the researcher's work. In recent decades, my senior colleagues have carried through many projects from beginning to end with only encouragement and advice from me.

The best way to provide an overview of our long-term research program is to emphasize that it has been shaped by two discrete sets of forces, one intellectual, the other a responsiveness to changing conditions in the labor market. These interacting forces were already involved in our initial efforts, which were concerned with studying the problems of the long-term unemployed in South Wales and New York City. Intellectually, we wanted to learn more than was then known about the effects of long-term unemployment on a man, his wife, and their children, and in South Wales, on such key institutions as the trade union, the chapel, and the coal-mining community.

It was no accident that we picked the long-term unemployed as our first foray into research in "economics and group behavior." Unemployment was the great scourge of the 1930s. It prepared the way for Hitler. It buffeted the United States to a point where many basic institutions had to be radically changed to prevent the country from falling into chaos. It extracted a high toll in human misery.

The following were among the important findings that emerged from our research. Personal failure had little or nothing to do with the explosive growth of the long-term unemployed; when the demand for labor strengthened in World War II, most of the unemployed succeeded in getting back to work; while the worker's life was undermined by loss of a job, his unemployment also had negative impacts on his wife and children. In the short term, the dole required fewer tax dollars than work relief, but over the long term it was more destructive of human skills and morale. It made little sense to provide skill training for the unemployed unless there were jobs for them at the end of their training. Government-sponsored emigration schemes to move young people from depressed areas into metropolitan areas, such as from South Wales to London, where they could be placed into jobs, were a positive intervention but often led to adverse reactions.

My associates and I were so impressed with the centrality of work in the life of adult men that at the end of World War II, when we restructured our interdisciplinary research team, we selected "occupational choice" as the preferred entry into the study of the larger phenomenon of "work." With regard to policy, we recognized that because of the absence of a conceptual framework, the field of occupational and career guidance was floundering. Most practitioners spent their time testing people to learn about their aptitudes and interests, and then they offered advice to their clients that was seldom useful and was often counterproductive.

Our 1951 book *Occupational Choice: An Approach to a General Theory* turned out to be one of our most successful undertakings. It provided the first tentative "general theory" about the process of occupational choice. Two decades later, we returned to the theme, but at that time we focused on the key institutions that have an impact on the choice process and we analyzed how improved early interventions could result in better career outcomes. This later study was published under the title *Career Guidance: Who Needs It, Who Provides It, Who Can Improve It* (1971).

As noted in the last chapter, we directed most of our efforts during the 1950s to studies aimed at extracting the principal lessons from the manpower experience of World War II. Access to the records of the Selective Service System, the armed forces, and the Veterans Administration afforded us the opportunity to construct a unique data base of over seventy thousand soldiers to study the interactions among individuals' strengths and weaknesses, the army's policies and procedures that affected the utilization of its personnel, and societal needs and values that affected the performance of soldiers under stress. Our major findings were published in 1959 in a three-volume work entitled *The Ineffective Soldier: Lessons for Management and the Nation:* volume 1, *The Lost Divisions*; volume 2, *Breakdown and Recovery*; volume 3, *Patterns of Performance*.

A few highlights: There were about 2.5 million rejections and premature separations from the armed services based on criteria of ineffectiveness. (At the peak, there were over twelve million men on active duty.) The principal reasons for rejection and premature separations were illiteracy, psychoneurosis, and behavioral problems. Psychiatrists went far beyond their knowledge base and recommended rejection of certain selectees or approved premature separations, often to accommodate the strong preferences of the military, who believed that if they could add "better" recruits they would be able to increase the quality of their fighting forces. But our data revealed that if men were kept at the front for excessive periods of time, even the strongest among them would break down. The armed forces' personnel policies fluctuated widely, sometimes pushing capable servicemen out, at other periods retaining even the totally unfit. Although a person's adjustment prior to service provided a clue to his (future) performance in the military, many recruits did better or worse than their earlier records suggested. Much the same was true when one looked at the performance of veterans after they returned to civilian life compared with their earlier service in the military. Some did better; some performed at about the same level; some performed worse.

We carried through our analysis by looking at the interactions among the individual, the organization (the armed services' personnel policies and procedures), and the value system of the larger society. We concluded that, from a policy perspective, a society should adopt and follow criteria for effective performance—a man's ability to hold a job, stay out of trouble with the criminal justice system, marry and support his dependents, and, in the event of mobilization, respond to the call to military service.

We ended this major effort with a chapter entitled "The Management of Men," which extracted the most important lessons relevant to large corporate enterprises as they experimented with designing more up-to-date and sophisticated human resources policies. The study also addressed the ways in which government could help strengthen the nation's human resources, particularly by improving the educational system and in providing second-choice opportunities for young people who initially encountered difficulties in finding a place for themselves in the world of work.

In addition to *The Ineffective Soldier*, the Eisenhower studies also included a detailed analysis of *The Uneducated*, both in and outside of the military, which called attention to the serious shortcomings of the nation's public educational system in the low-income states in the South, particularly among minorities, primarily blacks. This study also called attention to major policy problems that the nation's leaders have been slow to recognize: advancing technology, both in agriculture and in industry, threatened the future employability prospects of persons with limited literacy, an issue that is once again, in the 1990s, very much at the forefront of current national concern.

A related by-product of the military manpower experience of World War II was our pioneering volume on *The Negro Potential*, which organized and analyzed important new data about the performance of black men in both the military and civilian spheres. The analysis not only highlighted the substantial costs to black men and to the black community from the persistence of segregation and discrimination in all sectors of American life, particularly in education and the labor market, but it also pointed up the costs that such actions inflict on the larger society. Moreover, the volume noted that with discrimination beginning to ease in the world of work, blacks urgently needed access to more and better educational preparation if they were to take advantage of the broadened employment opportunities.

In the 1950s, the research group also opened up a second line of investigation focused on those on the top rungs of the occupational ladder. This effort is reflected by the titles of our two monographs— *What Makes an Executive?* and *Effecting Change in Large Organizations.* While we recognized the importance of continuing to focus a great deal of our efforts on persons at the lower end of the human resources pool, on those who were encountering special difficulties in obtaining jobs and performing effectively at work, we recognized early on that any comprehensive approach to the study of human resources required that we also pay attention to those at the top of the job hierarchy, with special attention to the development and utilization of talent.

In the decade of the 1960s, CHR's staff grew, as did the breadth and depth of its inquiries. Once again, the focus that propelled us was in part intellectual, based on what we had learned from our earlier investigations, and was in part our response to the changing national policy agenda.

The Golden Anniversary of the White House Conference on Children and Youth (1960) was the precipitating event that led me, in my role as director of studies, to edit a three-volume work on *The Nation's Children* (volume 1, *The Family and Social Change*; volume 2, *Development and Education*; and volume 3, *Problems and Prospects*) which served as the basic preparatory documents for the more than four thousand conference participants.

In the 1960s CHR's staff also responded to other external forces and events, as suggested by the following titles: *Scientific and Managerial Manpower in Nuclear Industry* (James W. Kuhn); *Manpower and the Growth of Producer Services* (Harry I. Greenfield); *Electronic Data Processing in New York City: Lessons for Metropolitan Economics* (Boris Yavitz and Thomas M. Stanback, Jr.). With the advantage of hindsight, we can recognize that in the 1960s the Conservation Project took the initial steps of looking at the nation's manpower problems from the vantagepoint of the growth of the service sector as well as from a metropolitan-urban perspective. These two directions informed much of our work in the following two decades.

In the mid-1960s, in collaboration with my colleagues Dale L. Hiestand and Beatrice G. Reubens, I published *The Pluralistic Economy*, which challenged the conventional two-sector model of the U.S. economy—the private, for-profit sector and government—by introducing a third sector, the non-profit sector, which, according to our calculations, accounted for a significant proportion of the GNP and total employment. We calculated that the not-for-profit sector, government plus nonprofit together, accounted for at least one-third of all jobs, and possibly as much as two-fifths. Even a quarter-century later, American economists remain standoffish if not antagonistic to this revisionist view.

During the decade of the 1960s, the staff continued to be involved with the preparation for employment and the employment of vulnerable groups, particularly members of the black minority. *The Negro Challenge to the Business Community, The Middle Class Negro in the White Man's World, The Peripheral Worker,* and still other investigations speak to this continuing concern. In association with Alfred S. Eichner, I wrote *The Troublesome Presence: American Democracy and the Negro,* a historical-political analysis that sought out the roots for the special treatment, or, more correctly mistreatment, of blacks in the American saga. I was looking to find out why the United States, which had successfully absorbed all sorts of immigrants, could not accept blacks.

How little even educated Americans know about the history and fate of the black minority is reflected in my continuing offer to pay anyone who could identify the origin and meaning of the phrase "the troublesome presence." My challenge, repeated hundreds of times since the book was first published in 1964, was never met, not even after I offered the clue that the words were used by Abraham Lincoln on the memorable occasion when he eulogized Henry Clay, the great compromiser and advocate of the repatriation of blacks to Africa. Lincoln stressed that it was the "troublesome presence" of the "free Negro" that led Clay to advocate emigration to Africa.

To underscore this crucial insight of the depth of white antagonism to living in a biracial society with free blacks: from George Washington to William Howard Taft, who was president when I was born in 1911, almost every president, including, it should be emphasized, Abraham Lincoln, proposed the large-scale out-migration of free blacks to Africa.

In 1966 the Conservation staff published a two-volume study of *Life Styles of Educated Women* and *Educated American Women.* This study traced the lives of several hundred women graduate students at Columbia University who had won scholarships or fellowships in the immediate post-World War II period. The findings demonstrated that many prevailing assumptions and presumptions about women and the world of work had been overtaken by events, but the study also emphasized that once a woman had more than one child she was likely to encounter severe difficulties in pursuing her career, even if her husband was supportive and cooperative. Many unsolved problems facing women who are trying to balance career goals and family obligations in the 1990s were first highlighted in this breakthrough study. When the *New York Times* asked me to summarize the first book's message, I replied that American industry operates on the principle that it prefers dumb men to smart women.

The decade of the 1970s saw the further expansion of the Conservation Project in terms of both collaborators and the range of their research investigations. Beatrice Reubens published the first of her significant cross-national studies in 1970 in *The Hard-To-Employ: European Programs*, which she followed up with several more: *Bridges to Work*, *Preparation for Work*, and *The Youth Labor Market*. Her comparative studies noted that European efforts directed to assisting special groups experiencing difficulties negotiating their respective labor markets had to be assessed in terms of the distinctive characteristics of each nation. Moreover, there was much that the United States could learn and borrow from these diverse experiences.

Thomas Stanback, Jr., and Richard Knight undertook a series of investigations into urban, suburban, and metropolitan economies, with particular attention to the role that the expanding service sector was playing in altering, generally for the better, these several labor markets. Dale Hiestand published a study, *Changing Careers after 35*, which was CHR's first effort to explore the problems of mature and older workers.

Many of CHR's studies in the 1970s had a distinct institutional orientation. Several addressed the structures and operations of the labor market both at a conceptual level and in terms of parallels and differences among discrete metropolitan labor markets. Together with my colleagues, Schnee, Kuhn, and Yavitz, I wrote a volume on *The Economic Impact of Large Public Programs: The NASA Story*. This joint effort resulted from an ongoing seminar that we held with Dr. George Low, the deputy director of NASA, who had sought our collaboration. Hiestand looked at *High-Level Manpower and Technological Change: The Steel Industry*, which provided telling evidence of severe trouble in U.S. manufacturing, evidence that at the time was hard to evaluate because of the continuing strength of our economy. Ostow and Dutka investigated *Work and Welfare in New York City*, in which they identified the importance of singling out young mothers as a priority group for broad-scale remedial educational and employment assistance.

The staff also produced a series of books and monographs that explored new linkages among local economic development, public sector programs, and employment, such as Charles Brecher's work on *Where Have All the Dollars Gone? Public Expenditures for Human Resources Development in New York City*, and the major CHR collaborative study on *New York Is Very Much Alive: A Manpower View*.

In the mid-1970s, Marcia Freedman and Gretchen Maclachlan completed an important study that broke new ground in conceptualizing the ways in which labor markets operate—*Labor Markets: Segments and Shelters*. And I sought, in *The Human Economy*, to pull together into a systematic account the work that we had been carrying on for more than a third of a century. The reach of this latter effort is considerable, since I dealt with both developed and developing nations and offered a new model for the systematic study of human resources based on four interacting sets of institutions: societal values, government institutions, the economy, and the complex of manpower institutions.

We also continued our long-term interests in the more vulnerable members of the labor force, with studies of *Unemployment in the Urban Core: An Analysis of Thirty Cities with Policy Recommendations*; *Upgrading Blue Collar and Service Workers*; and *Pride against Prejudice: Labor Market Experiences of Young Puerto Ricans and Older Blacks*.

In reviewing the record it is clear that the Conservation Project was at the peak of its research productivity in the 1970s—thirty principal authors published forty-four books, or the equivalent of more than one new book every three months throughout the decade.

As noted in the last chapter, the substantial reduction in federal financing for externally supported research by the Department of Labor and other federal agencies after the election of Ronald Reagan resulted in a substantial reduction in the scale and scope of the Conservation Project's research staff and research agenda. Nevertheless during the 1980s there were some important new departures and new emphases for CHR: additional or new research into the service economy, retirement, technology, computerization, the transformation of cities, globalization, immigration, and comparative metropolitan analysis.

To be more specific: In 1980 Dean Morse and Susan Grey published *Early Retirement: Boon or Bane?* based on the detailed analysis of a questionnaire survey of middle managers and technical personnel who had taken, or had been encouraged to take, early retirement. In contrast to the conventional wisdom, the authors did not find widespread or deep discontent among these early retirees. For the most part, they had sufficient income and other assets with which to pursue a life-style that on balance proved satisfactory to them.

In 1981 Stanback, together with his colleagues Peter Bearse, Thierry Noyelle, and Robert Karasek, returned to the theme of the expanding role of services, and in *Services/The New Economy* sought to inform the reader of the magnitude and implications of the transformations that the growth of services were bringing about, both as a source of jobs and a source of income.

In the following year, 1982, Stanback and Noyelle in their *Cities in Transition* looked at the changing job structures in Atlanta, Buffalo, Denver, Phoenix, Columbus, Nashville, and Charlotte to concretize some of the broader generalizations that had been formulated in earlier CHR studies of urban transformations.

Morse, Dutka, and Grey returned to the retirement theme in their book *Life after Early Retirement: The Experience of Lower Level Workers*. As the book's title suggests, this inquiry was centered around blue-collar, clerical, and service workers, who, when they found themselves confronting retirement, had less personal and financial resources than the group of middle managers studied earlier. But once again, the results pointed to a reasonable level of adjustment for most, if not for all, of the members in this second group. If they, or their spouses, were not afflicted with serious illness or disability, they were able to make do with their savings plus Social Security, and many of those who wanted to continue working were able to do so.

In 1984, Noyelle and Stanback returned once again to the earlier theme of *The Economic Transformation of American Cities*, but with a more ambitious approach. They developed a typology that enabled them to group the more than two hundred largest American cities according to their distinctive characteristics, from the largest nodal centers, such as New York, Chicago, and Los Angeles, to highly specialized population centers, such as cities whose economic base was closely tied to government employment, education, or recreation.

Starting in 1980 and continuing throughout the decade, Charles Brecher and Raymond Horton published annually or biannually *Setting Municipal Priorities*, in which they examined the changing fiscal position of New York City and explored selected implications of its changing financial future on the development of the city's human resources and employment profile.

In 1985, Matthew Drennan, who had been working in close association with Brecher and Horton, published *Modeling Metropolitan Economies for Forecasting and Policy Analysis*, in which he presented the details of his econometric model for calculating the short- and middle-term trends, including the trends in employment, that were likely to shape a city's future.

In 1986, *Technology and Employment: Concepts and Clarifications* appeared under the joint authorship of Noyelle, Stanback, and me. We reconceptualized the relationships between technology and employment that differed from the conventional wisdom. In particular, we challenged the widespread belief that the new technology deskilled work, arguing that this occurred neither in the factory nor in the office. We argued instead that the new technology often resulted in the enhancement of an individual's scope of work.

In the following year, both Noyelle and Stanback published the results of larger research investigations that carried the analysis deeper and further. Noyelle's book carried the title *Beyond Industrial Dualism: Market and Job Segmentation in the New Economy*; and Stanback's was called *Computerization and the Transformation of Employment: Government, Hospitals and Universities.*

Noyelle concluded, from his case studies of a major retailer, a communications company, and an insurer, that the new technology was pervasively influencing all aspects of these companies' labor forces. He traced how the new technology was altering the ways in which work was organized, performed, and supervised. Next he analyzed the impact of these changes on the type of employees hired, how they were trained, and how workers were promoted and rewarded. In Noyelle's view, the internal labor market, so long characteristic of large companies, was rapidly disappearing.

Stanback's study of computerization concluded on a more moderate note. His field and data analyses led him to see computerization as less revolutionary, in part because the costs and complications of introducing new technology in the not-for-profit sector slowed the challenges that the workforce had to face; moreover he noted that the new skills that workers had to master were not so difficult to acquire. But Stanback noted that even in the not-for-profit sector, the progress of the new technology was impressive and the results were on balance positive.

In the same year, 1987, Thomas Bailey authored *Immigrants and Native Workers: Contrasts and Competition*, which was CHR's first effort to assess the significance of large-scale influxes of newcomers to the United States, both in terms of their absorption into the labor force and as a preliminary assessment of what this substantial and continuing flow meant for indigenous workers, particularly youths, minorities (blacks), and women. There were many in academe and political life who believed that the large immigrant flow was disadvantageous for the employment prospects of at-risk native workers, but Bailey's results revealed that for the most part the two groups did not compete head-on and that the negative assessment of large-scale immigration was unjustified.

In 1988, Noyelle published two books that ushered in CHR's explorations into the impacts of globalization on the U.S. economy and labor force. The first, coauthored with Anna Dutka, *International Trade in Business Services: Accounting, Advertising, Law, and Management Consulting*, looked in considerable depth at how key U.S. companies were responding to the opportunities offered them by increased international trade to establish and expand their specialized services abroad, and the extent to which host countries responded positively or negatively.

In association with his French colleague, Olivier Bertrand, Noyelle also published a volume on *Human Resources and Corporate Strategy: A Comparison of Banks and Insurance Companies in Five OECD Countries*, the principal thrust of which was to uncover the parallels and differences in the five countries as they sought to adapt their strategies as the forces of globalization became ever-more potent.

At the end of the decade, a number of additional studies were nearing publication. Bailey has carried through a major case study of how new technology has helped to transform the textile and garment industries in the United States; he has traced, in considerable detail, the consequences of these transformations on the recruitment, training, and work patterns of their employees. Bailey, together with colleagues in New York, Chicago, Los Angeles, and Philadelphia, is also in the last stages of a manuscript that assesses the parallels and differences among these four metropolitan areas in the adaptation of their educational and training infrastructures in response to the technological and economic transformations of these urban economies, particularly as they bear on the employment and career opportunities for vulnerable groups—youths, women, minorities.

Noyelle has explored selected impacts of globalization on the banking industry in New York City and has initiated studies of the role of the software industry, both in New York and abroad. Stanback, returning to his earlier interest in suburbanization, has looked anew at inner city-suburban interactions, with particular attention to the extent to which inner-city minority youth are at particular risk because of the rapid growth of retailing in suburban areas, a critical entrance into the job market that they are unable to penetrate.

In the mid-1980s, in collaboration with George Vojta, the executive vice-president of Bankers Trust, I published *Beyond Human Scale: The Large Corporation at Risk*, which had roots in my early interests in large corporations and their human resources policies. We emphasized an inherent paradox: good management and good fortune lead to high profitability and rapid growth; but as organizations expand they inevitably become bureaucratized and fail to use their human resources effectively, which foreshadows their eventual decline. In 1988, I planned and edited a book with specialists from academe and business, *Executive Talent: Attracting and Retaining the Best People*, which focused on the unmet challenges that human resources specialists face in making a place for their discipline at the highest levels of the large corporation and in gaining support for policies and programs to assure the more effective utilization of the organization's talent.

In response to a suggestion by my friend Clark Abt, I arranged in the mid-1980s to collect representative selections from the more important books in human resources that I had authored, so that interested readers could find the essence of my contribution within the confines of a single work; the result was *Understanding Human Resources: Perspectives, People, and Policy*. The titles of the ten principal sections of this huge tome (more than seven hundred pages) provide an overview of the five decades of my research:

- Ideas and Reality
- Career Choice and Performance Potential
- The Unsuccessful
- Women
- Older Persons
- Blacks
- Technology and the Changing Economy
- Human Resources Management in Large Organizations
- Metropolitanism: Focus on New York
- Programs and Policy

It would be not only inappropriate but fatuous for me to venture an evaluation of my own work, or of the work of the Conservation Project as a whole. That is a task for others. But I can say without fear of contradiction that once my mentor Wesley Clair Mitchell had convinced me to embark on a career of empirical research in the border area between economics and psychology, I stayed with the challenge.

Throughout the ensuing five decades I have kept my eye on the place of work in modern society in an attempt to understand the respective roles of family, school, the armed services, and employers in providing opportunities for employment and training, the prerequisites for leading a satisfying life and being able to help one's children get a decent start. Our successive investigations have contributed a great deal to our understanding about the role of human resources in the modern economy, as well as about the role of governmental and nongovernmental policies in contributing to the improved development and utilization of human resources.

However, although we have learned a lot, much remains to be learned, for modern economies confront accelerating changes. But knowledge, once gained, does not lose its relevance, even if the economy undergoes rapid change. The challenge that researchers face is not to apply yesterday's knowledge to today's problems, but rather to take advantage of the enlarged pool of theory and technique to explore the new issues that call for analysis and solution. Both society and human resources research face an open-ended future.

In this chapter, I referred to fifty-three books that resulted from the research efforts of my collaborators and myself. Let me suggest a few dominant themes that helped to inform and direct this half-century of research into human resources.

First and foremost, we sought to recognize emerging policy issues that mainline analysts had not yet come to recognize, much less given them their due, from the consequences of long-term unemployment to the expansion of the service economy.

A second strong impetus was to frame questions and to search for answers that went far beyond the model of the competitive market and made room for studying both individual development and societal opportunities and barriers. The impact of the family and the school on the development of the individual could not in our opinion be ignored or given short shrift.

Another theme: The overriding importance of gender and race in the United States—as in most other advanced and developing countries—must always be reflected in any and all models used to analyze preparation for and performance in the world of work.

Since people must work in close proximity to where they live—at least until they decide and are able to relocate their residence—the issue of location must play a large role in any and all studies of the labor market, a lesson that first impressed itself on me in 1939 in South Wales and that remains of critical importance for inner-city minority youth faced with the continuing suburbanization of the U.S. economy.

The two-sector model of modern economics is inadequate, and a three-sector model—private, nonprofit, and government—is required because many of the key services on which the population depends, such as education, medical care, science and the arts, religion, and others, are deeply rooted in the voluntary nonprofit sector.

In a world that is being rapidly transformed as a consequence of changes in technology, demography, and markets, it is questionable, to say the least, whether we need ever-more refinements in the theory of competitive markets, considering the restricted explanatory power of competition in the development and utilization of human resources. Honesty requires that I acknowledge that more relevant approaches are not easy to design and implement, but so long as we recognize that a deepened understanding of human resources extends far beyond the principle of utility maximization, we need to push more broadly and more deeply into the complex processes that govern how people prepare for and perform in the world of work. This is the broadened challenge that we set ourselves a half-century ago and that we have pursued from that day to this with, we hope, some modest success. And modest successes are all that one could hope for in an ever-changing world with changing people and institutions in constant flux.

6

Health Policy Research

My interest in medical matters started in my seventeenth year, when I was a student at Heidelberg and took a course on the history of medicine, and where I listened for hours to my starry-eyed friend, Irwin Sobel, M.D., from New York City, recently graduated from Columbia's College of Physicians and Surgeons, who was pursuing graduate studies with the head of Heidelberg's Pediatrics Department.

The following year I had a more personal exposure to the medical world: My father had a close call. A distinguished physician in Frankfurt am Main, performing a routine urological examination on my father, had set off a raging cystitis attack with high fever, which he could not bring under control. In desperation, he decided to operate, but fortunately I had a cousin who was an experienced internist and she fought a winning battle to prevent his operating. After three months of hospitalization, my father was able to make the trip back to the United States.

The following year my cousin-physician visited the United States as my father's guest. She wanted to see the great Harvey Cushing operate at Peter Bent Brigham Hospital, and through another relative on the staff of the Harvard Medical School it was arranged that I would accompany her, although Cushing discouraged laymen from being present when he operated.

The operation that day was on a patient with a diseased pituitary gland. Cushing's assistant had spent three hours opening the cranial cavity before the master arrived. We were able to see next to nothing of Cushing at work. The next morning I inquired about the condition of the patient and was told, "Of course he died." Neurosurgery at the time, even with Cushing performing the operation, was largely experimental. I recently learned that today the procedure can sometimes be performed on an outpatient basis via the nasal cavity and usually requires less than an hour, from start to finish.

One more recollection from the 1930s about a number of friends who were recent medical school graduates and who were starting in practice: The way many of them went about setting up a practice was to borrow the office of an older colleague during the evening hours, 7 p.m. to 10 p.m., in the hope that some relative or friend might direct a patient to them. Others did not even make an effort to start a practice; they worked in the Post Office or drove a cab, waiting for the depression to lift. Most physicians at the end of the prosperity in 1929 had only modest incomes; on the average, they earned about $5,000 a year. In contrast, full professors at leading universities earned about half again as much.

It is possible, but surely no more than possible, that my research interests could have led me to the health-policy arena. As chapter 8 makes clear, my deep immersion in medical matters was a direct consequence of my experiences in World War II. Once the war was over, or, more correctly, after I left the Pentagon to return to Columbia in mid-1946, I continued to have only occasional contacts with the health-policy arena until the passage of Medicare, after which I settled into a long-term, continuing relationship. In the early years, I took special care to avoid letting the health arena deflect much of my interest and energies away from human resources. More recently, I have worked closely with colleagues in the design and execution of our more than two score health-policy studies, but over the last three decades I have had only one close collaborator in the arena of health, Miriam Ostow.

World War II marked a watershed for American medicine, which had up to that point been largely supportive activity, but thereafter became high-tech medicine, increasingly focused on curing. But the war and the immediate postwar years led to other major transformations. Physicians increasingly shifted from family practice to specialist or subspecialist practice. Federal dollars became available to help smaller communities build or improve their local hospitals. Congress decided to invest large sums in biomedical research. Academic health centers (AHCs) were the beneficiaries of most of the new research funding. Private health insurance took off during the war and expanded rapidly thereafter. The American people wanted and obtained more and better access to health care services.

Our first publication in the health-policy arena was in 1948; it consisted of a report by the Committee on the Future of Nursing, which I chaired, and was entitled *A Program for the Nursing Profession*. The committee members represented a broad cross section from the fields of nursing, medicine, and the social sciences. Herbert E. Klarman, at the time a member of the Economics Department of Brooklyn College, served as executive secretary. The initiator of the project was R. Louise McManus, the then head of the Department of Nursing Education at Teachers College, Columbia University, who, recognizing that the war and its aftermath had loosened many of the foundations of nursing education, was seeking guidance for the redirection of her department, one of the first in the nation to offer a doctoral degree in nursing education.

Among the important conclusions of the committee's report were that diploma schools, which still dominated the nursing educational scene, were inherently exploitative, since they provided no more than nine months of didactic training during a three-year apprenticeship; that the nursing profession could gain true professional status only if it had a well-educated leadership cadre who had earned master's or doctoral degrees and who were able to pursue research in nursing; and that the best prospects for meeting the growing demand for ever-larger numbers of bedside nurses would be to differentiate between the leadership group with advanced degrees and the much-larger group of bedside nurses, who could be trained in two-year programs.

Nursing underwent many transformations in the succeeding decades, but only a few of the transformations were congruent with the committee's recommendations. Four decades later, many problems that the committee had identified are still awaiting resolution.

The first substantial health policy study that CHR undertook was launched in the fall of 1948 and was completed the following year. The study was undertaken at the request of the Joint Hospital Survey and Planning Commission of the State of New York, which confronted two pressing problems: many voluntary hospitals were looking to the state for supplemental financial support, and the state had to sort out a great many questions about future hospital construction to assure that hospitals could discharge their responsibilities to the entire citizenry. Our task was to submit a detailed report to the commission for the guidance of the governor and the legislature. In order to insulate us from the many pressure groups, it was arranged that the State of New York would enter into a contract with Columbia University.

With respect to the financing issue, we advised the commission and the governor (Thomas E. Dewey) that the ominous trend of the immediate postwar years, in which hospital expenditures outpaced hospital revenues, had begun to reverse; insurance payments had begun to catch up with hospital expenditures. In our view, there was no basis for the state to start subsidizing voluntary hospitals, a practice that, once begun, could not readily be discontinued. In the absence of our strong findings, backed by careful analyses, it is likely that the governor and the legislature would have moved as planned to assist the voluntary-hospital sector. Even if the original subsidy had been small, the cumulative subsidies would by now have been in the high tens of billions of dollars. The avoidance of such a large expenditure was no small return for a study that carried a price tag of around $65,000!

With respect to bed requirements and future construction needs we were less prescient, but we had some sensible as well as some not so sensible advice. Our worst error stemmed from our recommendation that the tuberculosis hospitals be expanded just shortly before the new drug therapy, isoniazid, radically transformed the treatment of TB patients from in-patient to ambulatory settings. But our recommendations also encouraged the state to expand ambulatory clinics at upstate hospitals; we emphasized the potential for more home care services for the chronically ill and fragile elderly; we called attention to the need for strengthening regional planning authorities to avoid duplication of costly services and to assure that existing hospital capacity would be more fully utilized. We adopted a cautious position about the large-scale expansion of psychiatric units at general hospitals and advised the state to expand its mental hospitals, particularly in urban areas, where staff would be easier to attract and retain.

At a time when private health insurance covered fewer than 40 percent of the state's population, we estimated that the goal of optimal coverage be set at 85 percent, which turned out to be a sound projection; we urged that insurance benefits be structured away from first-dollar coverage so that persons who encountered catastrophic hospital stays could be protected; we called attention to a number of problems in the interface between the public and private sectors, such as increasing reimbursements for voluntary hospitals that cared for welfare clients.

In the early 1950s, I had arranged a symposium at the annual meeting of the American Economic Association on health economics at the request of Milton Friedman who had undertaken to structure the association's program for his teacher and mentor, Frank H. Knight. A leading British observer, A. S. Culyer, has written that this symposium marked the beginning of health economics in the United States, a flattering if exaggerated statement.

I gave an occasional lecture on health policy and participated in some meetings of the New York Academy of Medicine, but basically kept my distance from things medical until I was appointed in 1959 to a four-year term on the Advisory Committee to the National Institutes of Mental Health (NIMH).

In 1960 the trustees of the Federation of Jewish Philanthropies, which was involved in the support of ten acute-care hospitals in New York City, decided that the time was ripe for a major reassessment of its philanthropic support program, particularly as it related to its support for hospital care. The federation trustees were interested in a number of specific questions: What were the likely future trends in hospital costs? To what extent were payments by third-party payers covering all or most of the annual budgets of acute-care hospitals? How were demographic changes in New York City altering the composition of needy patients? To what extent were the leading federation hospitals in the forefront of hospital care, and what would assure that they remain at the cutting edge?

On the eve of World War II, philanthropy still played a major role in helping to balance the operating budgets of the federation's ten hospitals. Two decades later it had only marginal importance. In the interim, private insurance had come to pay for most acute care. My coauthor Dr. Peter Rogatz and I (*Planning for Better Hospital Care* [1961]) foresaw a continuation of increases in hospital costs, by about 50 percent in the next five years, which foreshadowed a further relative decline in the role for philanthropy. Lawrence Wien, then president of the federation, questioned our figures, but we stuck to them and time proved us right. In fact we had underestimated the increase in costs for hospital care.

Our report made specific recommendations that addressed each of the concerns of the federation's trustees, relating to institutional closures, mergers, affiliations. But it had one unexpected result. A throw-away sentence, about the importance of teaching hospitals having a close affiliation with a medical school, had unforeseen consequences. The staff of Mt. Sinai Hospital, increasingly restive about its lack of a close affiliation with an existing medical school and seeing little prospect of developing such a satisfactory affiliation in the near future, used the sentence to support a proposal to establish a medical school under its own auspices.

I was startled to find myself cited as an authority in the attempt to create a new medical school at Mt. Sinai. I had looked with considerable misgiving on the earlier effort by Yeshiva University to start Einstein Medical School and I was opposed, for a variety of reasons, to a further Jewish philanthropic effort in New York City directed at establishing a second private medical school. I knew that a quality medical school would absorb a great amount of philanthropic dollars. I saw no shortage of physicians in the New York area, and it was clear that there was a rapid lessening of the pervasive anti-Semitism characteristic of medical school admissions policies and appointments to hospital staffs in the pre-World War II era. True, a strong teaching hospital needed an affiliation with a strong medical school, but until all alternatives had been exhausted, I remained skeptical about the Mt. Sinai proposal.

I learned several important lessons from my four-year term on the Advisory Committee to the National Institutes of Mental Health: that most bureaucrats measure their success by the amount of money they are able to extract from Congress; that these bureaucrats pay inadequate attention to the uses to which they put the money and that they fail to consider that Congress will sooner or later ask for an accounting of what they had accomplished with their much-expanded budgets; that there was a cozy relationship between the senior officials of NIMH and the academic medical leadership, much like the relationship of senior procurement officers in the Pentagon and the aerospace companies; that fashion and enthusiasm dominate the world of medical ideas and policy as much as they do other fields.

Impressed by what they had learned in the United Kingdom about the care of the mentally ill in community settings, senior NIMH staff assumed a leadership role in proposing to empty our crowded state mental hospitals without taking a hard look at the adequacy or potential for improved ambulatory care in urban centers. With relatively few exceptions, the Community Mental Health Centers, which were supposed to become the centerpieces for community psychiatry, proved to be stillborn. Hundreds of thousands of the senile elderly are now wasting away in nursing homes, and many others are found on the streets of our big cities without proper housing or custodial care, not to mention access to supportive mental health services.

I did my best at our quarterly meetings to raise warnings, but the combined enthusiasm of the staff and most of the Advisory Committee members for speeding the onset of the brave new world assured that action would win out over deliberation. The NIMH was so action oriented that it later succeeded in separating itself from the National Institutes of Health. In obtaining its independence, it lost its identity, since it was eventually joined with the drug and alcohol agencies to form a new agency (ADAMHA).

The early 1960s set the stage for two major health care reforms—the initiation of direct federal funding to expand the physician supply (1963), and the passage of Medicare and Medicaid (1965). Both developments had a long history, which the Conservation Project had been monitoring. For reasons that will become clear in the next chapter, I had had the opportunity to become deeply involved in the logistical operation of the single largest health care delivery system in the nation's history—the Medical Department of the U.S. Army in World War II. My responsibilities involved planning and allocating all resources, personnel as well as beds and equipment, to assure that the battle casualties would receive quality specialized treatment.

As noted earlier, in the immediate post-World War II decades I had avoided becoming deeply involved in health-policy issues. But the federal interventions in the mid-1960s convinced me that the United States had entered on new efforts to provide quality medical care to the entire population, a commitment easier to establish than to implement. Since the outcome of the new experiment would depend in no small measure on the nation's success in expanding the supply of physicians and other groups of health professionals, a linkage between the Conservation Project's major focus on human resources and prospective health care reforms was easy to forge.

The speed and intensity of our broadened research interests in health policy are indicated by the fact that *Men, Money, and Medicine*, which I published in 1969 with the help of Miriam Ostow, represented a collection of nineteen pieces most of which I had prepared for oral or written presentation in the preceding four years, since the enactment of Medicare. The following calls attention to some of the more important themes on which my opinions dissented from those of the majority.

The presumption that the nation faced a crisis in physician personnel and that major governmental interventions were required to expand the supply was just that—a presumption; there was no proof. I warned that even a much-enlarged supply would not necessarily lead physicians to practice among underserved populations; that attention should be paid to adding more paraprofessionals and at the same time to directing efforts to restructuring health care delivery to the poor; that potential dangers, both to health and pocketbook, loomed ahead if, because of a surfeit of physicians and money, the population were to be overtreated.

One chapter was devoted to the "woman physician." At the end of the 1960s, women accounted for only 9 percent of the total number of U.S. physicians, which was among the lowest ratio in any community in the Western world. But the U.S. trend was up from the 5 percent level only a few years earlier. With more women entering and reentering the labor force; with women accounting for four out of every ten college graduates; with new medical schools being established largely outside the conservative Eastern seaboard; with governmental support for medical students, the odds favored a continuing increase—although I did not foresee two decades down the road that women would account for almost forty percent of the entering class in medical schools.

Another major theme emphasized that the analysis of the health delivery system could not proceed without close attention to macroeconomic trends. I noted that many of the poor faced a greater need for food than for medicines; that physicians are willing to practice only in locations where they can make a satisfactory living; that modern hospitals cannot be built and maintained in isolated low-income areas. Further, I argued strongly that the competitive market model could not be relied upon for efficient resource allocation or policy guidance.

In 1971, in association with six colleagues on the CHR staff, I published *Urban Health Services: The Case of New York*, which explored a number of challenging issues in health care delivery in New York City resulting from the continuing presence of two largely independent hospital systems, voluntary and municipal. We explored the reasons that successive efforts to integrate the two had not succeeded, and the different ways in which each system used the new funds made available by Medicare and Medicaid. We also explored the evolution of the "affiliation system," whereby the major medical schools and teaching hospitals were providing professional staff for the municipal hospital system, which alone made it possible for the latter hospitals to obtain the specialists they needed to treat their patients. The volume ends with fifteen guidelines for planners, ranging from an explanation of how "pluralism" operates as both a potential and restraint on reforms, to a warning that "there is a danger that the input of additional resources will be equated with the output of additional services."

In the mid-1970s the Conservation Project, in association with the Josiah Macy, Jr. Foundation, sponsored a conference on *The University Medical Center and the Metropolis*, the proceedings of which Alice Yohalem and I edited. Yohalem and Charles Brecher had prepared a working paper outlining the changing relationships of the university medical center to its immediate community as well as to the larger metropolis in which it is located. The writers focused on such questions as whether, and how far, the medical center should go in designing and putting in new systems of health care delivery to low-income groups in their neighborhoods; the financing of such schemes; and the desirability that medical centers broaden their educational and training missions to do much more in the preparation of allied health personnel. In my concluding chapter, I reviewed the range of positions that had surfaced with respect to each of the foregoing themes. On two points the conferees were in broad agreement: The medical centers would remain in the city, and they would have to become more responsive to the problems of the metropolis and their immediate neighborhood, if only because of the much-enlarged influxes of public money. And the events of the subsequent decade-and-a-half validated this forecast, at least in part.

In 1977 I published *The Limits of Health Reform: The Search for Realism*. It was the one and only time in my life that I wrote a book specifically for one reader, Jimmy Carter, who had recently been elected president on a platform that included his commitment to introduce legislation aimed at national health insurance (NHI). After a long period of quiescence, some thirty years or so, NHI had reemerged on the nation's political agenda with sufficient strength that the chairman of the House of Representative's Ways and Means Committee, Congressman Albert Conrad Ullman, prophesied in 1976 that Congress would pass such a bill and that President Ford would not dare to veto it, since 1976 was an election year. Congressman Ullman was twice wrong: Not only did Congress not pass NHI, but it did not mark up a bill. But Carter announced that, if elected, he would press for the passage of NHI.

I believed that the president was on soft ground: The remedy was disproportionate to the deficiencies of the U.S. health care system, NHI would not perform as expected, many defects in the delivery of health care would remain, and, finally, the costs of NHI would be substantially higher than currently estimated costs, although the latter were substantial. By the time my book was published and I was able to forward a copy to the president, NHI was no longer a live issue. The projected costs, all other issues aside, had pushed it onto the back burner.

The nub of my argument was summarized in the penultimate paragraph, which identified four reasons for my skepticism about NHI: "Three out of every five dollars spent on health care still originate from outside the governmental arena; the regional and area distribution of health resources is grossly uneven; most members of the medical profession prefer to live and work in large metropolitan communities; it will be difficult to assure future large inputs of new resources for the health care system."

With the advantage of a lengthened perspective, I find that the first three points have held up well, but the fourth surely needs to be modified. National health care expenditures in 1979 totaled $170 billion, or 8.5 percent of GNP; the comparable figures for 1992 will be in excess of $800 billion, or 14 percent of GNP. Even after a correction is made for the intervening inflation, it is clear that the U.S. health care system was able to attract a great many additional resources during the past decade.

In the same year, 1977, I published a monograph on *Regionalization and Health Policy* for the Department of Health, Education, and Welfare in collaboration with a group of American and foreign experts. The concept of regionalizing a health care system had first been advanced by Lord Bertrand Edward Dawson in 1920. How could one explain that, except for the period of the Second World War, and then only within the army, the approach had been more talked about than acted on?

While the volume presented case illustrations of regionalization in action (for example, in the United Kingdom under the National Health Service, or in the establishment of trauma center networks in the United States), the weight of the analysis pointed to substantial barriers in the path of regionalization. Lack of political will, resistance by bureaucrats, shortcomings in the data base, and above all the power of providers, particularly physicians and hospitals, who preferred to continue in their own ways in pursuit of their own goals, largely accounted for the slow progress. The persistence of large differences in incomes among occupational groups, between urban and rural communities, and between whites and blacks were additional roadblocks to the growth of regionalization.

In 1978 *Health Manpower and Health Policy* was published. I had written all but one of its twenty-five chapters in the 1970s, and they provided the backup for the analysis in *The Limits of Health Reform*, which had appeared in 1977. The closing sections of the "Afterword" are quoted, not only because they offer a summary of the approach that had helped me to tie the discrete chapters together but because of their relevance more than a decade later:

> The American people may long endure the imperfections to which they have become accustomed, primarily because they are afraid of the consequences of radical intervention. On the other hand, the people may decide that the cost-benefit ratio has shifted so adversely that there is no option but to take the risks involved in remodeling the system. . . . The question that remains open is when.

The 1980s was a period of high productivity in health policy research for the CHR staff. We dealt with wide-ranging issues, including home health care; the evaluation of the Robert Wood Johnson Foundation's Municipal Health Services Program; the transformation of New York City's health care system as a result of the threefold increase in real per capita expenditures between 1965 and 1985; an assessment of the potential of prevention to moderate the risks facing young people in the areas of drunken driving, drug use, pregnancy, and dropping out of school; a systematic analysis of the post-World War II trends in the financing of biomedical research, the total expenditures for which exploded from $45 million in 1940 to $16.4 billion in 1987; and an assessment of the nursing shortage and what to do about it. Each of the foregoing, except the last, received book-length treatment.

A few highlights that emerge from these successive inquiries: The book on *Home Health Care: Its Role in the Changing Health Services Market*, which I carried out with my associates, Warren Balinsky and Miriam Ostow, was initiated at the request of Health Services Improvement Fund, an affiliate of the Blue Cross-Blue Shield of Greater New York. The fund was interested in learning whether more liberal home-care benefits were desirable from the vantage of patient care and controlling costs for acute care episodes. To answer these questions, we developed a seventeen-county study aimed at analyzing a representative group of acute-care patients who had utilized home-care. We also undertook a selected review of the agencies providing such care. What we found was that there was some scope to expand home care for patients who had been admitted and treated in a hospital for an acute episode, particularly those with orthopedic impairments, cancer, or heart disease. However, the real potential for a large-scale expansion of home health care services involved the growing numbers of the frail elderly, many of whom preferred remaining at home to being admitted to a nursing home. But such an expansion was related less to "health care" and more to "personal care," which in turn raised major financing problems both as to total funding and as to the distribution between public and private dollars.

In the late 1970s the Robert Wood Johnson Foundation selected five cities in which to finance demonstration projects aimed at establishing community health clinics in low-income areas, in the hope and expectation that such efforts would improve primary care for the local population and relieve pressures on the acute-care public hospitals, where most of the poor and medically indigent had previously sought care. The Conservation Project carried out the "institutional and management" evaluation; Ron Anderson and his staff at the University of Chicago undertook the data analysis. In our 1985 book *Local Health Policy in Action: The Municipal Health Services Program*, Edith Davis, Miriam Ostow, and I reached the following conclusions. The demonstration was well conceptualized and for the most part well implemented. But many of the foundation's expectations were not fulfilled: Most inner city people did not shift the locus of where they sought primary care; the new clinics simply added to the available treatment centers; for the most part the self-pay and insured population did not utilize the new clinics; the clinics had difficulty in reaching a volume of work where they could become self-supporting without benefit of a subsidy. The single most important finding was that the five years during which the experiment was underway (1978–1983) led to so many new and unanticipated developments in the health care delivery system that much of the original design and many of its goals were no longer relevant or achievable.

In *From Health Dollars to Health Services: New York City 1965– 1985*, my colleagues and I sought the answer to a basic question: What were the impacts on the quantity and quality of health services of a threefold increase in real dollar annual expenditures from $6 to $18 billion in these two decades, a period during which New York City's population had declined by at least half a million? The major answers that we came up with follow. Most hospitals were able to acquire more equipment and more specialized staff and therefore to provide more sophisticated care, including treating many more of the sick elderly. Nursing home capacity expanded greatly, and many more New Yorkers were able to utilize such care; ambulatory care clinics and emergency rooms expanded. The six academic health centers were able to broaden and deepen the entire range of their activities—educational, research, and patient care. The ratio of hospital staff per patient admitted increased substantially. The lower-paid hospital workers—clerical, dietary, security, housekeeping, and others—enjoyed substantial increases in wages and benefits; and the house staff received significantly more in the way of salaries and benefits. But it remained something of a mystery how the health care sector could have absorbed so many additional dollars without evidencing a more radical transformation in health care delivery than in fact had occurred.

Young People at Risk: Is Prevention Possible? was undertaken in response to a request from the Commonwealth Fund that we assess the potential of prevention to reduce the number of adolescents who get into serious trouble. The foundation had been supporting efforts to reduce drunken driving among adolescents and asked us to review the state of knowledge not only about that subject but also about teenage pregnancy, drug use, and school dropouts. Faced with mounting evidence of the rapid growth of social pathology among adolescents, grant-makers were increasingly attracted to "prevention" as a low-cost, effective intervention.

However, to everyone's disappointment, our monograph pointed to the limited potential of the medical model of prevention. As we analyzed the dynamics of high risks among young people, we became impressed by the major roles of racism, ineffective schooling, and unemployment in predisposing so many urban youth to aberrant and ineffective behavior; we also noted how various deleterious forces—the growth of single-parent families, the low self-esteem of minority children, neighborhood deterioration, adolescent risk-taking, and the low cost of crack—individually and collectively, were largely responsible for adolescent pathology. If we were right in our identification of the precipitating causes for the new pathologies, then the answer to the question "Is Prevention Possible" is self-evident. It is possible, but it is very costly and our society has given no evidence that it is willing to assume the high initial costs.

The last policy question that the Conservation Project pursued in depth during the 1980s was *The Financing of Biomedical Research*, a project carried out by Anna Dutka and me in response to a liberal grant from the Lucille P. Markey Charitable Trust, which is dedicated solely to the support of biomedical research and researchers and which must expend its entire corpus of $300 to $500 million by 1997.

In our book, published in 1989, we presented the first comprehensive analysis of the sources of funding for and the performers of biomedical research during the post-World War II decades, when the federal government made steadily rising annual appropriations for the support of basic research, and comparably large investments were made by private industry to finance applied research. Since most of the federal dollars, which exceeded $7.2 billion in 1987, went to universities and medical schools, the role of academe in biomedical research in the post-World War II era has been radically transformed, and this transformation has had major impacts on medical education, on the specialization of the medical profession, and on patient care.

The Markey Foundation had a particular interest in our assessing the potential for greater philanthropic support for biomedical research, particularly because of the continuing budgetary difficulties facing the federal government. We found that philanthropy accounts directly for no more than 3 to 4 percent of the $16 billion annual outlay for biomedical R&D. But with the Howard Hughes Institute expanding its level of support substantially and with more deans of medical schools seeking out the new millionaires in an effort to interest them in supporting biomedical research, the role of philanthropy is likely to grow. There is little or no prospect, however, of anybody in the wings who can act as an understudy for the dominant role of the federal government.

The following are some of the priority issues that currently command attention: the relatively small proportion of approved new investigator grants that the federal government is able to fund (30 percent or less); the backlog of laboratory construction projects characteristic of even our best-endowed universities; the steadily rising costs of university overhead, which reduce the amount of money from government grants available to the bench scientist; the demographic outlook, which threatens to depress the number of well-qualified biomedical researchers.

Under the leadership of the Commonwealth Fund, Miriam Ostow and I collaborated with two nurse specialists on the staff of the American Hospital Association and a health economist from Harvard to assess the growing nursing shortage, especially as it affected hospital nursing, thereby closing the loop that started with our monograph on *A Program for the Nursing Profession*, which marked our debut into health-policy research in 1948. I was struck with the fact that one way that we could have met our recent assignment would have been to reprint the earlier volume, since many of its key recommendations are still pertinent and are still awaiting implementation. The 1989 Commonwealth Fund report, *What to Do about the Nurse Shortage*, emphasized the extent to which married women, many with children at home, had come to dominate the nursing field and the importance, therefore, for hospital administrators to provide greater flexibility in nurses' work schedules. Moreover, we emphasized the need for hospitals to establish salary levels that are competitive with other fields of employment for women and also to provide sufficient support personnel for nurses so that they can use their skills appropriately and justify the higher salaries that they must be paid.

Our other suggestions point to the responsibility of state governments to provide more financial assistance to nursing schools, so that they could recruit among persons who are exploring a second career as well as among men and women from lower-income families; the need for flexibility in the scheduling of course work so that many who are currently working could at the same time learn to become nurses; and the need for the educational authorities to introduce additional flexibility that would enable students to accumulate and transfer their educational credits.

In addition to these six substantive inquiries, I devoted considerable time and effort during the past decade to writing a series of articles about urgent and emergent health-policy issues, especially those that relate to such subjects as cost containment, for-profit medicine, competition, academic health centers, and other subjects that are at the center of public attention. A first collection of these essays was published in 1985 under the title *American Medicine: The Power Shift*; the second in 1990, with the title *The Medical Triangle: Physicians, Politicians, and the Public*. In the articles that are reprinted in these two collections, my aim was to identify and assess the unique characteristics of the U.S. health care sector, with its admixture of public funding, private insurance, and out-of-pocket expenditures; to point out the limited value of conventional paradigms of the competitive market or regulation in bringing about desirable changes; and the continuing shortfalls of our system because of its steeply rising costs and its disregard of large numbers of people in need of care who remain without ready access to physicians or hospitals.

Initially, in association with Dean Thomas H. Meikle of the Cornell University Medical College and later in collaboration with David E. Rogers, the Walsh McDermott Distinguished University Professor at Cornell, I edited or coedited six symposia dealing with important issues on the health policy agenda: *The U.S. Health Care System: A Look to the 1990s*; *From Physician Shortage to Patient Shortage: The Future of Medical Practice*; *Medicine and Society: Clinical Decisions and Societal Values*; *The AIDS Patient: An Action Agenda*; *Public and Professional Attitudes toward AIDS Patients: A National Dilemma*; and *Improving the Life Chances of Children at Risk.*

Each of the foregoing was focused on unsolved issues that require assessment and action such as the fact that many of the poor and the near poor do not have access to the health care system; the new imbalances that developed, especially among selected specialists and among selected communities, between the number of physicians in practice and the number of patients requiring care; the extent to which the United States has failed to look critically at the limitations—as well as the potentials— of high-tech medicine; the slow response of the political and health leadership in New York City to the ever-worsening AIDS crisis, which has left many seriously ill patients with inadequate and inappropriate care; and the extent to which prejudice, the fears of contact with AIDS patients, and hostility among all sectors of the community, including physicians, nurses, and paraprofessionals, have made it difficult to treat AIDS patients humanely.

As the foregoing makes clear, the 1980s provided multiple challenges to the health-policy researcher because, among other reasons, none of the critical issues recognized at the beginning of the decade were resolved by decade's end—not cost containment, not new forms of efficient health care delivery, not the expected surplus of physician personnel, not coverage for the uninsured, not care for the sick or frail elderly. The failure to develop effective solutions could hardly be blamed on inadequate health care expenditures: In 1980 total outlays came to $248 billion; in 1992 the estimated total is $800 billion, or an increase of 225 percent in ten years. The one safe conclusion is that the reform of the health care system, like the reform of the educational, criminal justice, and welfare systems, offers challenges that are easier to formulate than to resolve.

7

Crosscurrents in Academe

During the two-thirds of a century that I have been based at Columbia University, I have had the opportunity to become deeply involved in two of the university's three principal functions—teaching and research—and have had some minor but continuing exposure to administration, both as long-term director of the Eisenhower Center for the Conservation of Human Resources and more recently as director of the Revson Fellows Program for the Future of the City of New York.

A rough measure of the extent of my involvement in teaching is suggested by the facts that I have had about a hundred students enrolled in my classes each semester; that I have taught two semesters each academic year for fifty-three years; and that each student has been exposed to approximately twenty-five hours of my class instruction per semester. The foregoing adds up to a total of about ten thousand students for a quarter-million hours of classroom exposure.

With regard to research, in the more than fifty years during which I have directed the Conservation of Human Resources Project, I have been responsible for about a thousand years of employment of senior or junior research staff, with a cumulative budget expenditure of over $30 million and with a publication record of about 250 books and monographs. I was the sole or principal author of about a hundred of our publications.

During the six and a half decades of my presence on the campus, Columbia University has had nine presidents and acting presidents and, except for the forbidding Nicholas Murray Butler, I have had an ongoing relationship with all of them. And the Graduate School of Business, my long-term base, has had a total of thirteen deans and acting deans, with whom I have been more or less close friends, four of whom had been my students. Despite this considerable exposure to those in high administrative positions—and I note also ongoing relationships with other senior university officials, such as provosts, vice-presidents, and others—I have

95

been exposed to but know much less about the administrative-financial aspects of university life than about teaching and research. But I have had sufficient experience with all three sectors that I am able to identify and evaluate some of the important crosscurrents and tensions that are deeply embedded in the life of academe. By all odds, the single best account of the decision-making process in a major research university in the United States is Henry Rosovsky's *The University: An Owner's Manual* (Norton, 1989). The author, a distinguished professor of economics, had long served as Harvard's dean of Arts and Sciences.

I have recently reviewed the quality of the teaching to which I was exposed during my days as a graduate student at Columbia, where I took courses with an array of distinguished professors in a large number of different departments, including philosophy, anthropology, history, and sociology, as well as economics, which was my major. For the most part, the teaching left a great deal to be desired. One prestigious member of the faculty, about to retire, used notes that he must have prepared many decades earlier, since the paper had turned yellow. The notes of another leading professor had been transcribed and reproduced by an entrepreneurial student who sold them for five dollars for the first semester's notes, or ten dollars for the year's set. The professor had been presented with a complimentary set from which he lectured. Some pranksters, sitting in the back of the room, would say a phrase or a sentence ahead of the lecturer.

The course that I took in epistemology was over my head because I was inadequately prepared; I could barely follow where the lecturer was headed, and I certainly couldn't appreciate why he had chosen his particular route. Another of my professors came into class with two or three well-known tomes under his arm—which I suspect he had not looked at for more than a decade—and his ramblings, during which he often made incisive remarks, were unconnected to any of the contents of these books, which ostensibly included the themes and subthemes that the course was intended to cover.

I don't want to convey the impression that I never had a graduate course in which the professor was well organized and covered the materials in an interesting and in-depth manner, but such experiences were rare exceptions, not the rule. Many of the leading members of the Columbia faculty in the early 1930s did not seek to establish or strengthen their reputations by excellence in class room. They were first and foremost research scholars whose reputations rested on the quality of their contributions to advancing the frontiers of their disciplines.

In reflecting on the low estate of university's teaching, at least in the graduate departments, I identified several contributing factors. The Great Depression was dominating the land and graduate students were relatively few; their tuition, corrected for inflation, was approximately one-quarter of present-day charges; their career objectives were murky, and the senior faculty expected the good students to find their own way and were not concerned about the remainder.

The post-World War II era ushered in a new and different environment, with enrollments exploding, with tuition and living costs increasing rapidly, with a much closer linkage between higher education and career advancement in the professions, with time and performance criteria assuming much greater importance.

One of the important contributions that Dean Courtney C. Brown made to the Graduate School of Business at Columbia during his extended leadership in the 1950s and 1960s was his emphasis on raising the quality of classroom instruction. The message went out to the teaching staff that the nontenured members would be assessed for promotion to tenure based on the following three criteria: teaching, research contributions, and "service to the school." To give bite to the first criterion Brown introduced a system for student evaluations at the end of each semester, which provided his office with the "objective data" it needed to assess the instructor's success in engaging his students in a meaningful classroom experience. I recall the substantial restiveness of the faculty to student evaluations, but Brown insisted that the "customers" who were paying the bill were entitled to a quality product, and he knew no better way to judge customer satisfaction.

Junior faculty who received poor evaluations were visited by experienced seniors who counseled them on their performance, and the school provided remedial instruction for the staff in preparing and delivering lectures.

I believe that over the years the quality of teaching in the Graduate School of Business improved by an order of magnitude, first because it became a much more important consideration in adding new members to the faculty, and second, since the student evaluations were in the public domain, each faculty member decided to pay greater attention to the preparation of his lectures and to classroom performance.

Since candidates for the M.B.A. currently invest about $50,000 in the pursuit of their degrees, they are much more concerned that their education contribute to their career goals. The students want and need to make the most of their time and effort. Each class that they take is supposed to add to the skills and techniques for which prospective employers are willing to pay a premium.

While the vast majority of students who pursue a professional or graduate degree at a major research university are headed for employment off-campus, a number start out with or develop career goals that attract them to a life in academe. Once this becomes part of their occupational planning, they must confront the research imperative.

A prospective academic must feel driven to research, at least to the point where he or she can identify a challenging subject and devote the many months—often years—required to collecting and analyzing the source materials and writing them up in a scholarly product that will meet with the approval of the members of their dissertation committee. With a dissertation completed, many quickly get to work on their next research project, usually narrowly confined in order to develop the publication record they will need when, seven years after their initial appointment, they will be evaluated for tenure and the decision will be made: up or out.

The pressures on the young faculty members facing tenure have never been light, but I was startled to learn some years ago about the increasing constraints that they face. I had made a suggestion to a newly arrived colleague that she might like to join our research group, since her dissertation and interests appeared to be a good fit with our ongoing research agenda. She said that she appreciated the offer but had to decline because she needed the next five years to write, and have accepted for publication in refereed journals, a minimum number of scientific articles in order to achieve tenure. Joining an interdisciplinary research group engaged in policy research across disciplinary boundaries was impractical. I was so startled by her answer that I checked it out with the vice-dean for academic affairs, because I could not believe that the tenure process had become so constricted, but he assured me that it had and that my young colleague had made the right assessment of how to focus her energies in the years immediately ahead.

Although faculty members of major research universities seldom have more than four to six hours of classroom obligations per week, for about thirty weeks in the year, they must allocate time for lecture preparation and for administrative duties that range from reading dissertations to attending committee meetings. Even with a liberal allowance for the latter, their weekly commitments to the university are not likely to exceed two eight-hour days per week. Presumably that would leave them ample time to pursue their research, especially since the academic schedule includes at least three months of vacation in the summer.

But the problem of time is complicated by the fact that some professors, particularly those on the faculties of the professional schools such as schools of medicine, law, and business, have opportunities for consulting off-campus, which have the lure of permitting them to add significantly to their annual incomes. Although Columbia, like most research universities, has a rule that stipulates that when he or she is teaching a professor may devote no more than one day per week to outside (consulting) activities, the rule has never been enforced, and it appears that it has been continually breached by many of my colleagues.

The issue, however, is not as simple as it might at first appear. There is a lot to be said for a professor of business to be actively engaged in consulting on projects that provide him or her with significant insights into the processes of policy determination and decision making in the real world. Whether or not such consulting activities contribute substantially to the professor's annual income, the question that needs to be asked and answered is whether students would be better off if the professor engaged in little or no consulting.

The simple-minded answer would suggest that with time and energy limitations the busy professor-consultant will begin to skimp on his research, an ongoing commitment to his students, the university, and his profession. But once again the matter is not so simple or clear-cut. In fact nothing is simple or clear-cut in the university, a theme reflected by this chapter's title.

No graduate student who aspires to an academic career can possibly start down that path, much less secure a tenured position, unless he or she has some interest in and liking for undertaking scholarly research, which means identifying a problem, collecting and analyzing the relevant data, and writing up the results of the inquiry. Scholarly research is more frequently than not a lonesome activity, beset by frustrations, and, except for the truly gifted, it is likely to prove more of a burden than a pleasure. When the researcher's article or monograph is published, the odds are that it will be added to the ever-larger pool of existing publications and fail to attract more than passing attention, except from a few specialists. And there is always the danger that it may be singled out for criticism because of the investigator's errors in conceptualization or execution.

Small wonder, therefore, that if the junior professor has the good fortune to meet the publication requirements and to achieve tenure, he or she is likely to publish less and less over time. The exception is the small minority who are drawn to research and writing because they enjoy wrestling with intellectual problems and have been stimulated by the feedback from their earlier published work.

The teaching-research tension in the framework of the tenure decision after a trial period of seven years is at the heart of the strategic decision making of research universities. The leaders of these institutions are committed to making a wide-ranging search to identify the best candidates who are or may become available; Harvard boasts that it scours the entire world for the most promising person to fill a tenured opening. Most research universities make a serious national search, seeking help and counsel from all available sources. But what "best" means is not self-evident, since departments need to provide both breadth and depth to their offerings. And now, as in recent decades, they must also pay attention to diversity, as they seek to increase the number of women and minority members whom they appoint.

The tenure-selection process is further complicated and confused by at least three additional considerations: the state of the academic labor market, the bargaining power of the hiring institution, and the risks entailed in estimating the future research productivity of a thirty-five-year-old.

No dean or department chairman faced with a large-scale influx of new students, such as occurred at the end of World War II and again when the baby boom generation came of age, wants to be caught short by not having his classes covered. Often the supply of young academics is out of sync with the cycle of student enrollments. In such situations, the criteria for appointment to tenure tend to slip. Timing can play a major role, positive or negative, in the career of a young academic.

The tenure search-appointment process has become considerably more complicated in recent decades, especially for the older East Coast universities, because of the increasing competition they face from newer centers of excellence in other areas of the country, which are able to supplement attractive salary offers by quality-of-life benefits, particularly attractive housing at a reasonable cost. Columbia has been seriously handicapped in this intensified competitive environment because of the perceived and real deterioration in New York City's ambience, the high cost of its housing, and the difficulty of faculty members who must use the public schools for educating their children.

The third aspect of the tenure-selection process probably contains the highest element of uncertainty: Based on a young person's early record of scholarly output, roughly over a period of ten to twelve years, a judgment is made that commits the university to pay a salary and fringe benefits for the next thirty-five years, or, with the coming elimination of compulsory retirement at seventy, for an even longer period. There is a considerable risk projecting a scholar's productivity over the next three to four decades on the basis of his past decade's research. But if an error is made, tenured faculty members have opportunities to sort themselves out in a large research university by shifting their emphasis away from research to instruction or administration or consulting.

There is an underlying paradox about academe that invites attention and reflection. Research universities are committed to the discovery of new knowledge and new understanding. Hence their mission is to upset inherited doctrines. But universities are also the guardians of the great cultural achievements of the past and hence have as a primary mission the preservation and study of the old. The tension between the accepted and the new is kept within bounds by giving preference to the new when the results of research can be confirmed by experiment or theory. In the humanities, where matters of style and taste loom large, the tension between the inherited wisdom and the innovations in interpretation are greater. The greatest difficulties are found in the social sciences where the defense of the status quo, particularly in economics, has implications that go far beyond the ivory tower.

In my long academic career I have been exposed to three ideological revolutions—Marxism, Keynesianism, and neoconservatism, which also parades under the label of supply-side economics. Marxism hardly left a mark on Columbia, since so few Marxists had been appointed to the faculty in the 1930s and still fewer achieved tenure. Keynesianism, on the other hand, came to dominate American economics at Columbia and elsewhere until it suffered a serious setback in the 1970s, when stagnation, reflected in slow growth and high inflation, came to dominate the

American and world economies. The retreat of Keynesianism set the stage for supply-side economics, which has contributed to slow growth, small gains in productivity, growing inequality of incomes, horrendous increases in the national debt and in federal deficits, aggravated tensions between whites and blacks and between cities and suburbs, a deteriorated infrastructure, and all the other goodies that Ronald Reagan left behind.

Another revolution, this one more methodological than ideological, occurred in the post-World War II era and left its mark first on economics and later on the other social sciences. In short, mathematics came to dominate both the ways in which questions were formulated and the ways in which answers were developed. Modeling became the order of the day, and the more elegant the model, the more ingenious the solutions, the more the new methodology gained in recognition and prestige. The fact that economic, social, and political structures in which people live and interact do not lend themselves easily (if at all) to the simplifications that the mathematical-modeling exercises require did little to slow the interest in quantification. As Nobel Laureate Wassily Leontief has repeatedly emphasized, the leaders in academe were not slowed by the paucity of facts and figures, without which the results from their models cannot be judged. But mathematics is a powerful discipline, and it has an attraction for those who have a taste and a talent for it. Small wonder, therefore, that the mathematical fault-line has come to separate the older from the younger generation of academic social scientists, to a point where the former, using myself as an illustration, cannot understand the titles and the contents of the articles in most economic journals.

The quantification of the social sciences, the mathematization of their approaches, has also left its mark on the upcoming generation of students, both those whose goal is to become a professor and the less academically oriented who are preparing themselves for a career in business. The large numbers of graduate students who have received inadequate instruction in mathematics in high school and college spend a disproportionate part of their time and energies seeking to master the fundamentals in graduate or professional school, not because they want to but because they have little alternative if they are pursuing a Ph.D. or even an M.B.A.

The tensions between technique and analysis, exemplified by the almost complete victory of mathematical approaches first to economics and later to the other social sciences, is not the first nor will it be the last conflict to arise in the halls of academe. Technique and theory can be taught. The effective deployment of both to important problems, where the results can make a real difference to the functioning of institutions and the larger society, is something else again. Informed teachers can point their students to areas of inquiry and specific questions where carefully designed and executed research may make a large difference. But the primary responsibility for accomplishing more than mundane results rests with the investigator, not the teacher. Small wonder that most teachers, even in graduate schools, are busy teaching technique.

Some, like Nobel Laureate George Stigler, believe that the advancement of knowledge in the social sciences, as in the natural sciences and the humanities, is by the slow and steady accretion of bits and pieces of new information. It is a slow and tortuous process, and only a rare contribution results in a substantial step forward. But I have serious reservations about Stigler's approach, because I see scholarly refinements in methodology far outdistancing the pool of relevant information we need about how the economy and society operate. We need alternative models, beyond Adam Smith's great contribution of the efficiency of the competitive market.

Since breakthrough contributions are few and far between, it should come as no surprise that most faculty members, even those at our leading universities, pursue a course dedicated to making improvements in their inherited body of technique rather than risking explorations into the unknown, where the odds of failing far outdistance the likelihood of success.

The raison d'être of the research university is to enable its staff to explore, experiment, and innovate in the hope and expectation that by pursuing such activities they will succeed, some sooner, some later, and some not at all, in pushing back the veil of ignorance. But most men and women are not gamblers, and, presented with a choice between taking one small step forward or venturing a big leap into the unknown, they opt for the security of the former.

But once again there are important crosscurrents at work, the most potent stemming from the extraordinarily large amounts of governmental research funding that became available in recent decades to facilitate research, primarily in the physical and biomedical sciences, but with modest amounts also available to social scientists. The existence and expansion of such funding created a new academic type—the entrepreneurial professor—who has been able to put together a strong team that can build the track record to attract the millions and often the tens of millions of dollars of external research funding. Based at the university, many of these research directors see one of their principal tasks to be strengthening their linkages with the decision makers in their discipline and in the funding agencies that will determine whether they will continue to receive large amounts of support. With scores and sometimes hundreds of coworkers dependent on the director's ability to keep attracting these large amounts of external funds, the work of these key research enterprises often becomes the equivalent of established departments or divisions. Medical schools at research universities provide the most telling examples of this new development.

So far we have identified a number of tensions and crosscurrents that have come to characterize the modern research community. But we have not looked specifically at the administration and financing of the research university, which is a sine qua non for its continued existence and survival.

The major research universities on the East Coast are almost without exception nonprofit institutions where final responsibility rests with a self-perpetuating board of trustees. In the other regions of the country, the majority of major research universities are creations of state governments, which provide them with a significant portion of their annual budgetary requirements for teaching, though not for research. In both cases, the president is usually a former academic who moved over onto the administrative track some years prior to being selected for the top position. Eisenhower's appointment to head Columbia University in 1948 was one of the last times that a major research university appointed a president with no former academic experience.

Oversimplified, the major research universities have a great deal in common when it comes both to financing and to administration. They rely on three major sources of their financing—tuition, governmental grants and contracts (primarily federal, except at state universities), and philanthropy. Harvard leads the pack, with over $4 billion of endowment income. Columbia's endowment, which ranks fourth, is about $1.2 billion. In addition to earnings from endowments, the major universities rely on fund-raising in which recurrent gifts by alumni, particularly former undergraduates, play a significant role. When it comes to income from tuition, the so-called private institutions charge about the same, about $15,000 per year, and tuition at the state universities for in-state residents is usually less than half this rate.

Columbia, with a current budget in excess of $900 million, receives about $200 million from all outside grants and contracts, to which the federal government is by far the leading contributor.

The principal tasks of a university president are to spearhead the never-ending search for additional funding; to stimulate and support his deans in the same effort; to contribute to moderating the inevitable centrifugal forces that operate on every campus and that reflect professors' preoccupation with what is happening to them in terms of salaries, benefits, and perquisites; to consider from time to time, when the opportunity offers, whether to enter upon new activities or to eliminate departments and schools that can no longer justify themselves; and to invest some special university funds in attracting a few stars.

In the early 1990s no university president is likely to imitate Robert Hutchins's actions when he was chosen to head the University of Chicago in 1929. He set new goals and new methods of instruction despite instant and continuing opposition from many of his faculty. The fact that he was successful, at least in part, in restructuring the university helps to underscore how much academe has changed in the interim. The day of large-scale presidentially initiated change is over.

There is a deep seated antagonism between many professors and their colleagues who have become administrators. This antagonism grows out of ignorance about the administrative tasks that must be performed, envy of the administrators' higher salaries and perquisites, and a displacement of their own career disappointments. Occasionally professors' criticisms are well taken, as when they see weak administrators place the university at increasing risk. In four decades of attending faculty meetings, I never was able to reconcile myself to the low average of sensible talk. After long reflection, I concluded that a disproportionate number of the professoriat live in a make-believe world of their own construction. Even if my explanation is faulty, it would not alter my low evaluation of most discourse at faculty meetings.

I consider myself extremely fortunate to have been anchored in a major research university for all of my adult life. Hence I cannot possibly submit an unfavorable balance sheet. What I can do is to call attention to the many different and even contradictory forces that are at play in a major university and to point up how they accommodate each other.

Large research universities, like other large organizations with which I am acquainted, such as the army, the federal government, corporations, and foundations, have room to accommodate a wide variety of persons and talents, including individuals who undergo major changes in their goals and aspirations over extended life-cycles.

There is a basic paradox about a research community, in that its principal ambition and goal is to contribute to the discovery of important new knowledge. That ambition and goal determine whom it seeks to add to its tenured faculty. But by definition the number of significant contributions to research is much smaller than the number of faculty members that the fifty major research universities appoint, and must appoint, to discharge their teaching functions. Hence the inherent tension that is embedded in the twofold function of the university—research and teaching.

But, as we have seen, that is only the beginning of the tensions that exist. No matter how much care the university takes to offer tenure only to the talented young researcher with a good track record, there is no way to guess who will lose their enthusiasm and their steam after they have acquired tenure. All we know is that a high proportion will become less productive, often sooner rather than later. Fortunately, a reasonable number of those whose research interests weaken will find ways of justifying, at least in part, their continuing role on the campus by expanded work with junior colleagues, students, and administration, as well as by other activities.

We took note of the tensions between technical advances and significant intellectual breakthroughs and noted that most faculty, even at the leading universities, are more engaged in the former than in the latter. In the sciences, where the principle of accretion is at work, the contribution of one small building block on top of another may be the way to steady progress. But in the social sciences, it appears that technique can get so far ahead of conceptualization and understanding that what goes on within the halls of academe has at best marginal impact on the guidance that the leaders and the public require to improve the operations of the economy and the society. But as we noted, technique can be taught and professors have the obligation to send their students out better prepared than when they arrived. They may not be able to give them a vision or a key to unlock the secrets of the unknown, but at least they will have given them some useful and powerful analytical tools.

I want to draw this introspective reassessment to an end by noting that the administration and financing of the research university must be adjudged to be a reasonable success if the university has demonstrated its capacity to change, survive, and contribute to a society that is itself continually changing. No sensible person inside or outside the university would claim that the university is functioning at an optimal level, but that is a criterion that no long-lived institution has been able to meet—not the government, the church, the military, or the corporation. The research university has no reason to apologize. It performs a number of useful, in fact essential, functions. As is true of all institutions it must aim to do better.

PART II

The World of Affairs

8

Learning about the World Outside

My first recollections of the world outside, that is, the world beyond
my family, friends, and school, date from the entrance of the United
States into World War I, when I was six. As I reported earlier, I recall,
still with considerable discomfiture, my mother's walking with me
through the streets of Avon-by-the-Sea in New Jersey in the summer of
1917 loudly singing German lieder to register her annoyance with the
proscription of all things German, including music and speech. The
extent of that jingoism is underscored by the tale that I heard repeated
many times later: I came home from school that spring and announced
that unless we stopped speaking German at home I would leave.

I have a few other recollections tied to the war. I distinctly recall my
amazement at seeing women conductors on street cars. And in late
October 1918, school was suddenly dismissed one morning at around
10:30, after the principal heard a report that the armistice had been signed.
This report turned out to be about two weeks premature.

My broadening awareness of the larger world dates from the spring
and summer of 1922 when, together with my parents and sister, I spent
four months in Germany, Holland, and England. I had turned eleven in
April of that year and, as my colleagues and I demonstrated in our study
of *Occupational Choice*, by eleven most young people begin to be aware
of their interests and to recognize that they must sooner or later play an
active role in shaping themselves and in making the choices that will
affect their future studies and careers.

The three months—June, July, and August—that we spent in Germany, first in Berlin and later in Wildbad in the Black Forest and in
Frankfurt am Main, were memorable on several counts. My sister and I
were almost on the exact spot in Berlin where, twenty-four hours later,
Walter Rathenau, Germany's foreign minister, was murdered by right-
wing extremists, an act that many of my parents' friends interpreted as

motivated in no small part by anti-Semitism (Rathenau was a Jew) that had moved from words to deeds, a harbinger of the Nazis' victory eleven years later.

Inflation had taken off, and by June 1922 the mark had deteriorated to about 250 to the dollar, a depreciation of sixty-fold. When I got into arguments with Germans whom I didn't like—and there were many such—who believed that children should be seen and not heard and whose ideas and values I found abhorrent, I warned them that much worse was yet to come and that the mark would surely drop to 1,000 to the dollar before very long. How and why I came to this correct conclusion is hard to say, other than a perverse understanding that it was an ominous forecast that would unsettle people whom I wanted to unsettle. My weeks in Berlin in 1922 left an indelible impression on me with respect to the power of inflation, and I have been way off base in my anticipations, not only during the New Deal when Roosevelt opted for unbalanced budgets but again in the 1980s when Reagan followed suit.

A second learning experience that summer, about which I have earlier written briefly, grew out of conversations with a German officer, with whom we shared our train compartment from Berlin to Wildbad, who had recently returned from the U.S.S.R. where he had been training German troops. He reported that he had just finished a fifteen-month assignment for the German Army in the U.S.S.R. My recollection is that he told us that his assignment was to train a group of handpicked recruits to provide the *Reichswehr* with an elite noncommissioned corps. It struck me at the time, and even more in retrospect, that the assignment—and the entire undertaking—was clearly in violation of the Treaty of Versailles, but our traveling companion saw no reason to hide what he had been doing. Clearly, German militarism was far from dead.

During the four weeks or so during which my family was in Wildbad, I had occasion to take long walks through the Black Forest and was deeply impressed by the condition of the trails and the state of their upkeep. Clearly, the Germans had respect for public property and did not abuse it. The government may have been hard up for revenue, but the minimum required for park maintenance had been appropriated. Of course, the walkers themselves played a big role in seeing that the parks and trails were kept in good condition.

During the 1980s I had occasion to visit West Berlin almost every year in connection with my membership on the Advisory Committee on Labor

Markets for the Research Center Berlin (WZB). The walk from my hotel on Kurfurstendamm to the old quarters of the center was close to four miles, a good part of it through low-income areas heavily populated by Turkish immigrants. I was impressed many times by the maintenance of the streets and of the open spaces of both public and private buildings. There are some national values that are so deeply ingrained that they survive both wars and revolutions, and they are values that foreigners assimilate.

One more recollection of our trip abroad in 1922: We visited my father's brother-in-law, who had for a long time been the proprietor of a successful music store in Cardiff, Wales. But the store had fallen on hard times as the coal-mining industry in the Rhondda Valley began to slip, even before the General Strike of 1926, from which it never recovered. While the British were not suffering from inflation, I was impressed that the economic circumstances of the victors were not all that much better than those of the vanquished. It was not until many years later when I read Keynes's *Economic Consequences of the Peace* that I acquired some understanding of the reasons that the victors were not likely to come out far ahead or to stay ahead for long.

This visit to Cardiff in 1922 did not presage a return visit to South Wales in 1939, which would mark the launching of my career as an empirical economist with a focused interest on the role of human resources in economic development.

The seventeen years between 1922 and 1939 were the years of my growing up, the years during which I developed a great many views about a great many subjects, views that came to form and re-form how I thought about the outside world and the choices I made about finding my place in that world. I had to come to terms with my upbringing in a religious home; I had to sort out, from the many disciplines that attracted me, one in which I thought I could do well and make a living; I had to decide whether to marry earlier or later, and about a great many other opportunities and choices.

In looking back, 1922 proved to be a definite turning point for me. For the only time in his life, my father had taken an initiative with respect to my schooling and had called on the principal of the new junior high school that I was slated to attend to inquire whether our return to the United States some three to four weeks after the start of the semester would be a source of trouble. The principal assured him that it would not, but pointed out in passing that the specially selected students at Speyer Junior High School were expected to read and report on one book per week. Up to this point in my life I had directed all of my time to playing ball and had avoided books as if they were the plague. Everything changed that fall: my baseball-stickball days ended; my book-reading days began.

At the graduation ceremonies from Speyer Junior High School I was awarded the medal for the best student in the social sciences, an award that I believe I received because the faculty did not want to give all of the prizes to my friend L. S., who carried off all of the other awards. L. S. and I attended different high schools but came together again in Columbia College. To the best of my recollection, L. S. divided his time in college between playing bridge and pursuing the ladies, activities that he continued during his years in the Law School. Later on, he took over his father's paint shop, after which I lost track of him.

This is not the time nor the place to speculate about the steps and missteps between endowment and performance, but I am reasonably certain that my 1922 trip to Europe reinforced my emerging interests and concerns about the social-political arena; that Speyer's rule that students had to read a book a week left its mark; and that my winning the social science medal served as important reinforcement for my early pull toward history and the social sciences.

I have recently engaged in some arithmetic calculations about the seventeen-year span between my first visit to Europe and the outbreak of World War II, when I was in Devon, in the company of a colleague, Lowell Harris, and his wife, whom I had met in Ireland in the home of a mutual friend. We had returned to England where I had left a rental car on the chance that I might come back to reclaim it if war did not break out immediately.

In addition to these two European visits in 1922 and 1939, I had visited Europe in 1938; I had spent a year and a half in 1928–29 as a student at Heidelberg University, where I was enrolled for two semesters, a summer session at Grenoble, and the rest of the time traveling through Italy or mountain climbing in the Bavarian Alps. In sum, I spent just under two calendar years in Western Europe during this seventeen-year span. A point worth emphasizing is that my stay at Heidelberg occurred during my seventeenth-eighteenth year, an impressionable period about which I have written in *My Brother's Keeper*. I had become acquainted with most of Western Europe, from the north of Norway to Sicily and from Ireland to Austria, the Iberian peninsula alone excepted.

During this seventeen-year span, I spent the academic year 1933-34, as noted earlier, visiting corporate headquarters and plants in forty of the forty-eight states.

Of lesser weight, but still of some importance, was the fact that throughout this seventeen-year span my family (including me) spent approximately three months of every year in central Maine (Belgrade Lakes), which exposed me to still another environment different from New York or Europe. When I added all of the above up, I was surprised to discover that close to half of my time during these formative years was spent outside of New York City, which I have always considered the environment that dominated my early years. I have often remarked that I belong to the purest of all Manhattanites; in fact I am a West Sider, since I was born and have lived almost all of my life within one square mile of where I was born, in the shadow of Columbia University, which I first entered in 1927 and at which I have been teaching since 1935.

I don't recall that it took special effort to figure out that working and making a living was the critical activity of most men in the twentieth century in the United States, or for that matter in any other country with which I was acquainted. I realized that my father invested little or no emotion in earning his livelihood: He was a dedicated scholar who taught classes twice a week, but he considered his serious work to consist exclusively of his research and writing. Although my own career has been considerably less constrained than his, with many more choices, including turning a small part of my time into money, I have not deviated much from his basic pattern, which was to use all, or at least most, of his time for doing what he most wanted to do.

I often remind my students that they should pay more attention to what they most want to do, since, no matter what choice they make, their children will be fed and will go to college. But I realized early on that most people are not in a position to define for themselves the work that they most want to do; that many of them have no special talents and settle therefore for work in organizations; and that, indifferent about the use of time, they seek large rather than small incomes.

In the United States, if one asks a new acquaintance what he does, he frequently frames his answer not in terms of his occupation but by his annual earnings. He makes $50,000 a year doing so and so. I have seldom if ever encountered such an inversion between occupation and earnings in other countries, because, among other reasons, outside of the United States, education and social status are closely linked to occupation. Unlike those sensitive souls who consider all references to money as crude and socially inappropriate, I find much to commend in the American approach, because it so clearly downplays the importance of class and family status. No informed person doubts that there is a marked difference between the quality of the college education available at one of the nation's elite institutions and that available at a poorly funded and staffed institution, public or private. But more frequently than not, one identifies a person as a "college graduate," not as a Harvard or Stanford graduate.

I have had no illusions about the doctrine of equality of opportunity to which we, as a nation, are broadly committed. Clearly those who are born and/or raised in poverty face formidable challenges in competing for the prizes that our society offers. But there is the other side to the doctrine. A great number of individuals, many more whites than blacks, have been able to move up the social and economic ladder within one or two generations. One can find parallels in other countries, but they are less common primarily because class and educational barriers are so prominent. I recall a brief conversation with the German housekeeper of a U.S. consular official in Frankfurt, Germany, in the late 1960s; she expressed her deep distaste for the fact that so many young Germans from the "lower class" were currently attending university.

By the end of the 1930s, however, even a conservative, steeped in the traditional American values of the strength of free markets and the virtues of democracy, would have reason for self-questioning and doubt about our basic belief in the individual's ability to change his circumstances as long as he was willing to work hard, save, and demonstrate an entrepreneurial drive.

By 1939—a disturbing year and the end of a disturbing decade—structural weaknesses in the U.S. economy were revealed. Despite far-reaching efforts at reform, the New Deal had been at best only moderately successful in getting the stricken economy back on track after its derailment in the fall of 1929. Unemployment had dropped from its high point of around 25 percent in 1933, but in 1939 it was still in the 10 to 15 percent range, and underemployment was rampant. In 1939, gross national income had not yet regained its 1929 levels either in total or per capita. Agriculture and many sectors of industry were operating at or below break-even levels. Although I did not buy into Alvin Hansen's theory of stagnation (which had so impressed the young Turks at Harvard that they authored a monograph elaborating this thesis), I was deeply concerned about the economy, the causes for its collapse, and the prospects for its recovery. In fact, I had spent the greater part of 1934–1938 writing *The Illusion of Economic Stability*, trying to sort out and make sense of this tumultuous decade in light of what had gone before.

History forgotten is as dangerous as history misapplied. It still remains to be seen whether the illusion of the 1920s will prove a forerunner of the illusion of the 1990s! I remember how shocked I was when Representative Henry Reuss, the chairman of the Joint Economic Committee, asked me in 1981 whether I thought that the 1980s would be a replay of what I had described in my *The Illusion of Economic Stability*, in which I wrote that foreign and domestic financial speculation prolonged the expansionary cycle only to bring on a deepened depression.

As one would expect of an academic economist, even one who spent much time in the world of affairs, I hedged my answer. I explored some of the major differences that had occurred in the intervening half-century that made a replay of the 1930s highly unlikely. But I refused to rule out the possibility that seriously faulty economic policies could once again precipitate the U.S. economy into a long period of low output and low employment. There are many among my colleagues, and still more among the American people, who have proved by their votes—if votes can prove anything—that they don't believe that Reagan's economic policy was in any form or shape disadvantageous. Just the reverse: The United States in the 1980s enjoyed its longest peacetime expansion. But I insist that more time must pass before a definitive verdict can be rendered. Reuss's question was not unreasonable.

By genes and inclination I was a skeptic, who began his graduate studies in economics simultaneously with the arrival of the Great Depression. I was not likely to be attracted to neoclassical economics, with its self-regulating marketplace in which adjustments in prices would assure that supply and demand would be rebalanced and the full utilization of the economy's resources assured. There were only a few signs of self-correcting actions in the marketplace in the 1930s. Most academic economists, including my distinguished teachers, Wesley C. Mitchell and John Maurice Clark, recognized that a large gap had opened between the old theory and the new reality. But Mitchell held on to his belief that the business cycle would eventually correct itself and the economy would once again begin to expand, while Clark explored alternative approaches for government intervention, which led him to support the New Deal initiatives.

In 1936, Keynes published his *General Theory of Employment, Interest, and Money*, in which he offered a new paradigm to explain both the severity of the collapse and the remedial actions (compensatory government spending) that could avert such a calamity in the future. Most of my contemporaries became Keynesians overnight, and many of the older members of the profession took only a little longer before they announced their conversion; but my *Illusion* book, completed in 1938 and published in 1939, made no use of Keynes's macro theory. For my taste, it sought to explain too much, too simply. I felt sure that business expectations, especially when reinforced by expansions or contractions in the supply of money and credit, could result in excessive booms or deep depressions—as in fact happened between 1929 and 1933. But the movements of the economy were in my opinion more than epiphenomena and were rooted in such real factors as the size and competencies of the labor force, industrial capacity, and the speed and directions of technological change.

Even the most rabid anti-Rooseveltians—and there were many of them in leadership positions during the 1930s—recognized that the role of the federal government could no longer be ignored in shaping and reshaping the U.S. economy. The New Deal, in the view of its critics, was poorly conceived and poorly implemented, with its plethora of innovations affecting agriculture, labor, and industry. But the 1930s did not see a flowering of neoconservatism or libertarianism. Rather the reverse: It was the decade during which many young and even some older American intellectuals and many in Western Europe became enamored of the promises of Communism under the leadership of Josef Stalin. This engagement with Moscow said more about their lack of faith in their own leadership than about their knowledge of what was transpiring in the far-flung Russian empire.

Once again, my skepticism stood me in good stead. I saw no evidence that the U.S.S.R. was showing the way on any front, and I kept my distance. A government of limited rather than unlimited powers appeared to me to be the safer bet. But, as indicated earlier, I did not believe in the self-regulating marketplace and saw considerable scope for government to intervene in economic matters. During my year's field study through the United States I had had ample opportunity to see first-hand the widespread limitations of corporate management and had learned of its periodic resort to naked power, even including murder, to prevent workers in steel, automobiles, and rubber from unionizing. Roosevelt's efforts to alter the former relationships among owners, workers, and farmers appeared to me to be moves in the right direction.

My first exposure to the South, with its overwhelming problem of racism, in the fall of 1933 alerted me to the heavy hand of history, which no government could afford to ignore and even less to challenge outright. In 1933, approximately nine out of every ten American blacks were still living in the South. Most of them eked out a bare living as tenant farmers, supplemented by the few dollars that the women earned as domestics and by such toting of food as they were able to manage. It seemed to me at the time, and it has become much clearer in the succeeding decades, that, after three-and-a-half centuries of powerful reinforcement, the curse of racism would yield ground only slowly and only against great resistance. I found the South that I first encountered in 1933 much more foreign than the countries that I had gotten to know in Western Europe.

The twelve months that I spent visiting large U.S. corporations in all regions of the country impressed me with what I have since come to recognize as the American paradox—the extent to which we share a common culture and a common set of values and the extent to which the several states and regions and their residents differ from one another. I have long been appalled by the naiveté of those who say, "Why don't we follow the example of the Swedes or the Canadians and commit ourselves to a policy of full employment or to a publicly funded system of health care?" Sweden has a population approximately the size of New York City's, and Canada's population is less than California's. We are the only advanced economy of continental proportions, and for better or worse we must seek answers to our problems only after taking into account our scale and differences. To neglect either can lead only to trouble.

There was one additional building block that I put into place as a result of my early experiences—my opinions about whether the United States should try to go it alone or whether it had to shape and reshape its policies with respect to regional and global military, economic, and political power constellations. I was not sure whether our involvement in World War I was either necessary or desirable. But it seemed clear to me by the mid-1930s that the interrelations among Europe, the United States and Japan had reached a point where America Firsters, whatever their motivations, had set themselves against the facts and against history. There was no effective way for the United States to ignore what was happening abroad and to pursue a policy of nonintervention. The Nazis and the Japanese militarists had set themselves goals that the United States could ignore only at its peril.

This, in brief, is how I came to view the world of affairs: I had the perspective of a native New Yorker whose development was deeply affected by the Great Depression of the 1930s superimposed upon first-hand experiences in Western Europe, where people were simultaneously still recovering from the ravages of World War I and arming or failing to arm for the still-greater conflagration that would be ignited in 1939.

The United States was more committed to a democratic ethos than any other country, particularly because of its strong belief in and support for the principle of equality of opportunity, limited though that was when it came to the poor and, particularly, the blacks. But status in the United States is a function of the money one earns, not the family from which one comes.

Second, the Depression was the overriding experience of my young adulthood. Capitalism might have a great many successes to its credit, but its deficits stood out loud and clear throughout the 1930s. Almost no one still believed that the market alone could be relied upon to keep the economy functioning effectively.

Third, there is a role for government to assure that the economy could function more effectively. Sensible men might disagree as to the specifics of the changes that are needed or desirable, but only the unreconstructed ideologist believes that government should keep its hands off entirely.

The matter of race and racism was less clear-cut, partly because blacks were so heavily concentrated in the South. People living north of the Mason-Dixon line had little first-hand knowledge of the South, and most Northerners shared the attitudes of southern whites. But the occasional Northerner like me who confronted the black problem head-on shortly after the Scottsboro incident knew instinctively that here was a national cancer that would weaken the body politic until it was excised, however long and difficult a prospect that would prove to be.

Two more beliefs came to dominate my view of the United States. The first was that size and scale had an enormous effect on American thought and actions; the second was that despite its distance from Europe and Asia, the United States could not pursue a policy of isolation, however great the costs of involvement. To recapitulate: That one should seek equity; that a self-regulatory economy is an oxymoron; that government played a critical role in regulating the economy and the society; that racism was an unsolved problem; that our continental dimensions had an important impact; and finally that we could no longer be an island unto ourselves, if ever we had been—these were the convictions that I held in 1939, when my initial learning years came to an end.

9

The Pentagon: World War II

My relations to the Pentagon were by far the most important and long-lasting of my activities away from the campus. They began in September 1942 when I reported for duty to the Control Division of the then Services of Supply (SOS), later the Army Service Forces (ASF), the largest organization ever put together in the United States, with approximately two million military and civilian employees, twice the size of AT&T at its peak. Only a few years earlier, the commanding general of the ASF, Lieutenant General Brehon B. Somervell (with the rank of lieutenant colonel), had served as the Works Programs Administrator for Mayor LaGuardia in New York City, where, during our study of the long-term unemployed, I had become acquainted with him and several of his senior staff.

My last involvement in things military came almost forty years later, as the Carter administration was winding down. Elmer Staats, the comptroller general, had put together a high-powered task force of retired senior generals and admirals, together with a few of us who had been of, but not in, the armed services, to assess the readiness of the U.S. forces to respond to a crisis. But in point of fact my active involvement in the military had ended when I submitted *Manpower Research and Management in Large Organizations: A Report on the Task Force on Manpower Research* (I was chairman of the task force) to the Defense Science Board of the Department of Defense in 1971, or more correctly, when my term on the Scientific Advisory Board to the Air Force ended in 1975. This last date indicates that I had had slightly more than three decades of involvement with the Pentagon. By far the most intensive years were from September 1942 until May 1946. During the first fifteen months or so I had focused on human resources issues for General Somervell; the remaining thirty months I had served as chief logistical adviser to the surgeon general of the army. I had set up and directed the Resources

Analysis Division, which had the responsibility for designing the specialized system of general hospitals that were responsible for providing optimal treatment for the returning battle casualties and other seriously ill or injured servicemen and servicewomen; the division also had oversight responsibility for the allocation and use of all critical resources—physicians, other health personnel, and hospital beds.

I will single out some of the principal assignments that I carried out during World War II and also in the subsequent two-and-a-half decades, during which I continued as an active consultant primarily with the army but also for the air force and the Department of Defense. I had only infrequent contact with the navy.

The Pentagon, with its clear-cut lines of authority and responsibility, was a vastly different environment from the one I had known at Columbia: the rapidity with which items were put on or taken off the commanding general's agenda; the need for horizontal coordination; the confusion resulting from the rapid buildup not only of the forces in the field but also of staffs at headquarters; the jockeying for position by both regulars and reservists; and the anomalous role of the small number of civilians, who like me were tolerated, but little more, in the upper echelons of the Pentagon.

My first assignment was to take a hard look at how the many different staff divisions of the SOS were dealing with their manpower problems and to identify where reforms were needed in the organization, planning, and execution of their personnel missions. I spent at least three weeks talking to a great many people holding different positions on the totem pole, most of whom were too busy to take the time and trouble to keep their problems hidden from me. There was no love lost between the staff divisions and the Control Division. It was reported that Somervell had once remarked that every organization needs an SOB, and Robbie was his (Major General Clinton F. Robinson was the head of the Control Division). My report ran to about forty pages and each page called attention to grievous defects—the minor ones I had ignored—and suggested radical changes. When I got the paper back with Robbie's marginal notes, I went into a funk. His comments, not less than three per page, consisted primarily of "ridiculous!" "stupid!" "impossible!" I don't recall that he approved of any single section of the report or any specific recommendation.

When I recovered my nerve and could look at my report with some objectivity, I realized that I had failed to take account of the political elements in the equation: namely, the time and other costs involved in altering the existing organizations; the risks attached to putting reforms in place and finding that many of them worked no better than the systems they had superseded; and still other basics that I had overlooked or minimized. At the war's end, when I was a much more seasoned analyst, I reviewed my report once again and found that my assessments of the weaknesses had been well taken—with the passage of time almost every one surfaced. But General Robinson's criticisms, while brutal, had been to the point. Because of my naiveté I had failed to provide him with recommendations that he could implement and that, if implemented, held reasonable promise of improving outcomes. Fortunately I was a quick learner, and, as a tyro, I profited greatly from this disturbing episode. My subsequent reports—all read, annotated, and acted on by Robbie—passed muster.

One of my early assignments was to assess how well the army was doing in bringing itself up to full strength from the then 5.5 million level to the 7.7 million authorized by Congress. I knew that Somervell and his staff were keeping the heat on General Hershey, the director of the Selective Service System (SSS), to speed up the processing of recruits, and I had participated in several meetings at SSS to explore how this objective could be achieved more quickly.

More or less by accident, I stumbled on the fact that while the army was pressing for a much increased inflow of recruits, it was contributing to a sizable outflow. The army, early on, had used psychiatrists to "screen out" selectees who in their opinion would not make good soldiers. Once we entered the war, the army transformed a large number of family physicians and other general practitioners into psychiatrists through its ninety-day conversion program and put them to work evaluating soldiers whose aberrant behavior had come to their superiors' attention. The doctrine gained credence that the best thing to do was to separate these "psychoneurotics" before they caused more trouble and surely before they were shipped overseas. The army was discharging almost as many servicemen as General Hershey was able to process for induction.

When the data and the analyses reached the top command, General Marshall issued an order that forbade, from that point forward, the premature separation of any serviceman who was capable of doing a

"day's work." The phrase was left to the interpretation of local commanders. At Camp Lee, Virginia, where I was on a field inspection, the camp
commander paraded a full company of misfits, the likes of whom I had
never encountered in civilian, much less military, life. When pressed to
explain why he had not separated these ineffectives, he referred to
Marshall's directive, which he had interpreted as "capable of one day's
work per month." I came to realize that army policy often went from one
extreme to the other because of the Pentagon's inability to know how the
"field" would interpret a new directive. Time alone would make that
clear; and with the passage of time, a new policy directive often had to
be issued.

A related point: The wide scope for local interpretation gave the
competent, aggressive officer the opportunity to do many things that the
Pentagon had not anticipated and—if his actions were reasonable—to
escape censure or discipline. On the other hand, the timid commander
could adopt, as he had done in Camp Lee, the most literal interpretation
and be sure that in playing it safe, he was not placing himself at risk.

My keeping a close watch on the macro flows of personnel into the
army paid off again some months later. In adding up the totals, I
discovered that, instead of reaching the ceiling of the 7.7 million that
Congress had set, the army had almost 8.3 million men and women on
active duty, about 9 percent above its authorized ceiling. One of the more
pleasant by-products of the nation's total involvement in the war was the
much-lowered concern about all forms of accounting by the armed
services. The excess manpower involved an unauthorized cost of several
billion dollars, but that was not the nub of the army's concern once the
overage came to the attention of the senior staff. The army recognized
that it could be subject to serious criticism for having disregarded a
congressionally imposed ceiling on its authorized strength.

I was given the assignment of coming up with a reconciliation between
the facts of life as they had been uncovered and the congressional ceiling.
I knew, without having to be told, that the army had no intention of
reducing its numbers by 600,000 not many months before launching the
invasion of Europe. My solution postulated that the congressional ceiling
referred to 7.7 million *active* duty soldiers. Accordingly I developed a
sufficient number of categories of inactive soldiers—in basic training, in
hospitals, in transit, in confinement—to account for the 600,000 overage.
My recollection is that the army had stumbled on the problem and

developed a plausible solution before Congress became aware of its existence. In fact, I am by no means sure that its existence ever became known to Congress; if it did it caused little, if any, trouble.

But if the total size of the army was not a matter of concern to Congress, the same could not be said about the size of the ASF. General Somervell called me in one day to say that General Marshall had told him of Congress's concern with the number of employees in the ASF. Somervell asked me what I thought could be done to get the numbers down. I suggested a 10 percent reduction, including at least 180,000 civilians and some additional tens of thousands of soldiers who could and should be transferred to the Army Ground Forces (AGF) for combat training and assignments. However, I added that it could not be an across-the-board reduction because, among other reasons, some organizations had only recently been activated and were currently building up their strengths. Somervell said to go ahead and set a goal of ninety days for accomplishing the reduction.

I developed an ad hoc approach that enabled me to make some rough calculations about the relations of personnel to output, the results of which were included in a monograph, *Work Load Studies for Personnel Strength Control*, that the ASF published with a directive from General Somervell setting the new personnel quota for each of the major divisions. The ninety-day target was met. In addition to taking 180,000 civilians off the rolls, the ASF was able to make 60,000 uniformed personnel available to AGF. There was a little noise from a few of the ASF divisions, but not much. And there were, as I recall, no complaints from the civilians who were let go. In 1943 a person who lost his job one day could find a new job the next.

My last major assignment as a member of the Control Division did not have such a felicitous ending. General Somervell had decided that the only prospect of clipping the wings of the seven technical services that reported to him—Ordnance, Engineers, Transportation, Quartermaster, Signal, Chemical Warfare, and the Medical Department—was to bring about a fundamental reform of the ASF while the war was on, since once peace returned the seven services would be able to hold on to their independence and power. Accordingly, a few of us were assigned to a secret task force to develop the detailed plans for a permanent restructuring of the ASF. When our report was completed and had been put into final shape, Somervell obtained the approval of the senior members of the establishment, military and civilian. His last hurdle was Secretary of War Henry L. Stimson, who, when presented with the proposal, refused to sign off on the ground that since the ASF was functioning more or less satisfactorily, there was no point in introducing a major reform while the war was still to be won. It was just too risky.

While Stimson had the proposal under review, one of the technical chiefs got wind of the effort and pulled out all the stops to derail it; he enlisted the help of some disgruntled congressmen, who decided that the proposed reform of the ASF was part of a much larger conspiracy led by Harry Hopkins in the White House. They saw Marshall shifted to command the troops for the European invasion; Somervell would succeed him as chief of staff; and the seven technical chiefs and nine service commanders would be removed. As the *Times-Herald* reported the story: "Such brain-trusting civilians as James P. Mitchell (head of the Civilian Personnel Division) and Dr. Eli Ginzberg of the Control Division, pupils of Felix Frankfurter, were slated to replace these trusted military leaders." This is the way some of the press handled the story.

I came away from this unexpected and uninvited publicity with one observation. Most of the officials in the Pentagon did not believe that the story was without any foundation and they were right. And many decided that since Mitchell and I had been mentioned for high posts, there might also be something to that leak; in Mitchell's case yes, but surely not in my case. Mitchell would have been a general but for his inability to pass the physical. Neither of us had been pupils of Felix Frankfurter. Mitchell had not attended college, and my sole contact with Frankfurter had been a twenty-minute conversation some years earlier about the distribution of Jewish philanthropic funds.

My initial contacts with the Surgeon General's Office (SGO) came about as a result of my critical reviews of the Medical Department's use of its personnel resources. Each of the technical services had to submit monthly progress reports to General Somervell, who believed in management by and with figures, and it was my task to analyze the SGO's reports. After several critical reviews, General Raymond Bliss, the assistant surgeon general in charge of operations, tracked down that I was the author of the critical memoranda and invited me to come by and talk with him. As a result of that conversation I found myself, some weeks later on a tour of selected Zone of the Interior (that is, continental U.S.A.) general and station hospitals; at the end of the tour, by prearrangement,

I was to stop by and share my impressions with General Bliss. I reported that I found conditions in the field even worse than I had suspected. Bliss asked me to get General Robinson's agreement to take on a special assignment of several weeks, so that I could design a new organizational structure for him that would enable him to exercise more effective control over his resources. Robbie agreed, and I put together a good plan that lacked only one critical ingredient: at the last minute the person I had selected to head the division balked, doubting that as a civilian and a nonphysician he would be able to function effectively in the SGO. Bliss was unperturbed: He suggested, in fact insisted, that I run the new division. I decided to give it a try, but I was careful not to sever my ties with the Control Division.

My first task was to staff the unit. I realized that to plan the medical backup for the invasion of Europe under severe time constraints, I needed a few strong analysts and a small but competent support staff. Specifically, I looked for and identified three potentially strong analysts and sought approval for a total staff of about twenty. The SGO/ASF personnel divisions quickly approved, but the Civil Service Commission held up approving the plan. The commission's staff had no objection to my hiring three persons at the top Civil Service pay scale (one was in uniform), but they would agree only if these three in turn supervised not twenty but seventy or eighty subordinates. I explained that I had no need for such a large staff and had no place to house them. But the commission refused to yield until I threatened to go to the press and lay the responsibility for future inadequate facilities for treating our battle casualties at the commission's doorstep. That was the only time in my long relationship with the federal government that I ever made a threat. It worked, and we had a functioning organization in no time flat.

The second challenge was to develop a range of estimates about the demands that would fall on the Zone of Interior general hospitals to which battle casualties would be returned for definitive treatment. We had the casualty analysis of World War I by Colonel Albert G. Love of the SGO. We had the recent but small-scale experience growing out of the campaign in North Africa. When we looked at the few available facts and figures about casualties in the Soviet armies, we discovered that the Russians made no provisions for hospitalizing nonsurgical patients. Such patients had to fend for themselves using civilian facilities if they could find them. In short, we had no guidance for estimating what was to come, and yet we had to develop not only estimates but plans and actions to be implemented before the invasion would be launched some months in the future.

I had no option but to move ahead, to make estimates of the number of casualties as well as the proportion that would eventually be transferred to the United States for definitive treatment and hope that, once the invasion began, if the estimates proved to be far off I could make corrections in time.

I had access to the General Staff's planning documents for the invasion, which made me very nervous even though I parceled out the data to members of my staff in a fashion that helped to assure security. But I breathed a sigh of relief when Eisenhower finally jumped off on 6 June 1944. I had estimated 181,000 patients in our general hospitals on D + 6 months. When that day arrived I remembered to check our experience against my estimate and found that we were less than a thousand patients off. Impressive, but I made a further check to see how well I had done with each of the factors in the forecasting equation and discovered that I was way off, having seriously overestimated the number of casualties and seriously underestimated their lengths of stay in the hospital system. And then I broke out in a cold sweat: Suppose that the errors had turned out to be cumulative rather than compensatory!

The calculation of the total number of battle casualties who would be returned to the United States for definitive treatment was only the first stage in effective planning. The second required the SGO to develop a plan for providing specialized care, which in turn required the designation of specialized services based on the existing supply of specialists and the potential number of patients requiring specialists' care. We also had to take into consideration the strong pressures to hospitalize patients as close to their homes as possible. But General Bliss's overwhelming concern was to assure that each patient was treated by a specialist best able to diagnose and treat his injury or disease. We ran into an early flap with Gen. Fred Rankin, the chief consultant in surgery, because we had decided to designate all our general hospitals as specialized centers for the treatment of orthopedic patients on the ground that such patients would account for the majority, or at least the plurality, of all patients. But Rankin remembered what we had overlooked: The surgeon general, Norman Kirk, was an orthopedic specialist and would not look approvingly on our failure to specifically designate some hospitals as specialty centers for orthopedic surgery. We absorbed Rankin's criticism but made no change.

As D-Day approached, the chief of transportation for the army, General Charles P. Gross, called a high-level conference to discuss the allocation of scarce tonnage to supply the troops after they had landed on the European mainland. I represented the SGO and made a strong plea for substantial tonnage to evacuate the seriously wounded. General Gross reminded me in no uncertain terms that if he met the SGO's request he would soon be using all of his ships to evacuate the wounded, because the U.S. troops would lack the ammunition they needed to fight. A sharp reminder that good medical care, while important, was not the only, or even the first, consideration in the allocation of scarce shipping.

In between the key planning exercises that kept my staff and me heavily engaged in the months before D-Day, I was able to direct some of my attention to selected management issues. For the approximately 450 station hospitals in the Zone of the Interior, I developed a simple monthly reporting form that provided me with basic data about patient flows, length of stay, personnel, and other key variables. My sole aim was to spot outliers—hospitals that were performing much better or much worse than the average on these crude indices so that our consultants in the field could be alerted to visit them and find out in more detail what was going on. My recollection is that we had a somewhat broader set of categories when it came to the reports from our sixty-five general hospitals. About a half-century later, and after eighteen years of Professional Service Review Organizations (PSROs) and Professional Review Organizations (PROs), we still have not instituted a standard reporting system for the Medicare system, with a consultant review mechanism, such as we had in place in early 1944 in the SGO.

Some of my energies and efforts were directed to various forms of bureaucratic negotiations and in-fighting, as for instance, persuading the Office of the Assistant Chief of Staff (Personnel) ASF to agree to relieve Lieutenant Colonel Basil McClean, whom Governor Dewey had requested to head up a special commission in New York State. McClean, an outstanding hospital administrator (Strong Memorial, Rochester, New York) couldn't function effectively in the military, and it made good sense to speed his release. But the ASF staff, alerted by the earlier shenanigans of physicians overseas who convened discharge boards to release each other back to civilian life, had taken over the responsibility for authorizing discharges for physicians. Because of my earlier relationships with the top command of ASF I was able, but only with difficulty, to get McClean released.

The Air Corps, then a part of the army, was engaged in a ceaseless struggle to achieve its independence at the earliest possible time, and in the process it pushed relentlessly to be authorized to establish general hospitals. I was on the firing line to thwart these efforts, because, if successful, they could result in personnel reassignments and other dislocations that would have an adverse effect on patient care for both Air Corps and army personnel. This ongoing maneuvering by the Air Corps, which required the alert opposition of the SGO, brought me into close contact with the assistant inspector general (medical), Major General Howard Snyder, who later became my contact with General Eisenhower, whose personal physician he had been since the early 1920s.

General Bliss felt strongly that the quality of care in the hospitals in or close to combat zones would be determined in large measure by the quality of the nursing staff. He asked me to be sure to send adequate numbers of nurses to the European theater of operations. In carrying out his request I ran into unexpected opposition from the general staff, which balked at sending any women over forty into a combat area. When I pressed for an explanation, I was told, "You know, they go crazy at that time of life!"

Another episode relating to women in the services: General Bliss, whose specialty was surgery and obstetrics, was determined that the army hospitals should provide prenatal care and delivery for WACs who had become pregnant while on active duty, without inquiring as to their marital status. The senior female physician in the army was Major Margaret Craighill, who had been dean of the only medical school for women, Woman's Medical College in Philadelphia (now called the Medical College of Pennsylvania). One day she asked me to accompany her to a meeting with Colonel Oveta Culp Hobby, the director of the Women's Army Corps, who was uncomfortable about the SGO's plans to care for all pregnant WACs who sought medical care. Colonel Hobby at the time was bucking for a star and feared adverse publicity. In mid-afternoon my phone rang with Colonel Hobby on the wire: "I understand, doctor [sic], that you know all about pregnancy in the army." My reply: "I'm flattered; I know something about it but not all!"

Shortly after my arrival in the SGO I had discovered that the senior planning officer kept three sets of books—one for himself, one for the surgeon general, and one for the ASF. I informed General Bliss that we had to move expeditiously to a single best set of figures that we would share in house and with higher echelons. He agreed forthwith, and much of my success in gaining broad support, especially from the Inspector General's Office and the General Staff resulted from their growing trust in our data, which we shared with them.

In the early fall of 1944, the SGO faced a major crisis. Four months had passed since Eisenhower had launched his troops across the English Channel, and our general hospitals in the Zone of the Interior were still operating at very low occupancy and were fully staffed—an invitation for criticism and action from higher headquarters. To make matters worse, the view was gaining ground that the Germans were getting ready to sue for peace and that the war would be over before Christmas. Somervell called General Kirk to discuss the downscaling of our general hospital system. Kirk asked me to accompany him, in part because of my long-term acquaintance with Somervell, as well as because I was the person responsible in the SGO for overseeing the hospitalization of battle casualties.

Somervell stressed two points: our low occupancy and the probable early end of the war. Kirk encouraged me to undertake the rebuttal, and I pressed Somervell to consider the circumstances in which he would find himself in the event that the Germans retreated rather than surrendered. If we closed fifteen of our sixty-five general hospitals, we could not reactivate them in time to cope with a much accelerated inflow of seriously wounded patients. I stayed with this single argument—the risks were disproportionate to the short-term gains. We should wait and see and reassess the situation sixty days later. Somervell agreed, and Kirk was greatly relieved.

The next morning I set up a communications channel with General Paul Hawley and his staff in the United Kingdom, to remind them that once they had determined that a battle casualty could not be returned to active duty in their theater, the rules prescribed that he be sent home. With the inflow into their hospitals not pressing against their capacity, the physicians in the U.K. were extending the period of treatment for many patients who sooner or later would have to be shipped back to the United States.

We had to talk to Hawley not once but several times, over a period of days, to get our point across, but he finally decided to increase the flow of patients back to the United States. Our hospitals slowly but steadily began to fill up.

Under army regulations, the SGO would provide treatment for battle casualties in the United States up to the point where the patient could no longer profit from a further stay in an acute-care institution. At that point, if he could not be discharged to his home, as was the case with most paraplegics, the patient was to be transferred to a Veterans Administration (VA) hospital. But we learned that when our hospitals requested beds from the Veterans Administration for such transfers, they were frequently stalled with the statement that the Veterans Administration was unable to accommodate additional transfers. I looked into the matter and discovered that the VA hospital system was in a state of severe disrepair, since early in the war it had lost most of its staff to the army and the navy; furthermore, it was suffering the consequences of many years of uninterested and poor management. It was clear that we were heading for a national scandal, and I decided that I had best inform the assistant director of the Bureau of the Budget (BOB) of the dangers lurking ahead for the president and the nation. Carrying bad news to harassed officials is never pleasant, but my reception was so negative—I was told to mind my own business—that I realized that my message had gotten across, even though the BOB official had no idea of how to initiate remedial action and even less of how to do so quickly enough to alleviate our problems. But beds did open up for us in the Veterans Administration system after my visit, although I suspected that many of our patients suffered a serious loss in the quality of the care that they received after transfer.

As October and November came and went, it became clear that the Germans were still a fighting force and that the war would not be over by Christmas. The steady increase in our occupancy was proof positive of this trend. In mid-December, Colonel John C. Fitzpatrick, the medical regulatory officer, whose responsibility it was to assign the returning patients to the appropriate hospital in terms of specialty care and closeness to their homes, requested an urgent conference with General Bliss and me, at which he made an impassioned plea for enlarging our general hospital system by redesignating and upgrading a score or two regional and large station hospitals. He was even willing to look to the Air Corps for help.

With the war accelerating in both Europe and the Pacific and with our capacity utilization approaching the danger level, I appreciated that Colonel Fitzpatrick had legitimate reasons for concern. But I was reluctant to agree to his solution until it became absolutely clear that the extant system had reached its limits. I knew from our consultants and from my own visits to the field that our specialized system of patient care was operating with a high degree of effectiveness. I was opposed to being party to its dismemberment. After an increasingly acrimonious debate, which went on for over two hours, General Bliss sided with me. I had won the skirmish but not the war. On New Year's morning at 4 A.M. my phone rang. Colonel Fitzpatrick was at the other end, informing me that he had just learned that about ten thousand hitherto unreported (radio silence for reasons of security) battle casualties would be arriving in New York City and in San Francisco within the next forty-eight hours, and that he was out of beds. I told him that I would be back to him before 10 A.M.

Fortunately I knew the system in sufficient detail to know where the margins were. I telexed all commanding officers of our general hospitals and instructed them to put all ambulatory patients on home leave or to send them to convalescent facilities such as the one in Atlantic City. Next I asked them to remove all psychiatric patients not in locked wards from the hospital proper to adjacent barracks thereby freeing an additional sizable number of beds. Furthermore, I suggested that all ambulatory patients awaiting a second- or third-stage surgical intervention (as with patients involved in plastic reconstruction) be put on temporary leave, along with any other category of patient who could be removed from the hospital proper to barracks, convalescent facilities, or home leave. I asked the commanding officers to report back the number of new patients that they would be able to accommodate.

Shortly before 10 A.M., I called Fitzpatrick and told him that I would have the additional beds that he needed later in the day. He remained skeptical, but he had to sit tight. The field came through and the unexpected patients were distributed within the extant system. Unfortunately some of the newly arrived patients had to be hospitalized quite far from their homes, but we did not have to compromise in the quality of their care. Once the German counterattack on the Western Front had spent itself and the Germans were again in retreat, the inflow of new patients into the U.K. hospital chain moderated, which in turn led to an easing of the pressure on our general hospitals in the Zone of the Interior. The bed crisis of 1 January was fortunately an event that was not repeated.

The army had developed an elaborate point system to guide its demobilization. After one or two mistaken efforts to bring the Medical Department within these guidelines, the General Staff decided to delegate full authority for the demobilization of physicians to the surgeon general. Once the Armistice in Europe was signed in April and MacArthur's island-hopping strategy in the Pacific proved successful, many physicians found themselves more or less disemployed. To heighten their tension, they were hearing from their wives, their patients, and their colleagues of the need for their services at home—the United States had earlier commissioned about 40 percent of the entire U.S. physician supply. Both the underutilized physicians and the leaders of underserved communities started writing to their representatives and senators about the sluggishness and inefficiency of the army in demobilizing physicians. It was decided that I would be the key witness on the hill for the SGO, and for the next four months—that is, from the Armistice in Europe until the end of the war. I believe that no week, and surely no fortnight, went by without my having to appear before one or another subcommittee looking into the matter.

This was my initiation in appearing before congressional committees, and in contrast to the common opinion that most congressmen are ill-informed and looking for publicity at any cost—and are therefore prone to browbeat witnesses—that was not my experience. The congressmen were uniformly courteous and fair. The single exception occurred in 1952, when I got into a bitter altercation with an intemperate congressman from Michigan, who couldn't understand my statement that, by all indices, the health of the American people appeared to improve during World War II, in spite of the fact that the armed services had withdrawn 40 percent of the physician supply. He could not grasp the fact that higher levels of employment, income, and morale might improve people's health more than additional visits to physicians. I have had only positive, or at worst passable, experiences in my more than four decades of testifying before congressional committees.

Faced with a large patient load in its general hospitals and with the war with Japan picking up momentum, the SGO would have preferred to declare "essential" any specialist returning from overseas, no matter how long he had served or how many points he had accumulated. It was clear to me, on the basis of my discussions with congressmen of all persuasions, that such a policy could not be sustained, because it was inherently unjust. The future needs of the SGO were critical factors in designing a demobilization policy, but so were the points that long-serving uniformed personnel had accumulated. And the strained medical resources of many communities could not be ignored.

I decided that many specialists were not in acutely short supply, and that those with a high point score should be discharged on their return to the United States. Others, with shorter and less-arduous overseas services, could be held for brief periods of time so that we could get on top of our peak patient load. Our real problem involved such esoteric specialists as board-certified plastic surgeons; if I remember correctly, we had no more than ten in the entire army.

Since many patients requiring plastic reconstruction might have to remain in the hospital from six to eighteen months for repeated surgery—and we had many such patients—I calculated that the small number of plastic surgeons might have to be declared "essential" for five to ten years—clearly not a feasible solution. Accordingly, we quickly identified a group of younger general surgeons whom we assigned to a speeded-up course of on-the-job training with the established plastic surgical groups so that we could, with the addition of skilled nurses and technicians, start additional plastic-surgery centers to reduce the backlog.

Because I was able to adjust the discharge criteria in consonance with the declines in our patient load and to put out revised guidelines every two months, and because the SGO had no intention of abusing its authority to declare physicians essential and to force them to remain for protracted periods of time on active duty, we won widespread support from physicians still in the service, from congressmen, who were being pressured to get physicians back to their communities, and from wives, some of whom had not seen their husbands for three or four years.

Two additional observations on managing the demobilization of physicians: The instinctive approach of the regular army, though definitely not General Bliss's approach, would have been to fall back on the criterion of essentiality in order to retain enough specialists to meet its obligations to the sick and the injured. But once the Germans sued for peace, the public's tolerance for giving first consideration to the needs of the military declined rapidly.

When our first criteria for demobilization were ready for release—and on all subsequent occasions—I took special care to prepare a carefully crafted memorandum setting out the specifics in considerable detail. As further insurance, I held a press conference to assist the members of the press by answering their questions before they wrote their stories. But the performance of the press, including the reporters from the *New York Times*, had to be rated somewhere between poor and bad. In their efforts to simplify, they mangled their write-ups of the criteria, thereby confusing rather than helping their interested and concerned readers.

One of the complications that interfered with an orderly and speedy demobilization of physician personnel was the result of the surgeon general's strong preference to cut back proportionately the operating capacity of his general and station hospitals. But it soon became clear that such a strategy, while helping to keep the expanded wartime empire in place, would significantly slow the demobilization of physicians and other personnel because of the need to keep basic and specialized staffs at each hospital. The only real prospect for significant, accelerated "savings" would come from the closure of entire institutions, with the release of the surplus personnel into the general pool for early demobilization or reassignment. It took some time, and many subtle briefings of the surgeon general, before General Bliss and I were able to convince him that his preferred approach of cutting back the system across the board was not feasible, in light of the ever-stronger pressures from the outside to speed demobilization.

Once the war ended in Europe, all of our attention was directed to bringing the war in the Pacific to an early close. But nobody expected that victory over Japan could be achieved except through the invasion of the home islands, which was certain to lead to large casualties. Accordingly, the SGO decided to hold a planning conference on medical support for the invasion of Japan, to be attended by all senior medical officers who had had experience in dealing with large numbers of injured soldiers under intense battle conditions. During the last week in July 1945, the conference, with about forty in attendance, convened to identify the key "lessons" that had been learned in North Africa, Europe, and the Pacific and to explore how they should be modified in light of the special combat problems that U.S. troops would face in the invasion of Japan.

It was a good working conference, which produced the information and evaluations that we sought, but it ended on a heavy note. No one could estimate with any degree of firmness the number of probable battle casualties, but the figure that elicited the broadest support was in the range of a half-million seriously wounded during the first month of the invasion. I believe that our lowest estimate was around 350,000, the highest in the 850,000 range.

There has been a running argument from that day to this about whether President Truman and his advisers should have dropped atomic bombs on Hiroshima and Nagasaki. One thing is clear: The decision to use the bomb to make certain that the war would be brought to an early end must have been greatly affected by the knowledge that, if Japan had to be invaded, our losses in dead and injured would be very large indeed.

At the end of this planning conference, General Bliss decided that he and I, possibly with a very few others from headquarters, would go out to the staging area in the Pacific at the onset of the invasion so that we could learn first-hand of the problems involved and modify our treatment and evacuation plans and procedures accordingly. But our proposed visit was scratched when Japan sued for peace on August 14.

However, General Bliss was determined to visit the Orient, and in early November he, Brigadier General William C. Menninger, the chief consultant for psychiatry, and I were on our way to Peking in Gen. Albert Wedemeyer's C-54 plane, together with General Wedemeyer and some of his senior and junior staff. Wedemeyer was the commanding general of U.S. Forces in the Far East, and he also served as chief of staff to Chiang Kai-shek.

A few "medical" highlights from that trip: We stopped at Guam for a day, and I had the opportunity to talk with senior U.S. medical officers about their experiences in overseeing a hospital for Japanese prisoners of war. The Japanese Army surgeons had to be threatened with a gun before they agreed to operate on privates. We were told that many of the severely disabled jumped overboard when they were being repatriated via troop ships to their homeland. The explanation: Japan had little tolerance for and offered little support to men who could not care for themselves.

In Tokyo, I visited one of the country's largest hospitals and encountered the following practice: When a patient was admitted, one or more members of the family came along and ensconced themselves on a mat in a corner of the room, having brought along cooking and washing utensils. It was the family's responsibility to feed and nurse the patient.

Diagnosis and determining the treatment regimen was the physician's responsibility.

In a psychiatric hospital, where the staff showed little if any awareness of the importance of engaging depressed patients in one or another form of therapeutic activity, I was informed that the hospital had a shock machine that was apparently in frequent use—an early indication of Japanese fascination with advanced technology.

In China, I learned about an interesting improvisation in recruiting manpower for the army. Without warning, the military police would close off two ends of a thoroughfare and would tie all males who appeared to be capable of military service onto a rope and then march them off to a processing center. My informants explained that, even though such selectees would be transferred by air to battle stations a thousand or more miles distant, within six months more than half would have deserted and made their way back home.

In Shanghai, our party caught up with Colonel George Armstrong, the chief medical officer on Wedemeyer's staff (whom Bliss picked later on, when he became surgeon general to be his deputy and who subsequently became the surgeon general himself. Among Armstrong's many duties was to supervise the cleanliness of restaurants available to the GIs, which in turn gave him the power to enrich or impoverish the owners. We were his guests at his favorite restaurant, where the owner sought to repay the favor of having the army's seal of approval by preparing a twenty-eight-course dinner. I ate a little of every sixth course and found that too much.

After stops in South Korea, the Philippines, and Hawaii, we returned to Washington just in time for the Christmas holidays, having been gone for the better part of seven weeks. Traveling with the high brass—we were house guests of General MacArthur in Tokyo—in areas where the U.S. military and naval forces are important players sets a standard that no civilian traveling on his own can ever hope to approach.

Shortly after my return, General Paul Hawley, who had joined General Bradley as his chief medical officer in order to modernize the Veterans Administration, asked me whether I would come over to the VA and establish and run for a period of years, a Resources Analysis Division, such as I had been directing for General Bliss. This was not an offer that I could reject out of hand. I was conscious of the fact that I was one of the very few (fewer than a hundred) whom the War Department had asked to have deferred from military service, and I knew even from a distance that Hawley and the Veterans Administration needed all the help they could get. But I realized that I could not request a further leave from Columbia and that saying yes to Hawley meant saying no to an academic career, surely for the time and possibly permanently. And that I was not willing to do, so I reluctantly and with more than a little self-doubt turned General Hawley down late in 1945. This was a much more difficult decision than the decision to turn down a position with a major communications company as vice-president for research, at a salary about seven times greater than my Columbia salary.

The winter and spring of 1946 was a cleanup period. General Bliss had asked me to help him speed the transition from war to peace, to be certain that my division could continue to function effectively, to identify the priority issues that the SGO faced, and to sketch out the policies that should be put in place to assure that the much-restricted number of specialists available for service in the Zone of the Interior and overseas would be adequate to cope effectively with the prospective patient load.

I remember one challenge in particular. The army had only one certified obstetrician-gynecologist available in the Munich area, where our troop concentration was scheduled to remain relatively high. He happened to be a black physician. I did not see how one could force southern white women, married to officers or enlisted men, to be delivered by a black obstetrician and therefore arranged that on request they could go to the Frankfurt area for their delivery. Checking into the matter a year later, I found that almost no one had requested transfer to Frankfurt. The black specialist had won acceptance by the quality of his performance.

In May the army made me available to the Department of State to represent the United States at the Five-Power Conference on Reparations for Non-Repatriable Refugees, and when I returned in late June, with mission accomplished, I ended my three years and ten months of full-time work for the army. This was followed by another quarter-century of uninterrupted consulting activity for the Pentagon, the highlights of which are reviewed in the following chapter.

10

The Pentagon: The Cold War

In preparing a list of points to be included in this chapter, I did some simple arithmetic and was startled to discover that in the quarter-century between my leaving the SGO in 1946 to return to Columbia and my last major assignment for the Defense Science Board in 1971, I had spent roughly one day in every two weeks on matters affecting the Pentagon; this added up to approximately two-and-a-half years of full-time work during the quarter-century.

It would make little sense to me (and even less to the reader) if I sought to recount in any detail the issues in which I was involved over these two-and-a-half decades. Rather, I will single out some of the more interesting events that impressed me at the time and that in retrospect may hold some interest even for readers who know little and care less about the problems of the armed services.

A good place to begin is in 1946 with Secretary of War Robert R. Patterson's appointment of a Secretary of War's Medical Advisory Committee, with a small distinguished membership. The committee's chair was Edwin D. Churchill, professor of surgery at Harvard, who had served as Eisenhower's chief surgical consultant in the European theater of operations. The other members, as I recall them, were Michael DeBakey, who had served as deputy to General Fred Rankin, the chief consultant in surgery in the SGO; Hugh Morgan and William C. Menninger, respectively chief consultants in medicine and psychiatry in the SGO; and Marcus Pincoffs, who had spent the war in the Pacific as medical advisor to MacArthur. I was the only member who was not a physician and who had not served in uniform, but I had worked closely and continuously with DeBakey, Morgan, and Menninger over the preceding several years.

I am reasonably certain that Tracy S. Voorhees, who later became undersecretary of the army, was the sparkplug who led to the establish-

143

ment of the Secretary's Committee. He found allies among those in the top ranks of physicians who were being demobilized and who suspected that the Medical Department of the Army would return to the mediocrity that characterized its performance in the 1930s, a feeling that was shared by a few of the regulars, such as General Bliss, who was determined to keep the demobilized leaders of American medicine interested and involved.

While the members of the Secretary's Committee were concerned about the future well-being of the SGO, I don't recall that we met often or that we were able to provide a great deal of useful advice about how the military could continue to attract and retain the number of specialists that it needed to provide quality medical care in times of peace. What I do recall is a Thanksgiving dinner at Churchill's home in the Boston area in 1946 or 1947, with DeBakey as the other guest. Pete Churchill, as he was known to his friends, offered Mike DeBakey the carving knife, but DeBakey, thanking him for the honor, turned it down, saying that he had no skill in that area! Pete then proved that he was a master carver.

Norman T. Kirk's four-year term as surgeon general was drawing to a close in 1947. Eisenhower, as chief of staff, had much to say about selecting his successor unless the secretary of war (as in Kirk's earlier selection) or the president (as with Kirk's predecessor) should decide to intervene. General Marshall had recommended Howard Snyder to be the surgeon general in 1939, but Roosevelt was persuaded by his political advisers that if he appointed a little-known member of the Medical Corps, Major General James C. Magee, he would assure himself of more political support among the Irish-Catholic population in the upcoming 1940 election. Bliss was vulnerable because he had not served with troops during the war, but he had won the confidence of many of the top civilian physicians who served in uniform, and General Snyder's strong support for Bliss overcame Eisenhower's preference to choose a general who had served on an active front.

Despite Congress's deep respect and admiration for General George C. Marshall, it was unwilling in the early postwar years to approve his plan for compulsory military training for all young men. The Pentagon, at least the army, was strongly in favor of such a plan, but Congress had always been shy about relying on compulsion in peacetime to secure recruits for military service. It had renewed the draft in 1941 by only a one-vote margin in the House of Representatives! It took the unexpected outbreak of hostilities in Korea in June 1950 to lead to the passage of the Universal Military Training and Service Act in 1951.

The outbreak of hostilities in Korea was surely unexpected, because Dean Acheson, Truman's secretary of state, only a few months earlier, in testimony before Congress, had not included the protection of South Korea among the nation's strategic interests. Based on my 1945 trip to the Orient, I was restive about how prepared we were to deal effectively with the governments and people in that part of the world. A few examples: I was one of the few non-Japanese present at the first meeting of the Diet, when the emperor appeared before the legislators in an elaborate ritual that marked the beginning of his new role, stripped of his previous heavenly attributes and powers. I suspected then—and my suspicions have never been completely silenced—that even the best-informed Westerners cannot fully penetrate or understand these distant cultures.

In Peking, I recall having breakfast one morning with General Wedemeyer, who called my attention to a number of nondescript civilians eating at a table in the far corner. He remarked that "for all I know, they are the generals of the Communist forces in the outlying areas." He said it as a joke, but later events suggested that he may have been closer to the truth than he knew. Later that morning returning from the large market, I heard what was clearly some shooting close by. My marine guide explained that it was nothing to worry about: the shooting resulted from the on-the-spot execution of a thief in a small market nearby. The thief had been caught, tried, and shot within a period of five minutes. The Chinese saw no point in long, drawn-out judicial proceedings.

At a dinner meeting between the senior Chinese and American generals at the Summer Palace a few evenings later, at which each of the guests had four bottles of liquor at his place (most of which disappeared during the long hours of eating and speech-making), Wedemeyer went out of his way to try to persuade the Chinese not to reject the knowledge and skills of the West because only by using these skills would they be able to catch up. The message did not seem to be well received. The following evening, at a reception at the university, I asked the rector a question that he considered out of place, and I was brushed off in a fashion that reminded me that the Chinese viewed all whites—in fact all foreigners—as barbarians.

In Shanghai, at a country-club reception for Admiral Thomas Cassin Kincaid of the Seventh Fleet and our party, I was reminded by a beautiful Eurasian with whom I was dancing that in her view, and in the view of her friends, there was no real difference between the Americans and the British, who had formerly been the city's masters, other than our failure to disguise our interest in making a buck. The British had usually protested that they were great civilizers.

We flew from Shanghai to Seoul, where we spent several days as the guests of the commanding general of the U.S. forces. While he did his best to share with us his understanding of his mission and how that mission related to the divided country's past and future, the overwhelming impression that I came away with was that neither he nor our group could see beyond the very near future: The United States was there because a line had been drawn at the time of the Armistice between North and South Korea. We were clearly beyond our depth, but in December 1945 it seemed as if we might be around for a time, and we were still there in 1950 when North Korea launched its invasion. We know with the advantage of hindsight that MacArthur could not have been more mistaken in estimating the intentions and the actions of Korea's neighbor, China.

Three other recollections of my first exposure to the mysterious East: Since we could not land in Chungking because of bad weather, we went on to Kunming, where we spent a couple of days during which I learned that the local chiefs, each commanding his own army, paid little or no attention to the generalissimo in Chungking. China was one country more in name than in fact.

On the way back from Korea to Hawaii we stopped in the Philippines. I remember most clearly the miles upon miles of supplies piled multistory high between Manila and Clark Field, matériel to back up the invasion of Japan. It was clear that General Somervell and the U.S. economy had done their jobs well. What remained obscure was how the wealthy, all-powerful United States was going to win the peace, now that it had won the war. In each of the four Asian countries that we had visited— Japan, China, South Korea, and the Philippines—I felt restive because I sensed the immensity of the gap between the needs and desires of these nations and their leaders and our confusion about our short- and longer-term missions.

Our group touched down at Honolulu just as General Marshall was departing on the second leg of his first journey to establish a modus vivendi between the generalissimo and his Communist opponents. Although I had the greatest admiration for General Marshall, I feared that he had taken on an assignment at which he could not be successful, not because of lack of skill on his part but because of the historical forces operating on both of the Chinese contestants, forces that necessitated that only one emerge victorious.

Once hostilities broke out in Korea, the U.S. Army found itself short of men in a number of different fields, both at home and in the fighting zone. My consulting work was centered in the Office of the Assistant Secretary of the Army Personnel and Reserve Affairs. The assistant secretary was Earl D. Johnson, who was a close friend of Frank Pace, Truman's former director of the Bureau of the Budget, who had been moved to the Pentagon as secretary of the army.

The army's first response was to move troops from Japan to South Korea, next to ship some reserves from the Zone of the Interior out to the Far East, then to call up a large number of reservists, and finally to seek an early reinstitution of the draft. I recall specifically a request by the Corps of Engineers for no fewer than fifteen hundred engineers, which we began to broker with Detroit where the Big Three auto makers were slowly forced to curtail civilian output in favor of producing war matériel. When Detroit provided us with a list of their surplus engineers, a quick inspection revealed that they were extremely narrowly specialized in one or another facet of automotive manufacturing and could not fill the requisition from the Corps of Engineers, surely not without considerable retraining. We then took a closer look at the requisition and discovered that the Engineers did not really need fully qualified mechanical or electrical engineers; what they did need were able soldiers who could be trained in ninety days to operate various types of specialized equipment.

This experience of engineers in civilian life who had lost their flexibility through excessive specialization and the tendency of the armed services to overstate their requirements for skilled and professional manpower, was to be repeated many times.

In 1951 we received an urgent request from Major General Matthew Ridgway in Korea for infantry replacements, but we had none. We worked hard, however, to come up with a solution and finally informed Ridgway that we could send some black soldiers, but we would do so only if he wanted them. We got a message back that he needed replacements and had not specified anything about their color! South Korea saw the first broad-scale integration of black soldiers into combat units in the history of the U.S. Army.

In the summer of 1951, Pace and Johnson asked me to visit Europe to talk with Commanding General Thomas Handy and his staff at Heidelberg about their moving expeditiously to desegregate the army in Europe. President Truman had sent a directive to the Pentagon to act promptly, and the army, more so than the navy or the air force, had a tradition of following orders from its commander in chief. That I was selected for this assignment reflected in part the disinclination of the chief of staff, J. Lawton Collins, a native of Louisiana, to assume a lead position; and the same was true of Pace, who was a native of Little Rock, Arkansas. Moreover, Anna Rosenberg, the assistant secretary of defense for manpower and reserve affairs, who had made a tour around the European Command some months earlier, had also soft-pedaled the issue, informing the generals and their staffs that I would be along with the details.

When I arrived at Heidelberg and informed the senior staff (Handy was away) that they had twelve months in which to start and complete the total integration of blacks into the army, including housing, recreational facilities, and everything else under army command, their rejoinder was that it couldn't be accomplished in less than a decade, some said two decades. I repeated my message and they repeated theirs. When I talked with General Handy the next day, he listened and said very little other than that he would do his best. The only positive response that I received was from Lieutenant General Manton T. Eddy, the commanding general of the Seventh Army, when I visited him at his headquarters in Stuttgart. He told me that the move was overdue, and he felt sure that over time it would contribute to both the productivity and the morale of the army.

As is so often the case in communications between the Pentagon and the field, those in the field often resort to informal channels to ascertain whether the formal information is for real or for show. Heidelberg checked with General "Nuts" McAuliffe of Bastogne fame, the assistant chief of staff for personnel, who confirmed my message. Just about a year later, when Earl Johnson and a group of military and civilian aides were making a tour of air force bases from North Africa to Thule, five hundred miles from the North Pole, we spent a day at Heidelberg, where General Handy reviewed the great success that he had had with *his* plan for desegregation which he had carried through successfully and on time. The army's experience with desegregation convinced me of the important role that committed leaders can play in moving large numbers of people in directions they would prefer not to go. The intelligent use of power can alter people's experience and can speed changes in their thoughts, emotions, and behavior.

The navy, the most segregated service, rationalized its policy on the ground that white men didn't want to share close shipboard sleeping quarters with black men, a reasonable but not sufficient explanation. The simple fact is that, throughout most of this century, the navy was the preferred service and had been able to exercise wider choice in selecting from among potential recruits. The air force was the next favored and the army the least. Robert B. Anderson, a Texan whom Eisenhower had appointed as his secretary of the navy and who had earlier served on the National Manpower Council at Columbia, told me of various strategems that he had to use to take even the first steps towards desegregating the navy, two years after the army had completed its reform, strategems such as painting over signs that said "for colored only."

Having mentioned briefly the inspection trip with Earl Johnson to the North African air force bases in the summer of 1952, I will add a few observations. My recollection is that the Corps of Engineers spent between $150 and $175 million to build each airfield, an outlay that must be multiplied by four to be converted to today's dollars. The sad but incontrovertible fact is that by the time we looked at these fields, they were suffering from severe buckling, which made them inoperative in whole or in part. Lots of people, Americans and locals, had gotten rich by participating in the fields' construction but speedy execution of faulty plans did not yield useful output.

I was impressed to learn that construction workers from the United States, over an eighteen- to twenty-four-month tour, working seven days a week (and earning double time on Saturdays and triple on Sundays and holidays), could accumulate a nest egg of $50,000 (currently $200,000) because of exceptionally low living expenses and freedom from income-tax liability.

I knew as little about the culture and politics of North Africa as about the Far East. And we had little to do with the senior representatives of the French government who held down the top administrative positions, and even less to do with the local leadership. But once again, I became uneasy about the ability of the French to maintain their dominant position much longer. And the U.S. presence was even more of an anomaly, since we were interlopers twice removed from the people and their culture, preoccupied primarily with strengthening our defensive position vis-à-vis the U.S.S.R.

In the early 1950s, I arranged to visit the War Office in London to discuss the reasons that the British lost so few men between induction and their assignment to their permanent units; we had much higher losses during the transitional stage from civilian to military life. I got a quick and simple answer to my question. I learned that the British, recognizing that the transition period would be stressful for many young men who had never before been separated from home and friends, decided to put in charge specially selected sergeants, who had, as my informant expressed it, "mothering" skills. How different in the United States, where the armed services were wedded to the doctrine that the greater the initial shock the quicker the recruit would be turned into a soldier. What we had failed to allow for in our approach was the cost in manpower of prematurely separating soldiers who could not cope with the period of initial stress but who, if supported over the transition, would perform well.

I learned something more on that visit. When I showed up for my first appointment, a senior War Office official asked me to spell out in some detail the questions I wanted answered. He made notes and suggested that I return the following morning at the same time. When I reappeared he had a number of files before him; he told me that he had reviewed the files and that he was now in a position to provide me with the answers that I was seeking. At the end of an hour, I had all the information that I needed and a little more for good measure.

On reflecting on this episode, I tried to imagine what would happen if a Britisher came to the Pentagon to get an answer to some questions of concern to the British Army. First he would wander around the Pentagon for several days, being directed from one office to another where friendly but not very helpful officers would explain that the question was outside their sphere of competence. If he were lucky, the British visitor might, after several days of wandering through the halls of the Pentagon, make contact with an officer who knew something, but not necessarily a lot, about the subject. However, that officer would arrange a meeting some time the following week between the Britisher and some of his colleagues, whom he would identify after doing a search. If he were lucky, the Britisher could go home at the end of a fortnight with his questions answered, in part if not in whole.

Let me quickly add that the foregoing is not made up out of whole cloth. I recall an Israeli visitor to my Pentagon office who told me that he had been trying for days to talk about the army's philosophy and practices governing induction but had been unable to locate anybody who was both interested and knowledgeable. Someone had referred him to the "Columbia economist who serves as a part-time consultant," and that was the explanation for his presence. I explained that the subject was of special interest to me and that the National Manpower Council had recently published a report on *Student Deferment and Military Manpower Policy*. We began to talk, and my visitor told me that the Israeli Army accepted about 93 percent of the age cohort for service. We seldom got as high as 70 percent! He went on to explain the critical role that the Israeli defense forces were playing in speeding the acculturation of newcomers, a success story that I was able to learn more about during my first visit to Israel in 1953 and on subsequent visits, during which I spent considerable time with the Israeli military. Here was but one more bit of evidence of how national and military policies are shaped by the looseness or tightness in the human resources pool.

I had been uneasy, both during World War II and in the early postwar era, that the army, seeking to imitate the navy, was raising its requirements for enlistment and induction to levels that were justified more by preference and prejudice than by performance criteria. It was no secret that blacks had on the average considerably less educational preparation than whites, so that one sure way to keep the numbers and proportions of black recruits under control was to raise the qualification criteria for service through a screening examination that gave heavy weight to literacy and other school-acquired skills. My unease with the new requirements was further heightened by the emerging findings from our military manpower studies at Columbia, which demonstrated that most of the 300,000 illiterates who were accepted for service in World War II (and provided with up to ninety days of remedial education) had a satisfactory performance record. My disagreement with the new doctrine that the army needed better-qualified recruits stemmed from my belief that a tour of duty for many white and black men who came from disadvantaged backgrounds could pay off big both for them and for the country.

I kept pressing Earl Johnson and Frank Pace about this issue, to the point where Pace offered me an opportunity to make a detailed presentation at one of his monthly staff meetings attended by his senior military and civilian advisors. I had no sooner finished my presentation than General Collins, the chief of staff, started to hammer away at my logic and conclusions. His attack was direct and to the point, and in desperation I put the following question to him: If he had to assemble a squad to go out on patrol in Korea, would he prefer to select it from a group of Tennessee hillbillies who had never gone beyond the sixth grade, or from a group of Columbia doctoral candidates who had never handled a gun or who had never gone hunting. I knew I had lost the debate when Collins opted for the Columbia doctoral candidates.

The issue reemerged during the days of the Great Society programs. President Johnson persuaded Secretary of Defense McNamara to induct several hundred thousand "special standard" recruits and to keep track of their performance. The Department of Defense followed the president's orders and discovered that the overwhelming proportion of the "new standards" men, about 90 percent, finished their tour of duty satisfactorily; this was just a few percentage points below the completion rate for recruits with a higher cutoff score. But the DOD was careful to keep these findings from being widely disseminated, as did General Collins. The senior military knew the answer they wanted and gave short shrift to any other.

In the last months of the Truman-Pace era, I tried my luck once again with the secretary of the army to reform a basic element of the army's human resources policy. The promotion of officers depended in part on the evaluations they received from successive commanding officers under whom they had served. But the army offered little guidance to the evaluators. I suggested to Pace that the official appraisal report be revised so that between a sixth and a seventh of an officer's grade (roughly 15 percent) would reflect the skills with which he had utilized the human resources under his direct supervision. This time I was able to win a modest victory: the reform was introduced, but human resources management accounted for five, not fifteen, points.

In discussing officer evaluations I am reminded of a point that General Eisenhower once made to me. He was always leery of an officer who had not received one critical evaluation. In his view, that meant that the officer had been unwilling to challenge his superiors. If the officer had a number of negative evaluations he might well be either incompetent or a trouble-maker. But to have escaped any negative evaluation meant to Eisenhower that the officer did not have the guts ever to take a strong stand.

Another perspective on the Pentagon: In 1954 Robert B. Anderson, who had been serving as secretary of the navy, was promoted to deputy secretary of defense. Eisenhower had great respect for Anderson and might have selected him to be his running mate in 1956 had he succeeded in moving Nixon aside. Eisenhower recognized shortly after he had appointed Charles Wilson of GM as secretary of defense that he had made a mistake. I recall a conversation in which the president pressed me to explain how a person of such limited capacity could have risen to the top of the nation's largest industrial concern. I argued that GM moved people to the top who had undergone a long period of testing to prove that they would not disturb the others in the senior ranks. It was a system of promotion based on "not rocking the boat." I don't think that my explanation made a great deal of sense to Eisenhower.

I made it a practice to stop by and chat with Anderson whenever I was in the Pentagon and his schedule permitted, surely once a month or once in six weeks. I treasured hearing his perspectives on how that behemoth organization operated, and I think he found my interruptions relaxing. On one occasion I had hardly been seated when Anderson had to talk with Dulles about whether the Department of Defense or the Department of State would make a public announcement on a subject of minor importance that involved both departments. Dulles was no sooner off the phone, than some deputy called. And so it went for the next thirty minutes or more on matters of no importance except to the bureaucrats to whom prestige and public relations were all-important. Anderson was apologetic that he kept me waiting, but he was upset that much of his working days was directed to such trivia.

On another visit, he had to usher me out at the end of twenty minutes because he had set aside fifteen minutes for a lieutenant general from the air force to review and sign off on a $5 billion procurement order. Clearly it made no sense to him to allocate so little time for such an important decision but he recognized that his signing off was really pro forma. Once a contract reached the very top of the department and all the staff work had been completed and all the compromises had been worked out, the secretary or deputy secretary was unlikely to upset the arrangement. Those at or close to the top might change the direction of the department slightly at the outset of a program, but not at the end. Not even Robert McNamara was able to put his formal stamp on the department, and once he left, most of his modest reforms eroded.

Sometime in the 1950s, I began to lecture at the Industrial College of the Armed Forces in Washington, D.C., on military manpower policy, and some time later I gave an annual lecture to the students at Carlisle Barracks in Pennsylvania, where the army elite were sent, usually prior to, but sometimes following, their promotion to brigadier general. I also lectured at West Point on a memorable date—when a U.S. nuclear aircraft carrier intercepted the Russian vessels heading for Cuba.

The military, far in advance of other societal sectors, had a philosophy and practice of continuing education, and in my view it served as a model for the explosive growth of management education in the post-World War II era. Many business executives had become familiar with the army and the navy schools during their wartime experiences, and, when they returned to their companies after demobilization, they sought to imitate and adapt what they had learned. Although some officers were sent to school because the personnel department couldn't find them suitable assignments, most were sent to speed their career development and to provide senior officers with greater opportunity to assess them. It is said that General Marshall, during his years at Fort Benning, kept a small black book with the names and evaluations of the officers who passed under his scrutiny. Once the war broke out he had a preferred list of candidates to be appointed division commanders.

I had concluded early in my Pentagon experience that the army, like any other organization—the university, the church, the corporation—contained men of varying qualities and competences, from the best to the worst, and it was a mistake to consider all regular officers as men from the same mold. True, the military environment left its mark on all, but these environmental forces were less determining than the variations in personality and intellect.

This early impression was repeatedly reinforced as a result of my classroom experiences at the Industrial College. I went out of my way to formulate positions that were unconventional, challenging, and even contrary to the prevailing military ethos and doctrine in the hope and belief that I could thereby engage the class more fully. And for a period of more than ten years this approach worked, even though the commanding general or admiral who sat through my lecture could not have found many of my observations to his liking. At the end of my tenth year, the commanding general made a short speech of appreciation, presented me with a certificate that made me an "honorary professor," and announced that henceforth my photo would be added to faculty row. But within a year or two my presentation must have upset the navy commandant who attended the lecture to a point where he struck my name from future invitees.

I was satisfied during the dozen years or so that I lectured at the Industrial College that each of the services had a pool of able, mentally alert, and self-critical officers who, if and when selected for senior command or staff positions, would do their service proud. I had no reason to believe that they were a cut below our senior civilian officialdom, our politicians, our leaders in the professions, or our senior executives in corporate life. My only question related to the weight exerted by the military establishment. My years in the Pentagon had alerted me not to underestimate its dominant influence even on the most talented.

In 1959 the Conservation of Human Resources Project at Columbia University completed its three-volume study on *The Ineffective Soldier: Lessons for Management and the Nation,* which was the capstone of our decade's research (sponsored by General Eisenhower) into the military manpower experience of World War II. The assistant secretary of the army for personnel took the initiative to arrange a day-long conference in which the highlights of our extended research effort would be presented to the key staffs of the three services and to the interested officials in the Department of Defense. General Snyder, the long-term advisor to the study, conveyed President Eisenhower's greetings and his conviction that the results should be of benefit to the armed services. The audience was attentive, even interested, but I suspected before the conference began and was certain when it had concluded that not a single one of our findings that cut to the core of military personnel practice would be accepted. The Pentagon simply did not respond to university research on military manpower, not even when the commander in chief had sponsored it.

Unlike the instructors at the Industrial College, where many civilians participated, the dominant faculty at Carlisle Barracks was military, which made me conspicuous among the presentors. In 1963 two students asked whether they could take a walk with me during the morning break, a request to which I immediately assented although I was puzzled by it.

But my puzzlement was soon dispelled. The two officers explained that they had recently completed a year's tour of duty in the delta in Vietnam, and they wanted me to know that General Hawkins, the top commander, was not communicating what was really happening to the top echelons of the Pentagon or to the White House. What is more, the visitors from Washington who were sent out to take a reading on the spot were being misled—the Communists were gaining, not losing. I made a note of what I was told but did nothing with the information. However, on my next appearance, in the fall of 1964, a repeat performance shook me up.

This time I wrote to President Johnson, with whom I had had some contact both when he was vice-president and after he became president, to the effect that he might want to invite a few of these returnees from Vietnam for Sunday supper at the White House and elicit their appraisal of what was happening there. I added that these officers were not ideologues opposed to U.S. intervention but were some of our best army regulars who were upset by the failure of the facts to get through. To the best of my knowledge the president did nothing about my suggestion; and with the advantage of hindsight I see that it is unlikely that an evening's probing conversation with a group of officers who had served in Vietnam would have made any real difference in the slow unfolding that followed.

In January-February 1967 I had an opportunity to see for myself. The Department of State thought it might be useful if I made a trip to the Far East in order to consult with several governments about their manpower policies and programs as well as to give some lectures to academic and business audiences. And the army thought it would be a good idea, since I would be in the area, to stop at Saigon and see how things were developing with regard to military manpower.

My wife and I arrived in Saigon from Singapore on Sunday evening. I had selected the window seat on the assumption that as the plane neared its destination there might be signs of fighting. And the sky was lit up, even though the airport was blacked out. My first appointment, the next morning at nine at the U.S. embassy, was listed as "Meeting on Military Manpower." I expected to find a group of four or five—army, air force, a representative of the local forces, possibly a civilian or two. I came into a room with sixty persons present. My opening remark was that a vast reduction in the overhead structure was clearly indicated.

I returned to the hotel for lunch and found that my wife, who had spent an hour or so on the streets, was thoroughly confused: our young men were in uniform; the local young men were in civvies trying to work currency swaps or propositioning women. It had taken her less time than it took me to realize that there was a lot seriously wrong in Vietnam. I had a slight acquaintance with General William Childs Westmoreland, whose office in the Pentagon had been but a door or two from mine. We had talked on infrequent occasions and I had not been particularly impressed. I knew that he was very busy in Saigon and saw no point in trying to set up an appointment. I spent most of my time talking to junior and middle-level personnel who had acquired reputations for knowing what the score was. I was startled to learn from both CIA and the civilian pacification staff that things were much worse than reported in the press, and that there was little or no prospect for the United States to accomplish more than an honorable withdrawal. The corruption of the Saigon government was beyond belief.

I had no special knowledge of this part of the world, but I had delayed my departure from Tokyo in order to catch Ambassador Alexis Johnson, a major architect of our Far East policy, when he returned to the embassy in the late afternoon from a trip to the countryside. During the more than two hours of talk I was startled and dismayed to learn that the ambassador continually referred to Vietnam in terms of Korea. I knew that Vietnam was very different from Korea in its history, demographics, and much more. The analogy disturbed me, since it put our involvement in Vietnam as just one more effort in our containment policy against the Communists.

On my return to the United States, I tried to identify some senior personnel in the Pentagon who might be interested in discussing Vietnam and was able to identify only one—Townsend Hoopes, assistant secretary of the air force, who was an early and strong critic of our policy there. The rest of the high command, military and civilian, had concluded that Vietnam was a country that could bring only grief—better to stay away from it.

In the spring of 1967, I was invited to a luncheon at the White House at which the prime minister of South Korea was the guest of honor. Senator Fulbright was among the dignitaries at the head table. I ran into Walter Rostow, whom I knew, and started to tell him that I was recently back from Vietnam. Before I could add another word, he told me how well we were doing there. To make matters worse, he seemed to believe his own optimistic statements.

I found the president's luncheon remarks unexceptionable, except that he picked on his guest, Senator Fulbright, who could do nothing to even the score. But I concluded that the difference between being the president and being a senator, even the chairman of the Senate Committee on Foreign Relations, was vast.

The erosion and corrosion that our involvement in Vietnam brought in its wake is well known. One reminder: I made it a practice at the beginning of each semester at Columbia to inquire how many of the male students were pursuing an M.B.A. because they wanted to remain out of the army. Never was the show of hands less than one-third of the men. If one assumes that another third were loath to admit in public why they were in school, one can see that the nation fought in Vietnam primarily with poor blacks and poor whites who didn't have the money or the educational prerequisites to escape the draft.

As the 1960s were nearing their close, candidate Nixon supported the idea of a voluntary force to replace the draft. In 1970, early in his presidency, he appointed a commission, headed by Thomas S. Gates, to review the possibility of instituting a solely volunteer force and estimating the costs that such a force would entail. I was told that the Department of Defense had sent my name to the White House to be a member of the commission but that President Nixon had substituted Milton Friedman, a long-time advocate of the volunteer force. I was much relieved, because I would not have gone along with what became a unanimous report. I was a firm believer that military service should be an obligation required of all men in a democracy, and that if the numbers of potential selectees exceeded requirements then a lottery should determine who should serve. But the Gates Committee proposed a volunteer service and the president and Congress supported it. If truth be told it has worked better than I imagined, but I still think we took the wrong turn.

My last two assignments for the Pentagon date from 1973. The less important was my appointment to a four-year term to the Scientific Advisory Board of the U.S. Air Force. Edward Teller was a fellow member, but since we met as a committee of the whole only on ceremonial occasions, I never had a clue about what Teller was recommending to the air force. I was grouped with those with an interest in human resources, the informal head of which was one of the air force's large research contractors, a sensible if narrow man. His major effort was directed to taking our entire group on extended field trips, including visits to a number of civilian and military installations, during which we had an opportunity to observe some of the most modern technology used for simulated training and other instructional purposes. My term came to an end with neither the air force nor I any better or worse as a consequence of the four-year consulting relationship.

But 1970 had an edge to it because of my assignment as Chair of a Defense Science Board's special committee established to assess the manpower research activities of the armed services. I played a key role in selecting the other members, and the committee had able and interested members who did not balk at frequent meetings. We wanted each of the services to make presentations, but we had great difficulty in explaining ahead of time that we were not interested in receiving standard briefings with multiple charts and uninterrupted presentations. Rather, we wanted to ask questions as the briefings developed. This did not make us popular with the services, but we surely learned more—and more quickly—than we would have with traditional briefings.

Our primary focus was on manpower research and what more and better research could contribute to the more effective utilization of the services' human resources. Our final report was entitled *Manpower Research and Manpower Management in Large Organizations*. Our conclusions were restrained; some would call them constrained. We had reluctantly but nonetheless surely reached the conclusion that the armed services were going to proceed to do what they wanted to do, and that there was little that outside advice and counsel, no matter how sound and sensible, could contribute. Aside from a few innovative suggestions, we concluded that real control over the human resources deployment of the armed services was embodied in the president's and Congress's power to restrict the amounts of money available to the services. Any other form of leverage was doomed to fail.

It was not an optimistic report, but it was the best that we could hammer out. I suspect that I had run out of the enthusiasm of my younger years, when I still believed that the military would respond to sensible suggestions that promised to improve their operations. By 1971 I had lost my innocence.

But I still had my cunning. I arranged to have published a thousand copies of our final report, in the belief that through wide distribution some of our observations might find their way sooner or later into Pentagon policy. Imagine my surprise when, in 1973, an assistant of the newly appointed secretary of defense, Elliott Richardson, called up to inquire whether I could lend the secretary a copy of our report, since he was unable to raise one in the Pentagon. Clearly the Pentagon had learned how to keep reports from being read, no matter how many copies had been printed.

11

Employment and Training Programs

Until October 1953, when James P. Mitchell was appointed secretary of labor to succeed Martin P. Durkin, the plumber among the millionaires in Eisenhower's cabinet, I had had only fleeting associations with the Department of Labor. In early 1982 when Secretary Donovan presented me with the department's Certificate of Merit, I was surprised to learn that I had served under thirteen secretaries of labor during the preceding three decades.

My relations with Jim Mitchell began in World War II, when he had served as director of the Civilian Personnel Division for General Somervell, and I had continued my relations with him and his staff while I was attached to the Control Division of the ASF. We continued to see each other in the postwar years, at least monthly at the Columbia Seminar for Labor, at which he was a regular attendee. Mitchell had become general manager of Bloomingdale's in New York City, a high position, but he never told me his specific duties. What I did know from our frequent meetings was that Mitchell missed the excitement of Washington and looked for an opportunity to return. In early 1953 I was able to be helpful by telling Robert T. Stevens, the newly appointed secretary of the army, that Mitchell was available and would make an excellent assistant secretary of the army for manpower and reserve affairs. Stevens must have checked him out, and shortly afterwards Mitchell was once again ensconced in the Pentagon. My recollection is that he found the Pentagon considerably less exciting in 1953 than he had in his wartime post a decade earlier.

When Durkin unexpectedly resigned, I didn't need any prompting to get in touch with President Eisenhower via General Snyder and to urge the president to offer Mitchell the job. The president at the time was in Denver, Colorado, on his way to or from a fishing expedition. A reply was speedily received from the Presidential Office to the effect that they were surprised at my recommendation, since John Mitchell appeared to have had little direct involvement in industrial relations. I quickly recognized that they had confused James P. with John P. The latter was a competent civil servant in the Department of Defense but by no stretch of the imagination suitable for the open post. I got the confusion cleared up and added the suggestion that Governor Dewey of New York would probably provide political support—if that was needed. Such support was forthcoming, and within a few days Eisenhower nominated Mitchell and the Senate readily confirmed him.

During the course of my long association with General Eisenhower (see chapter 12) I offered him all sorts of advice, but I took special care not to make recommendations about personnel. In retrospect I realize that the only three times that I broke that rule Mitchell was involved, directly or indirectly. When the position of secretary of defense became available, Mitchell asked me whether I would be willing to mention to the president his interest in being considered for the position. I said that I would be pleased to speak on his behalf because I knew how interested he was in the administrative problems of DOD and his considerable prior experience in the Pentagon. When the president heard this, he told me to tell Jim that he could find a number of candidates for the secretary of defense but he could not find another secretary of labor like James P. Mitchell.

On the third and last occasion, Mitchell asked me whether I would talk to the president about the opening on the Supreme Court. Mitchell, a New Jerseyite, knew Judge William Brennan of the state's top court and believed that he would make an excellent addition to the Supreme Court, for in addition to his legal knowledge his appointment would have political, religious, and ethnic advantages. I knew Mitchell well enough to appreciate that he would not ask me to help unless he had the highest regard for the candidate, and I was willing to bet on Mitchell's judgment and integrity. When I mentioned Mitchell's positive views of Brennan to the president, I had a feeling that Jim's recommendation was going to carry great weight—as apparently it did.

Shortly after Mitchell became secretary of labor, he told me that he planned to appoint a number of senior advisors and asked me for recommendations. Among others, I suggested an old friend, Professor Albert Abrahamson of Bowdoin College, who had previously undertaken periodic assignments for the department. When the appointments were announced, I was surprised to find myself included, along with Douglas Brown of Princeton, Clark Kerr of the University of California, Berkeley, and the distinguished labor arbitrator Cy Ching. Brown acted as our informal chairman and our primary task was to reassess the mission of the department.

We took our task seriously: we met frequently, we talked with a great number of the department's stalwarts, we wrote papers, and after more than a year's effort, we submitted a report to the secretary that recommended that the department shift away from its earlier role as the advocate of the "working man and working woman" and redefine itself as the manpower planning and policy agency of the federal government. Mitchell was enthusiastic about our report and moved to insure its early implementation.

Mitchell was fortunate in his choice of his undersecretary, James (Jack) O'Connell, a talented but self-effacing administrator who set himself the task of making the department run as smoothly as possible while impinging as little as possible on the secretary's time, so that Mitchell could concentrate on external affairs—his relations to the labor movement, employers, and other agencies of the federal government.

In 1958 Mitchell asked me to head the U.S. delegation to the International Labor Organization's meeting in Geneva, at which the principal agenda item would be "discrimination," which early intelligence indicated would be used by the U.S.S.R. to launch a broad-scale attack on the United States. I very much wanted to accept, and I recognized that Mitchell was convinced that I would make a good chairman because of my considerable sophistication in this area (he had been the luncheon speaker in New York City a few years earlier when my book on *The Negro Potential* had been published).

But I also recognized that if I were to finish our three-volume study on *The Ineffective Soldier*, for which the president was waiting and on which we had expended eight years of hard effort, I had no option but to stay home that summer and get the manuscript to the publisher. I asked General Snyder to explain to Mitchell my prior obligation, which had to take precedence. Much as I regretted at the time having to turn this opportunity down, I realized in later years that most international conferences are drama, slow or lively, but still drama, little more.

Mitchell was deeply concerned about and used his influence to move an uninterested Republican administration into a more active civil rights posture. He had reasonable success with Richard Nixon, who had become the chair of the federal body that was responsible for eliminating discrimination in government contracts. But as the second Eisenhower administration approached its end and as the nominating convention drew near, Nixon began to waffle, unclear whether Mitchell's advice to come out strongly for minority rights would cost him more votes than it would win him.

One of the steps that Mitchell decided upon to implement our Consultants' Report was to establish a Manpower Administration to give visibility to the department's new mission and direction. He asked me for the names of candidates who might head and staff it. I had remained in contact with a Columbia student of mine from the late 1930s, Seymour Wolfbein, who had been moving ahead in the Bureau of Labor Statistics. I recommended that Mitchell have a talk with him; they hit it off, and Wolfbein later became a senior official in the Manpower Administration.

As the decade drew to an end, the United Steel Workers were moving into a strike posture with the industry, which, for the first time, appeared to welcome a confrontation. I had the opportunity to chat at length with one of the senior executives of U.S. Steel; he revealed that, since his company and the others were sure that the Republican White House would intervene in their behalf, they had nothing to lose by holding firm during the negotiations and playing tough if a strike broke out. I tried to alert him to the errors in his thinking by telling him that Eisenhower would rely heavily on Jim Mitchell for guidance, and that I had every reason to believe that Mitchell would advise the White House to keep its distance. The industry leaders misread the situation completely, and the settlement, when it came, cost them dear. One must proceed cautiously in estimating how presidents are going to act in a crisis, and one should never place much weight on ideology. Hard-nosed politics is likely to win almost every time over ideology.

It was not easy to be an effective secretary of labor during the last seven years of Eisenhower's administrations. There were few White House initiatives, Congress was apathetic, and the national industrial relations scene had lost most of its sharp edges. Mitchell contributed in his quiet way to keeping the labor scene on an even keel and used the tranquil era to restructure the department so that it could function more effectively once Washington, on its own or on the initiative of others, returned to a more active role in national labor affairs.

To tell the end of the Mitchell story: He became the head of industrial relations for Crown Zellenbach and relocated on the West Coast for a period of years. He then returned East, entered politics in New Jersey, won the Republican gubernatorial nomination in 1972, but suffered a fatal heart attack while the campaign was still underway. Mitchell was respected by Democrats as well as Republicans, by employers as well as trade unionists, for his judgment and his decency.

The unemployment rate had started to climb at the end of the Eisenhower administration, and Senator Joseph Clark of Pennsylvania and Representative John Holland from the Pittsburgh area began to hold hearings on the causes and cures for the increasing numbers of people who were without jobs. Garth Mangum, of the University of Utah, was the staff director for Senator Clark, and he invited an array of labor economists and others to appear before the subcommittee during the 1960 hearings. This was my initial contact with the senator, but we kept in contact thereafter.

Shortly after Kennedy's razor-thin margin of victory in November 1960, Senator Clark asked me to assemble a group of leading academics and others with whom he could explore the best way of raising manpower to a more prominent place on the new administration's agenda. The meeting was scheduled for the Harvard Club in New York City, and it took place on the day that one of the prospective participants, Arthur Goldberg, was called to the White House and informed of his nomination as secretary of labor. I had asked my friend and colleague, Arthur F. Burns, to attend, not because he was particularly interested in manpower but because of his experience in the White House as Eisenhower's first chairman of the Council of Economic Advisors (CEA).

Senator Clark reviewed with us that afternoon a number of options that might contribute to raising manpower to greater visibility, such as making the subject the special concern of one of the three members of the Council of Economic Advisors, recommending that Kennedy appoint a special assistant for manpower, and still other organizational initiatives. Burns and I finally put forward the winning approach: to have Congress require that the president submit an annual report on manpower and to have Congress schedule hearings to review both the analysis and the recommendations submitted by the president. Such a formalized procedure was certain to attract a reasonable amount of attention by assuring that both the administration and Congress would have to look at the broad manpower situation at least annually. The group also recommended, not without self-interest, that Congress make some funds available to the department for external research on manpower issues.

The Kennedy administration got off to a relatively slow start, but in 1961 Congress passed the first manpower legislation, which created a role, albeit a modest one, for the federal government to provide training funds to assist the unemployed in Appalachia as part of a larger regional economic development program.

There were heated arguments in 1961 about the causes of the recent increases in the number of unemployed. One side blamed the weakness in over-all demand and looked to macrocorrections through fiscal and monetary policy, while the conservatives saw the rising unemployment as a consequence of "structural" factors, primarily a supply-side deficit that could best be remedied by providing unemployed workers with an opportunity for retraining and for the acquisition of new skills.

The Republicans took the lead in designing the Manpower Development and Training Act (MDTA) of 1962 which was passed in the spring of the year—after which the chairmen of the House and Senate Appropriations Committees began to feud over who was to call on whom to settle some minor differences in the respective bills. It was finally funded in the fall, and the first enrollments began in the winter of 1962-63.

Wolfbein had been discussing with Secretary Goldberg the questionable logic of the administration's supporting a training approach that was not tied to a job-expansion program to absorb the trainees when they had completed their skill-enhancement efforts. Since he got nowhere with the secretary, he suggested that I try my luck. Goldberg explained to me that Kennedy's White House was being very cautious and that it would support the training effort but nothing more. And he made it clear that, while he agreed with Wolfbein and me, he had no option but to follow the White House's approach.

By the end of twelve months it was clear that the sponsors of MDTA had misread the scene: a recession, not the acceleration of automation, had been the cause of rising unemployment, and with the pickup in business most of the skilled workers got their old jobs back or found new ones without retraining.

Senator Joseph Clark, who had helped steer MDTA through the Senate, remembered the advice that we gave him at our meeting in New York City and provided for the establishment of a National Manpower

Advisory Committee (NMAC), to be appointed by the secretary of labor, which would report to both the secretary of labor and the secretary of health, education, and welfare. Further, the new legislation authorized the Department of Labor to enter into external contracts for research. Wolfbein had negotiated an agreement with Goldberg that I would be appointed chairman of the NMAC, but because of the delay in appropriations he had to renegotiate it with W. Willard Wirtz, who took Goldberg's place when the secretary was nominated for the Supreme Court.

The NMAC was invited to meet with the president prior to its first formal meeting in September 1962, but the president's schedule was badly awry that day and he was running an hour-and-a-half late. Lyndon Johnson was in our waiting area in the White House, and after learning who we were, he offered some important insights into the legislative history of MDTA. He told us that he was concerned from the outset that poor blacks and other poor people would be kept out of the job market unless the federal government stepped in and helped them to get training. Johnson reported that he had worked out a deal with the southern leadership, Senator Donald Stuart Russell and others, that this was the basic goal of the act, even though the act itself made no reference to the black minority. One of my first actions when we met in formal session that afternoon was to make Johnson's legislative history part of our record.

Finally, Kennedy was ready to receive us, to say a few words, to have a group picture taken. Johnson came along for the photo-taking. My most striking recollection of what was a harried meeting with a harried president was Kennedy's inability to see the tremendous excitement of our only black member, an assistant superintendent of schools from Chicago, to whom the occasion was a dream come true. I was upset at the time about Kennedy's oversight, and even though I have long appreciated the pressures on presidents, I remain unhappy about this evidence of insensitivity.

Since a decade ago I edited and contributed to a book on *Employing the Unemployed*, which afforded me an opportunity to undertake a retrospective assessment of the major developments in federal manpower policy and programming between 1962 and 1979, I will not cover the same ground here. Rather, I will offer an insider's view on how this departure in federal legislation evolved over the two decades during which I played an active role first as chair of the NMAC, later as chair of the National Commission for Manpower Policy, and then as chair of the National Commission for Employment Policy, as the commission was renamed in 1978 when its director, Dr. Isabelle Sawhill, found the term "manpower" jarring and convinced a sympathetic congressional committee to change our name. I supported Dr. Sawhill's effort, but only distantly. I did not favor a major lobbying effort to achieve a semantic correction, but I was pleased when she succeeded in bringing it about largely on her own.

I must mention at the outset the ambiguities that attach to a standing "advisory committee." Who is the committee supposed to advise? In our case, the statutory answer was the secretary of labor and the secretary of health, education, and welfare. The latter was given a role in the MDTA legislation by virtue of the fact that the vocational educational establishment had been singled out to assist in training and retraining the unemployed. In fact, the vocational educational lobbyists had rallied much support for MDTA when it was making its way through Congress.

But W. Willard Wirtz, the secretary of labor, had little interest in or, to put it more bluntly, use for advisory committees. He found the federal bureaucracy overwhelming, and he had no interest in becoming further enmeshed in the bureaucratic web via advisory committees. My recollection is that he never attended any of our quarterly meetings during the almost eight years that he served as secretary, and if he made an appearance it was purely ceremonial. He never asked us to provide him with our views on any manpower issue that crossed his desk and on which he had to take action.

But Wirtz made an early decision about the membership of the committee that proved helpful. The authorizing legislation indicated that employers and labor should have equal representation, and the U.S. Chamber of Commerce and the AFL-CIO had, after an informal discussion, decided to claim six out of the available ten places. When the secretary heard of this plan he decided that two for each of the major parties would meet the congressional intent and would provide additional leeway for the appointment of individuals with broader interests and perspectives. Wirtz was right: One of the two labor representatives in the early days of the NMAC proved quite recalcitrant, because he feared that the training legislation might dilute the control that selected trade unions had over skill training (via apprenticeship, which determined who would get the preferred jobs with above-average pay and benefits). While the organized labor leadership in Washington had supported MDTA during its journey from congressional committee to enactment, there was unease, particularly among several state labor organizations, particularly in California, about the act's potential to dilute labor's control over the occupations where skill training was important. But these questions and doubts dissipated early on, and organized labor remained a strong supporter of all subsequent employment and training programs.

Early in the deliberations of the NMAC the members agreed to elicit the active cooperation of the employer community in providing training and employment opportunities for the hard-to-employ. I therefore appointed a subcommittee to explore this approach under the chairmanship of Felix Larson, a senior official of R. W. Grace and Company, who had recently resigned as chief counsel to the Department of Defense. Larson reported at a subsequent meeting that he had secured the cooperation of the Advertising Council to launch a large-scale public information campaign directed at informing the public about the needs of the unemployed for assistance in obtaining training and jobs. The secretary, however, decided to stop the campaign before it got started, on the ground that operating the program within the federal bureaucracy was complicated enough without bringing in outsiders, such as the Advertising Council and the employer community.

We had just reassembled after lunch to start our afternoon meeting on 22 November 1963, when a member of the housekeeping staff put his head into the meeting room and announced that the president had been shot. We moved quickly to the third floor, where the secretary's office was located, in the hope and expectation that the TV or a radio would provide us with more definitive information. Wirtz, together with several other cabinet officers, was at the moment en route to Japan so we had the run of his office, but it took at least fifteen minutes—which seemed like an eternity—before we found a live radio that confirmed our worst fears. At no time, before or after, was Washington as shell-shocked as on that Friday afternoon; people walked the streets, hither and yon, because they needed companionship—but not to the point of talking with those whom they encountered.

Once Johnson became president, the war on poverty accelerated and Congress began to respond on a great many fronts, including manpower. While Senator Hubert Humphrey did not succeed in gaining support to reestablish the Civilian Conservation Corps, the MDTA legislation was amended to provide for the establishment of the Job Corps and the Neighborhood Youth Corps, each specifically aimed at helping disadvantaged youth. The former was a high-cost, low-volume effort to provide "second chance" opportunities for the most seriously disadvantaged youths. They would be relocated from their homes and localities and provided with health, educational, and other remedial services over a twelve-month stretch while they acquired work experience and a skill. Unfortunately, a high proportion of those who were relocated could not cope with the stresses of separation and the commitment and discipline that the program required. But for those who did, Job Corps paid off, since most of them had a "positive termination," governmental legalese for their successful transition to the army, to school, to an apprenticeship program, or to a job.

It is worth pointing out that among the contractors who bid and won contracts to operate Job Corps Centers were several large aerospace companies, and in future years, when the continuation of the program was at risk, their political muscle helped to keep the opposition at bay and contributed to the long-term survival of the program.

In the summer of 1965 Watts exploded, and the NMAC faced the challenge of whether to recommend one or more special interventions. Some members believed that it would be a mistake to respond dramatically, because that might lead out-of-control adolescents and young adults to cause still more trouble in the hope and expectation that the federal government would be more forthcoming with new supportive programs. Others argued that the rioting reflected serious shortcomings in the opportunity structure available to ghetto youth and that an early and sensible program of expanded training and jobs should be quickly put in place.

The Summer Youth Program was first enacted in 1965, and in subsequent years it was substantially enlarged, with the aim of providing many disadvantaged youth with a reasonable alternative to rioting during their summer vacations by providing them with some work experience and, even more important, with a weekly wage.

But the program suffered from many weaknesses. Congress was repeatedly late in making the appropriations, which meant that local program operators were always late in recruiting enrollees, as well as in assuring appropriate training and work sites and recruiting staff. As the years passed, responsible local officials improved their planning and operations, but many summer youth programs continued to be little more than a camouflage to pay youngsters from low-income homes a stipend that would discourage them from engaging in violent actions during their summer vacations. It took more than a decade before the summer youth program became—and then only selectively—a part of a year-round strategy to assist disadvantaged youth who need special assistance to make the transition into a full-time job.

Shortly after the Watts riots, I visited the West Coast to gain some first-hand impressions as to the causes and possible remedies. Several points became clear. One, that there was a serious mismatch between what was happening in the typical ghetto high school and the needs of the youngsters. I recall one overgrown youth who sat at the back of the room with a big knife on his desk to remind both the teacher and his classmates not to bother him. I learned that the conventional wisdom that it was the backward youngsters who were dropping out of school was only partially correct. The drop-outs included some of the best students, who just couldn't and wouldn't put up any longer with what they considered to be an oppressive environment that contributed nothing constructive to them.

There were plenty of job openings in the Los Angeles area, and most employers were willing to hire minorities, blacks or Latinos, but most of these job openings were inaccessible to people living in Watts unless they had private transportation. The federal government later on sunk tens of millions of dollars into subsidizing bus lines to the outlying areas, but the dispersion of the plants was such that even with the subsidy the buses could not attract enough passengers even from among those who were willing to commute for one-and-a-half hours each way in order to work. Watts should have been an early warning that developing real solutions for the job problems of people living in low-income urban neighborhoods would require more than Congress's passing some amendments to MDTA and subsidizing transportation.

It is difficult to know what would have happened to the Great Society efforts if the nation had not become so deeply enmeshed in Vietnam, but one conclusion is incontrovertible. Because we became trapped in Vietnam, the budget available at home for reform and reconstruction became more or less frozen, and with an annual manpower appropriation of about $1 billion in the latter 1960s, there was not enough new federal money to make much of a dent. The money had to be doled out among the fifty states and then further subdivided among various groups of poor and disadvantaged people.

In 1968, convinced that he could expect little leadership from his secretary of labor, President Johnson decided to launch a private-sector initiative from the White House, directed at large employers, under the chairmanship of Henry Ford II. The National Alliance of Business (NAB) aimed to increase the hiring of blacks and other minorities. The labor market was favorable, since unemployment had dropped below 4 percent and the offshoots from affirmative action and civil rights activities had added energy and support. Since the NAB wanted to be free of bureaucratic red tape, the Department of Labor was in no position to keep tabs on how many were hired, but spot checks suggested that they exceeded 100,000 during the first year of the effort. Some years later, I obtained access to the experience of one of the big three automobile manufacturers, which revealed several interesting facts. Although the company had added sizable numbers of inner-city blacks to their assembly lines on the outskirts of Detroit, two to three years later only a handful of the men were still on the job. Some had quit after a short time, finding the work, their coworkers, their supervisors, and their commutes more than they could handle. Others stayed on but were vulnerable to layoff when production slackened in 1970. On the other hand, most of the black women who had been added to the clerical work force as a result of the NAB effort were still employed in the early 1970s, and, moreover, a considerable number had been promoted into more responsible positions. I had long believed that, while black women do suffer from discrimination, they face fewer hurdles than do black men.

The tension between the president and Secretary Wirtz reached a high point in the closing months of the administration. Rumor had it that the White House wanted the secretary to resign, but the secretary managed not to get the message. What I recall is the large turn-out at a testimonial dinner for the secretary at which George Meany was the principal speaker. I sat at a table with George and Mrs. Shultz. Everybody commented on the absence of the White House staff and even more at the absence of a presidential greeting. But the secretary, a gifted speaker and writer, rose to the occasion in his final remarks.

Arthur F. Burns told me on one occasion how George Shultz became Nixon's secretary of labor. Burns was talking with the president-elect, who remarked that he had no idea whom to appoint to that position. Burns brought up Shultz's name, told Nixon that Shultz had been a good staff man on the Council of Economic Advisors in the Eisenhower period, was the right kind of academic with considerable experience in labor negotiations, and was not a captive of the AFL-CIO. Shultz got the job.

Shultz appointed Arnold Weber, a colleague from Chicago—and with family roots in the labor movement—as assistant secretary and as manpower administrator. Weber, like Shultz, had the happy faculty of being able to bridge the world of ideas and the world of action, and I was not surprised by his post-Washington successes as a university president. (He is currently the head of Northwestern University.) Weber was interested in the work of the NMAC and took a leading role in most of its discussions. While we were never intimate, I liked and respected Weber and he had a friendly stance toward the NMAC.

As the decade drew to a close it became increasingly clear to everybody who had even a casual acquaintance with MDTA that it made no sense for the Department of Labor to continue to operate its training programs out of Washington. Decentralization was urgently needed. But there were dangers. After all, by the late 1960s the poor and the disadvantaged had become the primary target group that needed help—and that meant blacks in the first instance. But under a program of decentralization, the white governmental superstructure in the South, at both state and local levels, would be the recipients and distributors of the funds, which suggested that the blacks would be shortchanged. In retrospect, I am certain that the NMAC's reluctance to take a strong position on decentralization and, more important, on the slow pace of congressional action, reflected this fear. By 1970 Congress finally passed new legislation that, in addition to laying the groundwork for decentralization, also contained a federal job creation provision, which led President Nixon to veto the bill. He wanted no part of a "new leaf-raking program."

James O. Hodgson succeeded Shultz, who had been moved to the newly created post of director of the Office of Management and Budget. Hodgson and his senior advisors, including me, were at Camp David for a two-day retreat when the news arrived that the president had vetoed the new manpower legislation. This marked the first serious break in bipartisan support for MDTA since it was first passed early in the decade. Within six months of the veto, the economy had turned down and, with the troops returning from Vietnam being demobilized at an accelerating rate, Nixon became more flexible. He accepted the Emergency Employment Act of 1971, which carried a two-year appropriation of $2.2 billion, the price that the Democratic majority extracted for proceeding with decentralization.

I recall being visited in the summer of 1970 at Martha's Vineyard by an acquaintance who brought me a message from the top AFL-CIO leadership—at least he claimed he was speaking for the leaders—to the effect that they would remain strongly committed to supporting MDTA, but only if the NMAC would in turn strongly support a federal job-creation program.

Our advisory committee had addressed this issue as early as 1965 and had reported at that time to the secretary that, under a set of carefully specified criteria, it saw merit in adding a direct job-creation effort to MDTA. By the end of the decade, even aside from the rising unemployment incident to the recession, the committee was more strongly in favor of such action. They had realized that many of the seriously disadvantaged would have great difficulties in getting a private-sector job. Public service jobs might provide them with the work experience and the work record they would need to eventually make the transition into regular jobs.

No sooner had Nixon gained his overwhelming victory over Senator McGovern in the 1972 election than he decided to thoroughly shake up the federal government, asking for the resignation of all of his cabinet secretaries and also contemplating a major cutback in federal expenditures, looking to potentially large savings from the manpower programs. I recall a meeting of the senior Labor Department staff, to which I was invited, at which Haldeman was scheduled to give us the message but to which John D. Ehrlichman came in his place. The outlook was sufficiently bleak that Sar Levitan and I arranged to call on George Shultz, who had in the interim become secretary of the treasury, to seek his intervention in preventing the administration from gutting the manpower programs. There were a great many poorly educated, low-skilled persons who needed access to government training programs if they were ever to make it into the regular labor market. Shultz was sympathetic and promised to do what he could to protect the manpower programs.

In December 1973 William Kolberg, the assistant secretary of labor, who had been working quietly with the Republican and Democratic leadership in the House and Senate while the president and his White

House staff were increasingly preoccupied with the Watergate scandal, helped to fashion the long-delayed compromise, the Comprehensive Employment and Training Act (CETA), whereby the federal manpower programs would be decentralized to five hundred prime sponsors (primarily local governmental units of over 100,000 population) and decategorized.

Just as the transfer of responsibility was being effected in the summer of 1974, a recession was upon us, and Congress added a new Title VI to CETA, which made an additional 300,000 public service employment (PSE) jobs available to the newly unemployed. Eligibility required only seven days of prior unemployment! I testified that there should be a family-income criterion, or many of these PSE jobs would go to middle-class married women who would be reentering the labor force. Little did I know that my daughter, arriving in San Francisco with a letter of introduction to a senior local official, was told: Too bad you weren't here last week; we could have given you a CETA job!

The CETA legislation provided for the establishment of a National Commission for Manpower Policy (NCMP) with its own budget line and with sufficient funds to enable it to build up a modest administrative and technical staff. Moreover, the new legislation stipulated that the NCMP would report to the president and Congress and make recommendations to various cabinet departments. I had had long and friendly relations with Kolberg, and he wanted me to be the chairman of the new commission, subject to my receiving clearance from the White House. In my forty years of active involvement in the federal bureaucracy, this was the first and only time that I had to participate personally in obtaining political clearance. During the course of a short and friendly interrogation by the White House operative, I was asked about my political affiliations. I mentioned my close friendship with President Eisenhower, the fact that President Nixon had sent me a letter of commendation upon the tenth anniversary of my chairmanship of the NMAC, and the fact that, as a voter in New York State, I had never aligned myself with either party—I was an independent. The fact that I was no rabid Democrat apparently sufficed to get me the clearance I needed.

Kolberg told me that he had an excellent director lined up for me: Robert Hall, a sophisticated bureaucrat who had a deep interest in manpower and who had spent the preceding year working in Australia (he had left the country because of his distaste for the direction the Nixon administration was taking). A brief discussion with Hall was all that I needed, and with the bureaucratic finesse that he continued to demonstrate, the commission was ensconced in no time in its own quarters—a mile or more distant from the Department of Labor, to underscore its independence. When Professor Juanita Kreps, a member of the commission, was appointed by President Carter as secretary of commerce at the beginning of 1977, she arranged matters so that Hall would become the assistant secretary for economic development. That means that Hall had three full years as the commission's director and helped to establish it firmly on the Washington scene.

I took my time before selecting his successor, among other reasons because I recognized that the successor should be able to serve as a director of research in addition to being the commission's administrator, a combination of qualities not often found in the same person. The commission was increasingly involved in broad macroeconomic questions, including international trade, immigration, and regional economic development, as well as in more narrowly defined issues of employment and training.

I finally offered the position to Isabelle Sawhill, who was then on the staff of the Urban Institute in Washington, and sought to persuade her to accept by pointing to the opportunities that the position would afford her to move more broadly into the policy arena. We had met only once or twice, and Sawhill sought the advice of a mutual friend, Robert Solow of MIT, who apparently gave me a good mark as a potential boss. Sawhill came aboard for a two-year stint, having taken a leave of absence from the Urban Institute. She met all of my expectations and more, and I think my promise to her was also fulfilled. She has since become a major scholar and policy advisor on the Washington and national scene.

I was lucky a third time, when I persuaded Daniel Saks, a senior member of the Council of Economic Advisors, who didn't want to return to Michigan State University, to accept the position of director for a two- or three-year stint, during which time I was sure that an alternative academic position would open up (as in fact it did at Vanderbilt University in Nashville). But Saks, who performed his duties with consummate skill, had the misfortune to be stricken with cancer shortly after his relocation to Nashville, and thus one of the nation's most talented labor economists was cut down in his prime.

In the six years between the passage of CETA and the election of President Reagan in November 1980, the National Commission for Employment Policy (NCEP) published eight annual reports; four interim reports to the president and the Congress; and a total of thirty-eight special reports, which covered such a wide range of subjects as *Recent European Manpower Policy Initiatives*; *The Role of the Business Sector in Manpower Policy*; *The Economic Position of Black America: 1976*; *Employment Impacts of Health Policy Developments*; *The Transformation of the Urban Economic Base*; *Women's Changing Roles in Home and on the Job: Education, Sex, Equity*; and *Occupational Stereotyping.*

In addition, four books were published commercially for the NCEP: *From School to Work*; *Employability, Employment, and Income*; *Jobs for Americans*; and *Youth Employment and Public Policy.*

In sum, within a six-year span the published output of the NCEP totaled six annual reports, four interim reports, thirty-eight special reports, and four books, for a total of fifty-two publications, or about nine per year. Since the staff never had more than three or four senior members and an equal number of junior researchers, the chairman-directors had to draw on their academic and manpower policy connections to the greatest possible extent to engage the range and depth of talent needed to probe the complex employment issues that were the NCEP's primary concern. This strategy and modus operandi alone account for the commission's high productivity.

To return to the last important era of active manpower policy—the Carter years. I recall having dinner very early in the Carter administration with the newly appointed secretary of labor, Ray Marshall, at the home of Howard Rosen, the far-sighted, energetic head of the Research and Development Office of the U.S. Department of Labor, who had done so much to create the field of manpower by providing both grants to graduate students for the writing of doctoral dissertations, and longer-term grants to established scholars for basic and applied research. Marshall gave me a lift back into town that evening, and I recall our agreeing that this was the last opportunity we were likely to have to prove that a large-scale PSE program could really work. Carter had decided to use job creation as a major mechanism to stimulate the economy, and he asked for 725,000 PSE jobs. Marshall remarked in passing that the president would have asked for more, but Marshall doubted that the federal-state-local bureaucracies could handle more within the brief time frame. It turned out that Marshall's caution was justified, for as the numbers on the public payroll grew rapidly, so did newspaper and other reports about misappropriation of funds, jobs going to ineligible persons with political connections, low productivity by PSE workers, excessive overhead, and other ills, which the public was only too ready to believe about any large-scale, publicly financed program, especially one directed to the poor, minorities, and youth.

There were no easy ways, in fact there was no way, that the Department of Labor could moderate the increasingly shrill attacks on CETA. While it had decentralized and decategorized the program in early 1974, the department had failed to establish a reliable reporting system that would have provided routine evidence of how well, or how poorly, the program was meeting its objectives. But that was not an oversight. Putting in place a properly functioning reporting system would be time consuming and costly, and no cabinet officer would take the initiative to do so unless Congress insisted. But Congress was not really interested in learning what was going on. It was willing to take the credit for offering new opportunities to the poor and disadvantaged without taking the next step of analyzing the short- and long-term benefits that the disadvantaged received from the new programs. Had a reporting system and hard analysis been available, the results might have thrown cold water on some, if not all, of the programs, embarrassing the administration and the congressmen who had so far gained political capital from their support of these programs.

In 1963, the first full year of MDTA, appropriations totaled $81 million; in 1979 the manpower budget stood at roughly $11 billion. As the 1970s neared their end, I knew from my periodic testimony before various congressional committees that the bloom was off CETA: the questions directed to me by the Democrats became at least as critical as the comments made by Republican members. I had a great many reservations about CETA, particularly about the small number of persons who were moved into private-sector jobs. But I never believed the charges of widespread fraud and corruption. It was inevitable that, in a decentralized program with $11 billion in annual expenditures, there would be some mismanagement, even illegality. But the real challenge to CETA rested elsewhere: Was it meeting its primary task of increasing the employability of its enrollees? On that score I had serious misgivings. But I consoled myself with the knowledge that most of the enrollees were poor people who needed the money that they were receiving from the government.

Since we heard nothing from the Reagan White House during the first six months of 1981, the NCEP continued to assess selected employment and training issues and to report on them, although we realized that those in positions of power in the executive department could not have been less interested. In the fall, the staff picked up rumors that we were about to be liquidated, or at least that all of the members of the commission would be asked to resign. And that is what happened in early December.

The following day I received a call from the head of personnel, Mr. E. Pendleton James from the White House; he expressed chagrin and regret that he hadn't talked to me earlier and inquired what other position I might be interested in. And the secretary of labor made a similar phone call. Apparently my former colleague, Martin Anderson, on the White House staff, had made some inquiries as to how I had been treated, and the follow-up calls sought to smooth things over. I thanked my callers from Washington for their interest and concern but explained that I was ready for a respite after forty uninterrupted years of work for the federal government.

12

Eisenhower

I had met General Eisenhower when he was serving as chief of staff of the army early in 1947; I got to know him quite well during the three-and-a-half years when he was the active president of Columbia University; I spent some time with him and his staff in 1951 when he was serving as supreme commander, Allied Forces Europe; I saw him for a visit about once a month during his eight years in the White House; and I was one of the fifty or so friends who celebrated his birthday every year in the Gettysburg area during his retirement.

However, the foregoing leaves out what was perhaps the most import-ant aspect of my relationship to Eisenhower over these more than two decades. The missing link was the close relation that both of us had with Major General Howard McCrum Snyder. During the greater part of those two decades Snyder and I were in constant contact. At Columbia, he served as medical adviser to the New York State Hospital Study that I directed for Governor Dewey; he was an active member at our staff conferences; he attended my class on Human Resources and Economic Welfare. We spent time together every day except when he went home to Washington for the weekend.

When he became president of Columbia, Eisenhower had asked me whether I could work out an arrangement that would enable General Snyder to spend the week in New York, living with Mamie and him at 60 Morningside Drive, the residence of the president of Columbia. Eisenhower explained that he was loath to add another military man, even if retired, to his staff, which already included his long-term valet and his military aide Major (later General) Robert L. Schulz. My research contract with New York State made it easy for me to meet General Eisenhower's request. I arranged to pay Snyder a modest consulting fee, probably not much more than the amount required to cover his traveling expenses to and from Washington. He earned his modest consulting fee many times over by his insightful contributions to the issues with which we were grappling, as well as by his skill in moderating the tensions among the members of my staff, some of whom were out of their intellectual or emotional depth since we had to produce a major policy report within thirteen months.

During the eight years when Eisenhower was in the White House, my principal contact there was General Snyder. Except for the summer months I was in Washington almost every other week. The president frequently stopped by Snyder's office to chat on his way between his living quarters and the Oval Office.

Snyder had been the Eisenhowers' physician since the early 1920s, and he played a major role in their lives as physician, counselor, and friend from that time until his last illness and death in 1969. They valued his friendship especially because his discretion equaled his judgment. But having said that, I must quickly add that Snyder found it helpful over the years to talk to me, in confidence, about many aspects of the Eisenhowers' lives because he understood that I would respect that confidence. And even at this late date I have no intention of doing anything else. At the request of the Eisenhower Library in Abilene, Kansas, I agreed to provide an oral history of my relationship to the president but I held off until both the president and Mamie had died. And I was flattered that, after Mamie died, Barbara Eisenhower, John's wife and the Eisenhowers' daughter-in-law, asked to have lunch with me at Columbia to pursue some matters that I had alluded to in my oral history.

When I visited SHAPE in the early and again in the late summer of 1951, my wife and I stayed at the Palace Trianon in Versailles at the suggestion of General Snyder, who was living there with his wife Alice, as were the Eisenhowers. This was the critical summer when Henry Cabot Lodge, Clay, and others—in fact a steady stream of East Coast Republicans—visited Eisenhower seeking to nail down his agreement to their plan to step up their efforts to assure that he would become the Republican standard-bearer in 1952.

Although I talked with Eisenhower about the mission that I was carrying out for the secretary of the army involving the desegregation of the U.S. Army in Europe (see *My Brother's Keeper*), I kept my distance from all matters involving his political plans. Those were beyond my area of confidence or competence.

However, Snyder briefed me at length about the mounting pressures that Eisenhower's friends and advisers were putting on Eisenhower to declare himself a candidate, or at least not to call them off if they proceeded more energetically to make him a candidate. Mamie had serious doubts about the wisdom of Ike's running and thought there was much merit to his original plan (to retire to San Antonio, where he could play golf most of the year, where he would find many congenial bridge players, and where Brooke General Hospital could, if necessary, provide high quality medical support).

Snyder told me that the stream of visitors from the United States kept making a number of points in their discussions with Eisenhower. First, they felt it was essential, if the two-party system in the United States were to survive, that the Republicans come up with a winning candidate in 1952. After all, the Democrats had controlled the White House for the last two decades. Second, they stressed that, unless Eisenhower were to run, nobody could deny the nomination to Senator Robert Taft; and if Taft were the candidate he might lose or, equally bad, if he won, he might lead the country down an isolationist path that would make a mockery of our participation in World War II and would jeopardize the fragile peace that was currently in place. Further, they played on Eisenhower's patriotism, told him it was his "duty" to run; they added that he would be so popular with the vast majority of the citizenry that he would find the job of being president not particularly taxing.

Snyder was ambivalent about whether Eisenhower should run. We never probed the pluses and minuses that Snyder had identified, but I realized that he had identified many. I asked him whether he thought it would be appropriate for me to set out in some detail the questions that I thought General Eisenhower should weigh before he said yes to his importuning friends.

I prepared a long discussion of the issues as I saw them and took extra pains to raise or elaborate on some that I suspected those pushing Eisenhower to commit himself were minimizing or ignoring. Specifically, I asked Eisenhower to assess the state of his physical and psychological health. He was in his sixties and had carried such a heavy burden during World War II. His responsibility for the final decision as to when the troops were to invade the continent and many subsequent decisions must have placed a heavy strain on his reserves.

I specifically addressed the view put forward by his friends that for Eisenhower the presidency would be an easy job, one that he would be able to perform with a modest expenditure of time, energy, and involvement because he was, and would remain, the idol of the American people, who would therefore follow wherever he wanted to lead. I argued that such a vision of the presidency was hogwash. No one who was elected, no matter by how wide a margin, would find it easy to gain and retain popular and legislative support for solutions to the vast array of domestic and international problems that the United States faced—and the many more problems that would arise in the years ahead. The idea that Eisenhower could lead the country and run the executive branch of the federal government by putting in a few hours of work each day was unrealistic. There were simply too many issues that required the president's direct involvement. Calvin Coolidge was the last president who had had the freedom to take an extended nap every afternoon.

But I directed my primary attention to the question that I felt was gnawing at Eisenhower—did he not have an obligation to the American people to use his accumulated experience to help them secure a safe future in a world sorely in need of strong leadership? I argued that while the office of the presidency provided the incumbent with considerable leverage to instruct and lead the nation, it was inevitable that each decision that a president makes would disappoint some part of the citizenry. Therefore, after four or eight years in office it was inevitable that he would face an erosion of a substantial amount of the good will and support with which he had entered office. It is a testimony to Eisenhower's skills that my forecast was proved wrong.

I pointed out that if he opted for retirement it did not mean that he could not continue, as occasions arose—and surely he could create such occasions—to inform the public about his views and recommendations on issues of transcendental importance.

General Snyder gave my paper to Eisenhower, but to the best of my recollection I had no feedback either from Eisenhower or from Snyder, which was not the case with most of later papers that I prepared.

During one of my meetings with Eisenhower that summer at SHAPE, he asked me for my views about the prospects of the French economy and whether I thought that the United States should make sizable grants and loans to speed its development. By no stretch of the imagination did I consider myself capable of answering on the spot. Hence I promised to send along a memorandum after I had thought about the matter and was able to do some focused reading and some talking with informed persons.

Some weeks later I wrote to Eisenhower that I was uneasy about any large-scale U.S. support program for the French on the ground that the oligarchy that controlled the French government, society, and economy would be more likely to hold on to most of the additional money rather than to pass it down to farmers, small manufacturers, and other business-men desperately in need of capital for modernization. But I had ignored the potential for good that one talented statesman-administrator, Jean Monnet, could make to upstage my pessimistic appraisal. In later years I concluded that, as remarkable as was West Germany's recovery, even more remarkable was the major transformation and growth of the long-stagnant French economy.

During my fortnight's visit to U.S. Army Headquarters at Heidelberg and the Seventh Army Headquarters in Stuttgart, I made time to visit local bookstores, and I picked up a copy of Hitler's *Tischgespräche* (Table Talk), which I read. When I talked with Eisenhower on my return to SHAPE, I told him about the book and my belief that it shed important light not only on Hitler but on Nazi alienation and its deep roots in German culture. He was interested in learning more about it, and I asked my father to translate the key passages that I had marked. I later sent these on to Eisenhower, who wrote my father a warm thank-you note.

There were many who believed at the time, and this holds for later interpreters, that Eisenhower had set his eye on the White House from the time that he first returned to the United States as the great hero of World War II. This interpretation holds that all of the denials and equivocal statements that he issued about his political intentions while at Columbia University and at SHAPE were just so much smoke. I have never shared this view, first, because, had it not been for Dewey's unexpected defeat in 1948, Eisenhower's first opportunity to run would have been in 1956, when he would have been sixty-six, an age that, in the pre-Reagan years, would have made his running highly problematic. Further, I believe that he was genuinely undecided about whether he should run. And it must be recalled that, earlier, Truman had put out feelers to discover whether Eisenhower would run as a Democrat.

I came to appreciate over the years that Eisenhower was highly critical of Truman, but I never gained a clear picture of the reasons for his antagonism. I know that he thought that Truman was taking advantage of him, but the when, how, and why never became clear to me. The depth of Eisenhower's feelings were such that the antagonism clearly had a large personal component.

The tension between the two surely predated the unedifying spectacle of Eisenhower's campaigning in Wisconsin after Senator McCarthy's slashing attack on General George C. Marshall (Truman's hero and Eisenhower's mentor) in which Eisenhower said nothing in Marshall's defense. I had dropped Eisenhower a note suggesting that he avoid Wisconsin on the ground that he would surely win, and win big, even if he avoided Wisconsin, and that he not do anything to yield the high ground.

Margaret Truman's recently edited book of her father's papers, *Where the Buck Stops: The Personal and Private Writings of Harry S. Truman* (N.Y.: Warner Books, 1989), contains a special chapter on Eisenhower that only deepens the mystery. It demonstrates that Truman had developed overwhelmingly negative views and judgments about Eisenhower, the man, the general, and the president, views that are as ill-tempered as they are unexplained. Some day a historian of the era should be able to illuminate what at present remains largely obscure.

As the presidential campaign of 1952 neared its end, the Columbia campus was a hotbed of anti-Eisenhower sentiments. Many of the faculty found Stevenson attractive because of his facility with words and his humor. The local sentiment was summed up in this phrase: "Columbia's gain will be the nation's loss." With relatively few exceptions, Eisenhower had never established close bonds with the faculty. They saw him as an outsider, not much interested in what they were doing, who had failed to enlarge the university's endowment. He was, and remained, a stranger in their midst, and they looked forward to his relocation to Washington.

I had seen enough of Eisenhower, both directly and through General Snyder, to know that this appraisal was seriously off base. While it was true he was not an intellectual and he had conservative values, he also had a great many strong qualities that pointed to a successful presidency, even if it would not be in the mode of the New Deal. Eisenhower let me know before leaving Columbia for Washington that I could continue to send him memos through General Snyder and that he would read them. For the next eight years, I would send him brief memos outlining the arguments "on the other side," that is, putting forth the considerations that I believed would often be omitted in the advice that he was getting from his staff and from his coterie of advisors and friends. One of the first dealt with the Rosenberg case. I did not presume to comment on whether or not they were guilty, but I suggested that if he commuted their sentences the United States was likely, sooner or later, to learn something about Soviet espionage that it would be deprived of if they were executed.

The early months of the new administration revealed a wide gap in trust, respect, and working relations between the new Republican political appointees and the established bureaucracy, that had long ago assumed control over their respective departments and agencies. The standoff was inevitable, since the newcomers believed, and with some justification, that most of the civil service establishment were committed New Dealers. But at the end of six months of estrangement the new political chiefs had no option but to work out an accommodation with the incumbents. At no time did one see the across-the-board assault on government employees and on government itself that came to characterize the Reagan years. Even McCarthy in his heyday went after "Communists" and Communist supporters, not the rank and file of government workers.

After Eisenhower had been in the White House for some months, I got a call from his aide, Colonel Schulz, who wanted to know whether "Jews were permitted to shave," a question that I had some difficulty understanding until he went on to say that the president had a file on his desk in which an aggrieved air force serviceman threatened to take the federal government into court for violating his religious liberties. I told Schulz to have the file ready for me to review when I was in Washington later that week.

The file, many inches thick, with quotations from the Talmud by Lieutenant Mary Quinn of the WACs and other military and religious experts (*sic!*), reported that the air force had forcibly removed the beard of a Hasidic Jew from Brooklyn, New York, who had served in civilian life—and planned to continue to serve—as a part-time rabbi. He claimed that the air force's action deprived him of his religious freedom and jeopardized his career. Consequently he planned to bring suit in federal court. My reading of the file alerted me to the dangers that can stem from pursuing administrative regulations to the point of no return.

I told Schulz that I wanted to talk with my father before making any recommendation. Somewhat (though not totally) to my surprise, I found my father in the air force's corner. He was afraid to recommend any exception to the air force's regulations in the belief that hundreds or even thousands of young Hasidic men might use the anti-shaving prohibition to avoid military service. Although respectful of my father's learning and wisdom, I thought a tough line was a mistake. My recommendation to Schulz was to squash the case by sending the serviceman to the most remote outpost in Japan, to order the commanding officer to permit him to regrow his beard, and to make him eligible for separation just as soon as the regulations permitted. To the best of my knowledge, the air force decided that my suggestion was the best way to close "The Case of the Bearded Serviceman."

Some time later, when I was on an early morning visit with Eisenhower in the Oval Office, he started cursing. He stated that Senator William Knowland, the Republican leader, was a _____ and that if it weren't for the good sense and help that he was getting from Senator Lyndon Johnson, the Democratic leader, he, Eisenhower, would like to tell them to take back his no-good job. The Republican diehards were obstructing him at every turn and he could get nothing accomplished.

Eisenhower had a short temper, except when he knew that he faced a complex and difficult problem and could prepare himself for a careful, in-depth assessment of the pros and cons. He also had a large vocabulary of curse words and used expletives with good effect. Moreover, when steamed up and exasperated he could get so red in the face that one wondered whether he was about to have a stroke or heart attack. But once the steam was vented, he returned quite quickly to his usual poised behavior and clear-cut speaking.

Few people recall that during his first administration Eisenhower suffered a major heart attack while on vacation in Colorado and that he had surgery for ileitis and a mild stroke during his second administration—no small amount of trouble for an incumbent chief executive. General Snyder, who saw the president every day and who always traveled with him, was at the fishing camp when Eisenhower was stricken with his heart attack and made the initial decision about his transfer to Fitzsimmons General Hospital in Denver and his initial treatment.

General Snyder dictated and mailed to me a detailed medical summary of each day (and night) of the president's condition and treatment. Although we never discussed what led him to write in such detail about the course of the president's illness, I suspect that Snyder wanted a record to exist in the event that the president did not survive, a real danger in the earliest days of his heart attack.

The conventional wisdom at the time was that Eisenhower, especially because of his extended convalescence, would be a one-term president. But I never bought into that theory on the ground that, if his health improved and stabilized, he would show the same disinclination as had former presidents to leave the White House voluntarily after one term.

On the day that Eisenhower was planning to go on TV to announce that he would run for reelection, I was visiting with General Snyder. The president stopped by, and Snyder asked him whether I could be in the Oval Office that evening when he talked to the American people; the president generously said yes. The only other persons present were Mamie and his son John. When the president finished, the TV crews turned their attention to Mamie and John, and I walked back with the president to his quarters. He was in a relaxed mood, now that he had announced the decision to stand for reelection, but he added, "I hope, Eli, that these doctors know what the hell they are talking about. I feel OK now, but this is no job that I or anybody else can handle unless they are in good shape. I sure hope that these damn doctors really know what they're talking about when they say I'm OK."

The doctors almost messed him up at the time of his ileitis attack. General Snyder, who lived only ten minutes from the White House, usually stopped by to see the president around 8 A.M. just before he went to the Oval Office; but on the morning of the attack General Snyder received a phone call to come by early because the president had had a fitful night. After examining the president and deciding that he had some sort of abdominal obstruction, Snyder called for an ambulance to take the president to Walter Reed Hospital, where the patient was bedded down by about 8:30 A.M.

After some consultations with the local staff, various tests were decided on, and at the same time an alert was put out to have the president's consultant in cardiology, Dr. Paul Dudley White, get down from Boston as quickly as possible and to have Dr. I. N. Ravdin, the distinguished University of Pennsylvania surgeon, called in. The commanding general of Walter Reed, Lieutenant General Leonard Heaton, was a distinguished surgeon fully capable of operating on the president if an operation were required.

White and Ravdin arrived around noon, which led to more consultations and more tests, repeated hour after hour until after midnight.
General Snyder, the source of this account, told me that he was getting
increasingly disturbed by the attending physicians' hesitancy to decide
that an operation was the only treatment. Snyder recognized that the
surgeons, cognizant of Eisenhower's earlier severe heart attack, were
fearful that they might lose him during the operation and accordingly
kept stalling looking for an alternative treatment.

Snyder finally forced the issue by stating that if they did not make up
their minds within fifteen minutes, he would personally have Eisenhower
prepared for surgery and would do the operation himself—although it
had probably been fifteen years since he had last operated on a patient!
Fortunately, Ravdin decided to perform the operation, which proceeded
without a hitch. Had Eisenhower not been president, he would have been
operated on more than twelve hours earlier!

The president had a routine and uneventful recovery, but he still had
to face what could have been a further, serious, challenge with respect to
his health, which fortunately turned out to be little more than a threat and
an inconvenience. The president had a mild stroke—a transient ischemic
attack (TIA)—which resulted in his slurring his words and sentences for
a few days; but after that his speech returned to normal. I was visiting
with General Snyder a day or two after the president's episode. It was
clear from the few words that he said to us as he passed Snyder's open
office that he was having some difficulty, but by the following week his
speech had cleared up.

Senator McCarthy's escalating charges about malfeasance in the
government eventually led him to embarrass and denigrate the U.S. Army
by his treatment of Secretary Stevens before the Senate Committee on
Government Operations. The president had no use for McCarthy, but he
had avoided any public expression of his views. Sherman Adams, his
chief of staff, had advised the president to go public in an attack, a
position that I had also been urging on the president for a considerable
period of time. I was convinced not only that many innocent people were
being falsely attacked and publicly smeared but that the successive
victories that the senator had scored strengthened his position from which
to launch additional attacks on innocent civil servants and responsible
government agencies.

The president opted for a different approach. He asked Vice-President Nixon to line up some responsible conservative senators to lower the ax on their unsavory colleague, and Nixon performed this task with skill and discretion. Eisenhower once said to me that I was wrong to advise him to get into "a pissing match" with McCarthy. A president who did that would simply assure that the senator got more attention and publicity, because he had successfully maneuvered himself into a position where he had the president as his opponent. With the advantage of hindsight it is clear that Eisenhower had a better sense about how to cope than those on his staff and outsiders like me who advised him to take on the senator directly.

But it would be a mistake to assume that Eisenhower did not pay a price for asking Nixon to do various favors such as this. The president's relationship with his vice-president was neither easy nor relaxed. Eisenhower would have much preferred to pick a new vice-presidential candidate when his first term was up, and at least for a time he considered Robert B. Anderson, former secretary of the navy, and deputy secretary of defense (and later secretary of the treasury), as a likely candidate. Shortly before taking off for SHAPE, Eisenhower had run into Anderson while on a speaking engagement in Texas and suggested to me that, in putting together a list of members for the soon-to-be-established National Manpower Council (a Columbia undertaking supported by the Ford Foundation), I carefully scrutinize Anderson's qualifications. I took counsel with a well-informed Texan who asked for a couple of weeks to do some probing and who came back with the comment that if we (Eisenhower and I) wanted to bet on the future, Anderson was our man, although he was not yet well known. Anderson was appointed to the council by Eisenhower and my positive readings of his participation on the council probably helped him to get the nod as secretary of the navy.

Irrespective of whether Anderson would be Nixon's replacement, Eisenhower did not want Nixon on the ticket in 1956. He offered Nixon all sorts of tempting assignments: He could broaden his acquaintance with international affairs by becoming ambassador to the Court of St. James, or he could increase his managerial know-how by becoming secretary of defense. But Nixon was politely nonresponsive, and Eisenhower could not bring himself to take unilateral action to make a change because of the many occasions when Nixon had carried out unpleasant assignments on the president's behalf.

Sometime during the president's first administration, Grayson Kirk, whom Eisenhower had selected as provost of Columbia and who succeeded him as president, stopped by at the White House to report his observations of a recent trip through Southeast Asia. As soon as Kirk got to reporting critically on U.S. foreign policy in the area, Eisenhower brought the conversation to a premature conclusion and told Kirk that he had better convey what he had learned to John Foster Dulles, who was in charge of our relationships abroad.

Eisenhower used his tightly organized staff system when it suited his purposes, but it would be a mistake to conclude that he left the big issues in foreign affairs to Dulles or that he never invited aberrant or uncomfortable views. He held stag dinners at the White House to which he invited private citizens who he believed could broaden and deepen his understanding about what was going on in different sections of our large country.

When I was a guest, we had no sooner assembled for cocktails than the president was called to the phone; he was gone for a good twenty minutes. I quickly became uneasy because I knew that nothing short of an emergency would call Eisenhower away from an affair in which he was the host, and when his absence stretched to twenty minutes all of the guests appreciated that something must be seriously awry.

When Eisenhower returned smiling, I realized that the crisis was contained, at least for the time being. It was the night of the flare-up with Communist China about the Comoy-Matsu islands. Eisenhower's first comment on his return is worth recalling: "I don't know how history will appraise Foster Dulles' period as secretary of state, but let me tell you that he is the hardest working son of a gun that I have ever known!"

I recall the evening for a bit of gaucherie when it came to table settings. The entrée was pheasant, and each of us had a color photograph of the pheasant that we would soon consume.

Eisenhower enjoyed male companionship, and among his close friends were some of the nation's top business executives, such as Robert Woodruff of Coca Cola, W. Alten (Pete) Jones of Cities Service, and Barry Leithead of Cluett Peabody. Eisenhower had tapped all three in the late 1940s to become sponsors of the Conservation of Human Resources Project at Columbia University. He visited the Woodruff plantation in Thomasville, Georgia. He enjoyed a round of golf or several rubbers of bridge with people with whom he was comfortable.

Woodruff was an enlightened southerner who served on the Tuskegee Institute board for many years and was also a generous contributor to that institution, as well as to other black educational and eleemosynary organizations. Eisenhower's Texan roots and the fact that he had lived for many years in the segregated army led him to see no quick, easy answer to the race issue. He looked to local leadership to slowly bring about changes in the ways in which white people thought and felt about blacks. I was reasonably sure that this was a theme that Woodruff stressed in their many private conversations.

The only time that Eisenhower put to one side his preferred policy of no federal action on the racial front was when Governor Orville Faubus of Arkansas decided to challenge the federal court's decision to desegregate the schools in Little Rock; Eisenhower sent troops to force the governor to comply with federal law. Eisenhower didn't relish the idea of calling on the military to control racial tensions but, faced with a direct challenge from the segregationist governor, he saw no alternative.

It is well known that Eisenhower considered his appointment of Earl Warren to the post of chief justice of the Supreme Court a serious political blunder. But Eisenhower felt trapped by other forces that led him to move in directions he would have preferred not to. He was dragged into supporting the National Defense Education Act of 1958, which was Congress's response to Sputnik. Eisenhower did not believe that the federal government had a role to play in the direct support of higher education, and he went along with the new legislation only because of the rationale that the act was intended to strengthen the nation's defenses. Near the end of his second administration, he failed to recommend legislation to enlarge the constrained physician supply, despite three separate reports from distinctly conservative committees: Bayne-Jones, Bane, and Boisfeuillet-Jones. And for many other challenges on the domestic front Eisenhower decided that he would do better to ignore the problem than to get the federal government overextended into areas where it had no legitimacy or competence.

Let's be clear: As a conservative political strategist, Eisenhower wanted to keep inflation low, taxes low, the role of the federal government restricted, and the Defense Department on a short leash to prevent it from wasting the taxpayer's hard-earned dollars. He was willing to use the federal government to moderate the ravages of unemployment, and he was a quasi-Keynesian who believed that the federal government could

risk an unbalanced budget for one year—but no longer. He felt comfortable, positioned as he was between Arthur F. Burns on the Left (*sic!*) and
George Humphrey on his Right. What really commanded and engaged
Eisenhower's interest was foreign policy. He was determined to keep the
Republican party from retrogressing into isolationism. He did his best to
avoid getting into minor or major wars, and he sought for an opening to
negotiate a nuclear arms agreement with the Russians, for which he
successfully set the stage (see Emanuel Piore's *Science and Academic
Life in Transition* [New Brunswick, N.J.: Transaction Publishers, 1990]).
His outrage at the British-French-Israeli military adventure to capture
Suez and topple Nasser (1956) had an element of personal pique, since
he deeply resented that these allies and beneficiaries of the United States
had not taken him into their confidence—and he was deeply upset that
their actions undermined that fragile structure of international peacemak-
ing machinery, the U.N. Their action was that much more reprehensible,
as he pointed out in correspondence with me, because of the U.S.S.R.'s
aggressive action in Hungary.

After Arthur Burns returned to Columbia in 1956, it was difficult,
when eating at the White House mess, to find a table where one could
have an exciting conversation. The staff was made up of competent
specialists who did their jobs effectively, but new ideas and new domestic
programs were not part of their work assignment or, in fact, on
Eisenhower's agenda. Straight ahead, steady on the tiller, were the
captain's orders.

In 1956, Secretary of Labor James P. Mitchell arranged to have me
brief the cabinet on *The Skills of the U.S. Work Force*, a chart book that
I had recently prepared for the department. For the one and only time in
my life, I had at my disposal excellent graphs to provide visual support
for my oral presentation. But I was less than ten minutes into my
half-hour presentation, when I realized that I had lost the interest and
attention of all the cabinet except for the president and Secretary Mitchell. From that point on, I paced myself by keeping a close watch on
Eisenhower's responsive features. Near the end, I told the cabinet of
some observations that I had made about U.S. foreign assistance efforts
during a recent visit to Turkey and Greece and suggested that we could
save perhaps as much as eighty-five cents on every dollar of our aid by
shifting from exporting sophisticated capital goods to providing instruction in various skills and some simple machinery. That one statement

about saving the U.S. taxpayer's money got and held all of the cabinet officials' attention to the end of my presentation. Aside from the president, no one asked any pertinent, much less penetrating, questions. Mitchell was disappointed but, as he told me later, not surprised.

Some time in the middle of his second administration, Eisenhower began to be lobbied by a number of his rich friends and cronies, including General Lucius Clay, who was at the time CEO of Continental Can Company, about some emerging antitrust matters. The president resented their importunings, and the more he was lobbied the more he seethed inside. He considered what his friends were doing an affront to him personally, as well as disrespectful to the presidency and a denigration of the role of the federal government in the life of the nation.

This was the impetus for his valedictory remarks—put together for him by Professor Malcolm Moos of Johns Hopkins University—on the military-industrial complex, which took so many of the president's friends and advisors as well as his critics by surprise by the incisiveness of its analysis and its explicit warnings about the dangers that lurked ahead from such nefarious alliances among the powerful. This was a subject about which Eisenhower knew a lot, and he had learned more during his eight years in the White House. He decided to share his concerns with his fellow citizens in the hope of alerting them to the dangers of such plutocratic linkages among generals in the Pentagon, members of Congress, and the CEOs of major aerospace companies. Eisenhower's valedictory was not an accident; it was an all-out national alert.

I had devoted considerable effort and energy during the eight years when Eisenhower was in the White House to being a messenger who called his attention to a wide array of unpleasant facts through memos and personal discussions in the hope that after considering them, the president might modify, at least in a small measure, the policies that he was planning to pursue. I had no way of telling at the time and have even less perspective now after thirty years whether my self-defined assignment, encouraged by General Snyder, proved helpful to the president. I like to believe it was, because while Eisenhower would, on occasion, get quite impatient and annoyed with me, he always welcomed my next effort. I am certain that Eisenhower tried to be the best president he knew how to be, and I think he appreciated that I, in calling the shots as I saw them, sought to help him accomplish his goal.

13

From FDR to Reagan

Although I was sworn into my first position in the federal government as a consultant to the executive office of the president in the same week that Pearl Harbor was bombed, I never saw President Roosevelt. Nor had I met him in the earlier stage of his second public career, which dated back to his close victory as governor of the State of New York in 1928. All of my impressions, perceptions, and judgments are based on information in the public domain, refined and distilled by my acquaintance with a dozen or so individuals who worked closely with him and with whom I had ongoing relationships.

In point of fact, I had never been in the White House, as a visitor or on business, until I was invited to an exhibition of paintings that was sponosred by Isadore Lubin, a staff assistant of the president and a close friend of mine. It was early in the afternoon on Friday, 12 April 1945. There were about twenty guests, distributed through two rooms, when I arrived. I was struck by the absence of any noise, but I decided that was a special characteristic of the White House.

I focused most of my attention on the paintings, not that they were striking, but I sensed that something unusual was afoot. People seemed to be vanishing, one at a time, without saying a word to anybody. Suddenly I realized that the twenty or so had dwindled to four or five. At that point I decided to ask one of those still remaining what was up and was told that rumor had it that the president had died. By the time I returned to my office, only a few blocks away, the rumor had been confirmed. The free world had lost its greatest leader; he had been at the helm for so long and during such difficult times that he and the position he held were viewed as one. Never before nor since did so many people suddenly feel bereft.

In the summer of 1942, I had spent several days lecturing to a group of students under the auspices of the International Students Association at President Roosevelt's summer home at Campobello, New Brunswick, in Canada. I had been assigned a bedroom that Franklin Roosevelt had used as a young man, and the bookcases still held many of the volumes that he had read.

Roosevelt was stricken with polio at Campobello, and only a person of extraordinary inner strength could have fought his way back from the total loss of both of his legs to gain and hold his unique position of political leadership. Even at this late date, I believe that most biographers have underplayed the courage that Roosevelt's return to an active political role required. When people ask me to rank the presidents I have known, I duck the question because unspecified, it is a question that I, at least, can't answer. But on the basis of my reading and reflection, I would say unequivocally that FDR is in a category separate and distinct from all other chief executives in this century.

Although Harry Truman appointed me minister plenipotentiary in 1946 to negotiate for the United States the second agreement dealing with "Reparations for Non-Repatriable Refugees," I had no personal contact with him before, during, or subsequent to his years in the White House. I recall that his scheduled arrival in the Pentagon as head of the Senate Preparedness Committee during World War II used to send shivers through the high command, and even more through their staffs. I decided that the senator and his committee members must have much to commend them because it was no small task to rattle the brass—who in the midst of the war were at the top of the heap.

I was deeply impressed with Truman's performance when he was forced to assume the onerous burdens that Roosevelt's death left at his doorstep. I shared with President Truman his idolization of General Marshall, even though, as noted earlier, I questioned whether even Marshall could work out a solution among the warring Chinese factions.

On most if not all of his major decisions in foreign affairs, Truman acted with determination—his ending the war with Japan; drawing a line in Iran; replacing the British in the Eastern Mediterranean; recognizing the State of Israel; getting the Marshall Plan through Congress; responding to the invasion of South Korea. I believe it would be hard to fault him on any of these momentous decisions.

But many of his appointments at cabinet and subcabinet level and many of his cronies around the White House left a great deal to be desired.

I have never before nor since seen the Pentagon in such disarray as during the secretaryship of Louis Johnson.

Surely one of the highlights of Truman's presidency was the campaign that he waged and won against Governor Dewey in 1948, when almost no one but Truman believed that he had even an outside chance to win. It took character and guts as well as much hard work and a few lucky breaks, to get that campaign to end the way it did. Truman himself was the key strategist and tactician.

Although, as I said above, I never met Truman, I surely got the benefit of invoking his name. My assistant at the Five-Power Conference, a member of the U.S. embassy staff in Paris, decided to make reservations for me at the Crillon. I was shown to a sizable suite, but it was in the back and dark. When I returned to the registration area, I told my assistant that I didn't much care for the accommodations. He asked that the manager be called, and when he arrived my assistant, in fluent French, accused him of insulting the personal representative of the president of the United States. In 1992 that might not lead a French (or any other European) hotel manager to blink an eye, but in June 1946 it got me the best suite in the Crillon.

Since the last chapter dealt at length with Eisenhower, we can here move directly to Kennedy. He was the first of the six presidents under whom I served over two decades (1962 to 1981) as the chair of the National Manpower Advisory Committee, the National Commission for Manpower Policy, and its successor, the National Commission for Employment Policy. I reported earlier (see chapter 10) on our meeting with President Kennedy in the White House in September 1962, which was also attended by Vice-President Lyndon Johnson.

From one point of view, the thousand or so days that Kennedy was president reminded one of the New Deal years because of the large-scale invasion of academics who came to Washington with the new administration and who were particularly prominent in the expanded executive office of the president, as well as on the enlarged staffs of the Council of Economic Advisors, the Bureau of the Budget, and some of the mainline departments. Possibly it had less to do with their numbers than with their quality. Kennedy was able to attract some of the best East Coast professors.

But having drawn this analogy between the early days of the New Deal and the Kennedy years, I must quickly add that almost everything else was different: the position of the United States in world affairs; the strength of the domestic economy; the narrow margin of Kennedy's election (there were some political analysts who believed that the election had been stolen and that Nixon could have demanded a recount). Most important, by temperament, as well as because of his narrow victory, Kennedy turned out to be a cautious, conservative president, at least as far as domestic policy was concerned. He dragged his feet with respect to race, poverty, and tax reduction. My friend, Arthur F. Burns, told me of Kennedy's consulting him on monetary and other policies.

The Kennedy entourage may have had reasons for their belief that Kennedy would have been a different second-term president had he run and won—more aggressive and more imaginative. But the odds do not favor such a projection, since second-term presidents seldom have the leverage that newcomers to the White House have. Reviewing my four decades of observing presidents, I think that Kennedy was the least effective of all, probably because of his innate conservatism, his preoccupation with foreign affairs, and the fact that in an era of Camelot it was easy for everyone, even the president, to get confused between form and content.

My first exposure to Lyndon Johnson in action was in the summer of 1963. I was at our summer home on Martha's Vineyard when I received a call from the Department of Labor announcing that I should attend a meeting on affirmative action in employment in St. Louis in mid-August. I told my informant that I knew of a competent economist on the faculty of Washington University in St. Louis who could handle whatever role they had in mind for me. But I was unable to make the swap. Finally, I asked who insisted that I be there, and I was told that the Vice-President's Office had specifically requested that I attend.

I went and, after the secretary of labor had said his piece, spoke to a hundred or so vice-presidents of human resources from among the nation's largest companies. And there were other speeches. Johnson had had an earlier appointment that day in Chicago, and it was unclear whether he would get to our meeting; but he not only came, he delivered the most powerful speech on affirmative action that I—and, probably, all the other members in the audience—had ever heard. I traveled back to New York with a group of the corporate executives, and they had been thoroughly shaken up. It was clear to them, as it was to me, that Johnson as the chair of the affirmative action committee meant business and would not stop until he got the results he wanted.

The contrast between Kennedy and Johnson in the domestic policy area was underscored for me by the efforts that Senator Joseph Clark initiated to strengthen the civil rights bill of 1963, which the Kennedy administration had earlier forwarded with a weak fair-employment section. Clark, testing the waters, decided that he had a reasonable chance to strengthen the section, in which effort he was unwittingly assisted by the error committed by Judge Howard Worth Smith, the chair of the House Rules Committee. Smith thought that by adding gender to race he could stymie the proposed legislation, if not permanently then at least for a long time. To his great surprise and to the surprise of many onlookers, his ploy backfired, and women as well as minorities got written into the protected categories. I recall that I testified at length before Senator Clark's committee, and the discussion was much friendlier than I had anticipated.

I remember that I had difficulty putting the pieces together when the amended bill was finally passed (with a comfortable margin). I tried to figure out why Kennedy had been timid in forwarding a strong fair-employment proposal, and my first explanation ascribed this finding to his conservatism: I knew that he wanted a civil rights bill passed and thought that by taking a strong fair-employment stand he might jeopardize the outcome. But on later reflection I concluded that his assassination had moved the country off the conservative terrain where it had been rooted since Eisenhower's first election of 1952. Admittedly, Johnson's strong leadership, especially his dealings with Congress, was an important factor in this shift, but Kennedy's assassination had played the key role in making the electorate more sympathetic to more radical approaches.

Some years later I got a special insight into President Johnson's working style from Robert T. Hall, who was the first director of the National Commission for Manpower Policy. Hall told me of an incident when he was a junior official in the Bureau of the Budget working on an expenditure item that had caught the president's attention. He was amazed to get a call from the president at close to midnight asking probing questions about the disputed item. A few days later, the president called at 2 A.M.; and when he did so again the following night, Hall's wife told the president that her husband wasn't available!

My first personal encounter with Johnson after he became president occurred in connection with his effort to assemble his own brain trust, an assignment that he had given to Eric Goldman, a Princeton history professor on leave as a member of the White House staff. The group consisted of about forty academics, and as one might have suspected, Goldman made a special effort to identify persons from places other than Cambridge. Each had an assigned specialty—mine was "children and youth," a result of the fact that I had served as director of studies for the Golden Anniversary of the White House Conference for Children and Youth that had taken place in the waning months of the Eisenhower administration.

The group was called together for an inaugural meeting in the White House so that the president could greet us, tell us of his plans, and instruct us about the type of assistance that he wanted. But at the outset of our meeting, Goldman informed us that the president was suffering from a severe upper respiratory ailment and that it was doubtful that he could keep the appointment. But a half-hour after the originally scheduled time, sneezing, wheezing, and blowing hard into tissues, Johnson outlined his great hopes and ambitions for the years ahead and instructed us specifically to come up with a name for his about-to-be-launched national effort to move the United States along a progressive path.

Each of us later received as a memento a framed scroll of the president's remarks, which contained the following interesting formulations:

Informal Remarks of President Lyndon Baines Johnson in Greeting Group of Experts in Domestic Affairs in the Fish Room of the White House, March 19, 1964

The tax bill which put twenty-five million dollars a day back into the pockets of American citizens . . .

The civil rights bill has come further along . . .

The farm bill which will save the nation four hundred million dollars, reduce our subsidies . . .

The poverty program . . . is now being presented to the House.

So I come to you this morning to say to you that we want a better world for all the billions of people.

Our first step toward that goal is to have a better deal for our own people.

After the president had concluded his brief remarks we reassembled, ready to respond to his request to find an appropriate name for his new program. We were seated alphabetically and I found myself next to Paul Freund of the Harvard Law School. At one point, after we had discussed various names such as the just, the equitable, the fair society, Freund pulled out of his memory the fact that the British sociologist, Graham Wallis, had once written a book with an interesting title, which he could not immediately recall. I fortunately remembered: It was *The Great Society*, and that was the name on which the group settled.

In 1966 I found myself a member of a "secret" White House task force that had as its agenda to recommend a new program to deal with the urban ghetto. George Shultz was the chair and John Coleman, president of Haverford College, was the vice-chair. The members included a number of prominent industrialists, a few representatives of the minority community, and an assortment of jurists, public officials, and academics. William Kolberg of the White House staff was assigned to work with us.

The secrecy reflected the president's desire not to build up hopes for a major effort that he might not be in a position to fulfill. But for those of us who were not in the know, the secrecy left us somewhat at sea, among other reasons because it involved our having to use special passes to get into and out of the White House.

I recall a discussion with Dr. Howard Rosen, the head of the Department of Labor's Research and Development program, who had a long record of concern and involvement and considerable experience in seeking to bring about changes in the ghetto. I asked him what suggestions he had for our committee, and he strongly urged that we consider the most radical of all solutions—move the people out and dynamite the neighborhood. I realized at the time—and later—that he may not have been kidding and that even if he were, it was advice worth considering.

The committee, under Shultz's leadership, took its assignment seriously and developed a comprehensive agenda, even if it stopped short of Rosen's proposal.

One of the sensible things that the committee decided to do was to organize itself into small groups and spend some time visiting selected ghetto neighborhoods, talking to the people who lived there about their problems, and asking them what the government might do to ease their lives. Our deliberations took on a special edge as a result of the impacts these visits had on the task force members.

As is so often the case, one member was sure that he knew the "cause" and "cure" for all the problems of the ghetto. In his view, all of the troubles stemmed from the large and growing numbers of teenage unwed mothers. No one challenged his contention that teenage motherhood was a serious liability for mother, child, and community, but no one bought into his view that this was the root cause of the ghetto's pervasive pathology.

I became so annoyed with this repeated explanation that I inquired of a fellow committee member, a distinguished authority on constitutional law, how long it might be before the Supreme Court ruled that the decision to terminate a pregnancy was a private matter that the pregnant woman had a right to determine for herself. After considering my hypothetical question, he told me that he thought the Court would stall and would probably not rule along these lines until the early 1990s—but would eventually support the woman's right to make the decision. To everybody's surprise, the Court adopted this view in 1973, which is surely one reason for the abortion battles that continue to rage. The Court was too far out front.

We realized that it would not be easy for the federal government to assure that people in the ghetto had access to decent housing, jobs, and recreational facilities, but the worst stumbling block that we were able to identify was how to reform the ghetto schools so that they could meet the needs of the upcoming generation. We gave up on the existing school bureaucracies and opted in favor of a demonstration approach that would give the responsibility for remodeling the whole system, from kindergarten to high school graduation, to a university-based School of Education.

When we added up the price tag for the most important new and expanded interventions, we came up with a total of between $12 and $18 billion per annum. A draft report was prepared, but after the White House staff had reviewed it Joseph Califano, acting for the president, came to our meeting and sequestered all of the copies. The president was caught in a rearguard action to save his existing Great Society programs from congressional cuts so that he could finance the escalating Vietnam conflict. What he didn't want or need was to broadcast a new program, especially one carrying such a high price tag. The dissolving of our secret task force, without so much as an acknowledgment that it had ever existed, was an early forerunner of the tragedy that befell President Johnson, whose many ambitious plans and projects were derailed by our ever-deeper involvement in Vietnam, an undertaking that was twice flawed—in conception and in execution.

But Johnson was tough and did not turn his back on his goals. Dissatisfied with the continuing high level of unemployment of urban blacks and having given up hoping that the Department of Labor would take the lead to remedy the situation, the president, as noted earlier, decided in 1968 to launch a new national effort that would be spearheaded by Henry Ford II and other leading businessmen. In an organizational meeting held at the White House to inaugurate this effort, the president talked from his heart and with poignancy about the plight of blacks in American society; his words could not have failed to move his listeners. He recalled a trip from Texas to Washington by the Johnson family, including its black housekeeper, who often was unable to find a place to relieve herself. Johnson was without question the first president who was unequivocally committed to the eradication of racism from the American scene, not in the indefinite future, but starting immediately and progressing as fast as possible.

The tragedy of the Johnson administration was more than the president's entrapment in the war in Vietnam, costly as that proved to be. I had an opportunity to observe this powerful, dedicated president seeking to lead, browbeat, or push Congress and the American people along the path of the Great Society. He was so set on achieving his goals that he failed to pay adequate attention to the growing distance between himself and his followers. A leader who gets too far out in front is a leader exposed. Johnson measured himself by his legislative victories, and they were many and important. But after 1965 he failed to read the growing signs that the American people didn't really want to make a continuing commitment to further large-scale reforms. I believe Johnson would have been in trouble even if we had not gotten trapped in Vietnam.

The American people were relieved when Johnson announced that he would not run for a second term. And it was a much-diminished Johnson who turned over the presidency to Nixon. But no sensible person will deny Johnson the credit for both the reach of his goals and the magnitude of his achievements during his early years in office. For a time, Johnson was surely an oversized president.

Richard Nixon's victory in 1968 was his and his alone. Never had a national politician risen from the ashes and by will and work reestablished himself as the leader of his party after having suffered the major defeats that Nixon experienced in the presidential election of 1960 and the California gubernatorial election of 1962. The fact that he accomplished a second national resurrection after his resignation from the presidency in 1973 further attests to the presence of reserve powers not readily visible to outsiders, who must infer their presence from events.

My first personal encounter with Richard Nixon dates back to the time near the end of Eisenhower's first administration when Secretary of the Cabinet Maxwell Rabb, with whom I was acquainted, threw one of those big Washington parties, attended by a thousand or more persons. I was about to leave to take General Snyder to his car so that he could return to Walter Reed Hospital, where he had been a patient for several weeks, recuperating from an operation. Rabb asked the general to delay his departure so that he could introduce me to the vice-president, who was working his way to our room, where he would arrive shortly.

When Nixon came abreast, General Snyder said that it gave him great pleasure to introduce "Professor Ginzberg." The word "professor" alerted me that something was awry, because Snyder always called me either Dr. Ginzberg or Eli. He then went on to say, in a quiet conversational tone, that "Professor Ginzberg believes that you have never done anything right; you are doing nothing right; and that you are incapable of ever doing anything right—Mr. Vice-President, Professor Ginzberg." I broke in first, saying to the vice-president that this was some type of test to see which of the two of us could respond more quickly to this outrageous statement. Before I had finished, Nixon had recovered enough to say something deflecting, although I don't recall that it was any more coherent than my attempted cover-up. I had known General Snyder well for over a decade, and never had he done anything even remotely aberrant.

In reconstructing the incident, I believe this is what happened: Snyder had stopped off at the White House and had encountered an upset, angry president who wanted to drop Nixon but couldn't find a way to do it and who unleashed his feelings on General Snyder, who was often the audience for Eisenhower's explosive remarks. But Snyder was at that moment below par physically and emotionally from his extended hospitalization, and he upset Nixon to help balance the president's upset. In retrospect I would not be surprised if Nixon made some or all of these same linkages. In all honesty, I must add that Snyder exaggerated when he quoted me, but not much!

In December 1968 I had taken my mother to Methodist Hospital, Houston, to have Dr. Michael DeBakey, my wartime friend, do an angiogram on her, a procedure that her New York physician did not want to trust to one of his local colleagues. On returning to the neighboring motel around 6:30 P.M. I found a note in my box instructing me to call the FBI immediately. I called even before going to my room, but I failed to raise anybody. After a few minutes I called again from my room. (In retrospect I am sure that in my excitement I simply misdialed the number the first time.) In the interim, I had begun to speculate as to the cause for the emergency and could not get beyond the hypothesis that my exchange student from Moscow had gotten into trouble. The agent who took my call was immensely relieved that I had made contact and quickly explained that the president-elect wanted to announce his cabinet at 9 P.M. on TV and that he could not do so unless the FBI talked with me about George Shultz, the secretary of labor designate, for whom I was a character witness. The agent told me that Washington and New York had been after him all day to contact me and that now that he had he would be right over. I explained that he was welcome to come but that all that I knew about George Shultz could be communicated over the phone. I had only positive information—not a shred of anything negative. I went through the agent's list of questions, and at the end he was so pleased that he wanted to know what he could do for me. He asked whether I would like to go out on the town, and when I said no thanks, he asked about getting me my ticket for my return to New York the next day. I explained I had my ticket. He then suggested an escort to the airport, but I explained that it really wasn't necessary. Never before or since have I encountered such a relieved agent. Nixon announced his cabinet at 9 P.M.

Fairly early in the new administration I went to supper at the White House mess with my friend, Arthur Burns, whom Nixon had appointed as counsellor to the president. We discussed a great many issues but no politics or personalities. As we were walking home, Arthur said that there was something strange going on in the White House, particularly Haldeman's and Ehrlichman's efforts to control everything, people and paper alike. Burns indicated that it was making him sufficiently uncomfortable that he would be getting out soon. Not long thereafter he became chairman of the Federal Reserve Board.

Nixon appeared to enjoy playing hardball. As noted in chapter 11, James Hodgson, the secretary of labor, had his senior advisors at Camp

David to figure out the next steps in federal manpower policy, since Congress had passed major new legislation that would decentralize most of the training programs to the prime sponsors, that is, to the larger local governments. To our surprise and consternation, we learned while we were there that Nixon had vetoed the bill on which the administration had worked hard because it contained a job-creation provision.

After the 1972 elections in which Nixon overwhelmingly defeated Senator McGovern, the president asked for the resignation of all cabinet officers, and his staff let it be known that they were working on a major reorganization of the executive department with the aim of creating a limited number of superdepartments. But the continuing shocks from Watergate derailed both these ambitious plans and, later, the Nixon presidency.

Tension developed after Burns was ensconced at the Federal Reserve Board, and the president demonstrated his displeasure by not inviting Burns and his wife to his weekly prayer meeting. American political life often leaves well-informed Europeans mystified. But the incident just cited would confuse even a Washington aficionado.

Another view of Nixon came from watching his participation during the 1960s at the birthday parties that we put on for President Eisenhower after his retirement. On occasion, Nixon would be among the most interesting and relaxed of the attendees, and his comments to the birthday celebrant were witty and perceptive. At other times, he was wooden, withdrawn, sulking—suggesting that he didn't enjoy participating in these festivities for a man who, by his delayed and reluctant participation in the campaign, probably cost Nixon the presidency in 1960. Nixon gave the impression of being under the spell of forces he could not control or master.

The Ford presidency turned out to be much better than anybody had reason to anticipate, since it was the first time in the nation's history that the incumbent in the White House had not been elected by the voters.

Ford alienated many of the electorate by his early pardon of Nixon, an action that in retrospect seems to have been the best of the alternatives. Further, within about a year of his succeeding to office, Ford found himself confronting the worst recession in the post-World War II era. He also had to avoid being caught in the gunsights of Nelson Rockefeller, his vice-president, whose sizable retinue were looking desperately for an opening that would enable their boss to have a try at the presidency.

Once the recession of 1974–75 gained momentum, President Ford was unable to stay out front and shape the interventions necessary to improve the situation. Congress decided to take the lead and moved quickly to expand public-service employment as the best way to ease the threat of rising unemployment.

At one point a meeting was arranged between the members of the National Commission for Manpower Policy and the president. The president asked a number of pertinent questions, which led to a relaxed discussion in which a number of the members, including me, helped to keep the discussion at a level that was neither so general as to be irrelevant nor so technical as to fall outside the president's competence. I came away from the meeting convinced that the president had more things going for him than most of his critics were willing to acknowledge. No man is ever prepared to be president, and Ford's preparation was more modest than that of many presidents. But I got the impression that Ford was aware of both his strengths and his weaknesses, and that this awareness turned out to be an important asset.

Ford had another asset. He was well served by his senior economic advisors. Arthur Burns arranged a lunch in my honor at the Federal Reserve Board at which William Seidman, who was located in the White House, Alan Greenspan, who headed the Council of Economic Advisors, William D. Eberle, who was in charge of international economic relations, and a senior official from the Treasury Department were present. Until they went off on a tangent and began to argue that what the United States really needed was a thousand-dollar car that would provide basic transportation (with Seidman the only dissenter), I found the conversation so sensible that I concluded that the president was being well served. And I believe he was.

The mid-1970s found the country not only in a serious recession but also in increasing trouble because of the underlying inflation, a subject of the deepest concern to Arthur Burns, who complained to me that the only advice that he could elicit from the left-of-center Brookings Institution staff was for the United States to spend its way out of the recession. As the high unemployment—high inflation dilemma came increasingly to the fore, I made Arthur a proposition. I said I would try to moderate the requests from the National Commission for Manpower Policy for increasingly large public-service job programs and work to persuade the members to see inflation as a serious threat to existing jobs and incomes, if Burns in turn would publicly favor a federal commitment for a job for everybody who was able and willing to work.

We talked about this several times in the ensuing months, and in an address at the University of Georgia at Athens in 1975, Burns came out in favor of public-service jobs for all, but with a modest twist, slightly below the minimum wage. This twist made him an anathema to George Meany of the AFL-CIO but not to Senator Hubert Humphrey, who realized how far Burns had come in espousing a program of full employment.

When Governor Jimmy Carter's name first surfaced as a possible Democratic candidate for the presidency, I gave the report little credence. I did not believe that the Democratic party would nominate a one-term southern governor who had had almost no national visibility until he started chasing the nomination. Nor did I believe that, with the recession in remission, he would be able to beat President Ford. But these were private opinions, privately held, since I had gone out of my way over the three decades not to become involved in party politics.

Consider my surprise when, shortly after the Democratic convention, I got a call from Judy Powell, on Governor Carter's staff, asking me to prepare a memorandum for the governor on work and welfare. I explained to Powell that I couldn't possibly get involved in the campaign since I was currently holding the chairmanship of the National Commission for Manpower Policy, which reported to both Congress and the president. Powell told me that the paper that Carter wanted would not be used in the campaign, but, in the event that he won the election, Carter wanted to move quickly to design some programs of reform. After going over the ground once again with Powell and being assured that my paper would not be used in the campaign, I prepared the requested document. The Georgians kept their word. Many years later, in 1988, Congress passed the work-welfare reform legislation that bore many resemblances to my memorandum. (The memorandum had never seen the light of day, but by 1988 I was much less sure about the validity of the ideas I had outlined for Carter. Of course, the long-term unemployed, including mothers of school-aged children, would be better off working than being on the dehumanizing welfare rolls, but in the interim I had begun to question seriously that our society would come up with the up-front money that such a policy required. It would involve money for child care, training, transportation expenses, and transitional Medicaid coverage).

Carter's win was probably due to the backlash to Watergate, since he had made points by promising to clean up the mess in Washington. But no other president, at least in my experience, was more distant from the Washington scene at the end as well as the beginning of his term in office than Jimmy Carter. He never was able to work out even a passable relationship with Congress and the press, without which no president can be effective.

From my perspective, Carter was also not well served by his senior staff, except for Stu Eisenstadt, who quickly learned his way around. The senior Georgians just didn't trust the Washingtonians, and their attitude was reciprocated by the local sophisticates. I recall my amazement and discomfort at seeing a sign hanging prominently in the office of a senior White House staffer, relatively early in the new administration, with the following message: "Califano Is Bad for Your Health."

I had dropped the president-elect a line after his victory and before his inauguration suggesting that he look carefully at the suitability of Juanita Kreps, a long-time professor of cconomics at Duke University, who was currently a member of my commission. I told him that I knew Juanita well; I considered her sensible, energetic, and politically savvy, and I thought he would find her a congenial cabinet officer. Carter appointed her secretary of commerce, but I never learned from him whether he found my assessment sound. The record shows that Kreps left the cabinet after having served for three years. I don't believe that she found her term in office particularly rewarding.

As noted earlier, Carter pursued a job-oriented economic expansion policy that was focused on both adults and youth. With Ray Marshall as labor secretary and William Spring on his White House staff, Carter had two deeply committed advisors who encouraged and reinforced his own preferences to base his economic policy on expanding jobs. Since I had close relations with both Marshall and Spring, I soon began to interact with the president with some regularity.

I began to send him memoranda, and I was surprised to find that he annotated them with approving or critical comments and sent them back, usually without an accompanying note, assuming correctly that his notations proved that he had read and considered what I had said. But I found it strange that the president, busy as he was, should proceed in this fashion. I was flattered, but I did not consider it an effective use of his time.

Our commission met with the president on a few occasions, and the interchanges were much livelier than had been the case with his predecessor. Carter was better briefed; he was more engaged; he made his points more sharply. But I started to become concerned quite early in his administration—and my concerns increased with time—that he was not in control of his agenda, but rather was responding to events that were forcing him to act. Three years and more into his term, he recognized that something was askew and decided on the several weeks of Camp David meetings to sharpen his goals, which, together with personnel changes, would let him conclude his term on an upbeat note and position him to win reelection.

I was included among the advisors who were invited to participate at Camp David, with the White House staff presumably looking to me to help hold the line against any serious cutbacks in funding for employment and training. On the day that I was at Camp David, key leaders of the House and Senate, some well-intentioned corporate executives, and the leadership of the American trade unions were also in attendance. I listened to a lot of special pleading that day, but few if any of the speakers addressed the president's problems. Finally I asked for the floor and told the president that in my opinion he had to focus on the containment of inflation, for that was the dominant challenge. If the anti-inflation program required a severe reduction in employment and training programs, then so be it. My only specific suggestion was that funding be continued to assist inner-city minority youth. Any shrinking of efforts in that direction would cost the nation dearly. By the time I returned from Camp David in mid-afternoon, my phone was ringing with outraged White House staffers saying that I had double-crossed them. My reply was simple. I thought the president was entitled to my honest appraisal of the options he faced.

About six months later, the president invited some of us to the White House for lunch so he could brief us about the progress he had made in the interim. I drew Mrs. Carter as my table companion, and at the end of what turned out to be a long luncheon, I was certain that the president was the recipient of lots of good advice from his First Lady, who clearly had an aptitude for the political jugular.

But inflation, the U.S.S.R., and Iran were more than Carter could cope with effectively. He was intelligent and hard-working, but a successful president needs presence and a strong staff; Carter lacked both of these essentials. As I reflected both at the time and since, on his predicament, I concluded that a one-term governorship of Georgia with prior service in the Navy was simply not adequate preparation to lead the country in the late 1970s. And one cannot lay the blame completely on a weak staff, for it was the president, nobody else, who appointed and kept the staff in place.

In 1978 Michael Dukakis, the Democratic governor of Massachusetts, was defeated in his bid for reelection, and I learned that Secretary Marshall was planning to recommend to President Carter that he replace me, as chair of the National Commission for Employment Policy with Dukakis. I had been in the chair since 1962, and Marshall was surely entitled to ask me to step down in favor of Dukakis or anyone else. But I had taken special pains over the years to operate the commission as a bipartisan body and had good working relations with both parties in the House and the Senate. I therefore suggested to the White House staff that, unless the president wanted to politicize the commission, it would be better to appoint Dukakis as a member and to let me remain as chair, which turned out to be the option the president chose.

I got to know Dukakis reasonably well, since we frequently breakfasted together before the commission meetings. I was impressed with the story he told me about his unexpected defeat for reelection and what he had learned about his mistakes as he reviewed his experiences. I have long believed that the strongest people are those who are not overwhelmed by defeat but who can profit from the errors that they have made. Moreover, Dukakis was an intelligent, constructive member of the commission. But when I first learned that he was going to make a serious run for the presidency in 1988, I was more than a little surprised. I did not believe that the country was ready to elect as president a Greek-American with a Jewish wife. Nor did I believe that Dukakis would be able to project himself as a strong leader. And I had some questions about how well he did after he returned to the governorship. Massachusetts was on a roll, but it was the private, not the public sector, that was in the lead.

My misgivings were confirmed by the outcome of the election, although the Bush campaign was much dirtier than I had anticipated. I don't believe that even a strong Democratic candidate would have won in the face of the continuation of the Reagan boom. But Dukakis turned out to be a much weaker candidate than I had anticipated, even though I never believed he had a real chance to win.

I knew that I would miss my involvement in Washington, but though a nonpolitical animal, I could not see myself working for the Reagan administration. Voodoo economics and neoconservatism were not my favorite dishes.

I had had an opportunity to observe nine presidents, and I had the good fortune to get to know one well—Eisenhower—and three others, Johnson, Ford, and Carter, reasonably well. Only two were truly failures: Nixon because he was too clever for his own and the country's good; and Reagan, former actor, trade union leader, and capitalist spokesman who was stage-managed by his staff during the eight years of his presidency.

14

Consulting Abroad: Europe

During the four-and-a-half decades since the end of World War II, I have done extensive consulting abroad, primarily for the U.S. government but also for foreign governments and for nongovernmental organizations both domestic and foreign. Almost all of my assignments have been related to my primary research and policy interests, involving human resources, the labor market, and employment. Occasional projects have focused on health policy. While my consulting activities have taken me to five of the seven continents—Australia and Antartica are the exception—most of my time overseas has been spent in Europe and Asia. A rough calculation suggests that I have spent about four man-years in carrying out these consulting tasks.

In addition to broadening and deepening my knowledge and understanding of foreign cultures and people, I have been happy to undertake these many study visits abroad primarily because they provided me an opportunity to get new and deepened perspective on what was happening at home. Without foreign travel and study, one is likely to develop exaggerated views of one's own culture's strengths since one has no basis for comparison. The same dangers of excessive parochialism confront the members of the U.S. foreign service if they are stationed for excessive periods of time in a country with whose concerns and interests they tend to overidentify.

Western Europe

With the exception of Denmark and Portugal, I have had repeated opportunities to become informed about the human resources and employment dimensions of the countries of Western Europe, particularly the big four—the United Kingdom, France, the Federal Republic of Germany, and Italy. Since all of these economies were more or less in the doldrums from the end of World War I until the outbreak of World War II, and since the latter war destroyed a great amount of their personal, business, and national wealth, it is striking how well they did in the quarter-century after the end of World War II. And nowhere was their success more impressive than in the low rates of unemployment that characterized their economies in the 1950s, the 1960s, and the early 1970s, until the first oil crisis of 1973.

As we might expect, economists and others hold all sorts of overlapping and contradictory viewpoints to explain this progress, ranging from theories that give the credit for economic recovery to Keynesian fiscal policy, to Moses Abramovitz's "catch-up" theory (a shorthand term for his theory crediting the narrowing of productivity between European and American workers). I want to call attention to some factors, generic and specific, that have been neglected or minimized but which appear to me to warrant more emphasis than they have so far received.

I noted earlier that I had little faith that the French would be able to make effective use of U.S. aid in the immediate post-World War II period, a conclusion based on the strength of the oligarchy that had for so long blocked the design and implementation of any major program of economic reform. Overstated, one could say that France had never completed its "glorious" Revolution of 1789. But this judgment failed to correctly assess the potential power and influence of the senior civil servants who, led by Jean Monnet, were able to conceptualize and implement a modernization program that proved highly successful. The French, possibly even more than the British, had long had in place the "great schools," which attracted and trained the country's intellectual elite, not only the bureaucrats but the engineers as well. Once the Communists were contained, the top level bureaucrats were given their head by the politicians, for they alone had the capacity to plan.

The Germans in the Federal Republic faced much greater challenges: The nation had been cut in half, the Allies remained as occupying powers, and the wartime devastation had been much greater than in France. The Germans had only one serious option: to work very hard. And that is what they did. I recall that on my visit to the U.S. Seventh Army Headquarters in Stuttgart in the spring of 1951, I was awakened by lots of hammering on a Saturday morning and learned that production was going on in bombed-out plants even while new structures were being erected. And two years later, while on a study visit to Turkey, I heard that German salesmen were out in the countryside looking up old customers and pursuing new ones.

The large influx of refugees from East Germany added to the pressures on the West Germans to find housing and work for many hundreds of thousands of newcomers. But the refugees brought valuable skills, which speeded their integration. Much of the German economy, like Japan's, had been turned into rubble by the bombing from the air and subsequent fires. But both countries had had sufficient experience in operating a modern technological economy that, as soon as they had renewed opportunities to use that knowledge—and to profit from critical grants and loans to refurbish their basic infrastructure—they were on their way to rebuild what had been destroyed.

Much credit for the German recovery has been given to Konrad Adenauer and Ludwig Erhard for their heavy reliance on market mechanisms, but I have never fully accepted that explanation. The German economy has never been that free. There are all sorts of powerful constraints on entrance into the market and on performance, constraints that grow out of the legal system, trade associations, trade union rules and regulations, local ordinances, the dominant role of the major banks, and other institutional arrangements. I recall a conversation with a young computer engineer who started his own software company in the mid-1970s; he told me that he had to secure over a hundred specific governmental licenses and permissions before he could start up, and he folded within less than two years because of the difficulties he encountered as a newcomer in obtaining a line of credit.

From many perspectives, Italy is the most unusual success story among the big four. At the outbreak of World War II, it was far behind the big three. The war had been fought by infantrymen from the heel to the Alps. The devastation had been widespread, and I recall that as late as 1950 many areas in the north were still relying on temporary bridges to connect them with their neighbors. The Christian Democratic party had to devote almost all of its efforts to containing the Communists, and it was left with little energy and few resources for any other activity. Later on, when public finances had improved in response to economic expansion, the government found it necessary to make sizable investments in the south, where unemployment was high and per capita income was very low. In the late 1960s or early 1970s, I participated in a symposium on the development plan for the south (Mezzogiorno) at the University of

Bari. The symposium led me to conclude that most of the investment had less to do with long-term economically viable projects than with short-term job and income creation. In the face of the disparities in the economies of the north and south, I could not fault the government for pursuing such an unpropitious development plan.

But the national government's preoccupation with the continuing threat from the Communists and the terrorists after the end of the Remo Gaspari era may have been a blessing in disguise. It was surely not an unmitigated liability. The entrepreneurially strong north encouraged all sorts of businessmen, small, medium, and large, to make their own way little bothered, much less constrained, by the actions of the government. At one point, the U.S. embassy arranged for me to lead a seminar with forty or fifty owners of small and medium-sized businesses in the Verona area who spent the opening hours denouncing the tax and other policies of the national government. At one point, I broke in and said, "Look, I know and you know that you pay very little attention to the government in Rome and that you have discovered ways of paying only a small part of the taxes that you owe. Let's stop kidding each other and talk about your real problems, which have little or nothing to do with Rome."

At a subsequent meeting with the minister of the budget, I inquired what his rough calculations were about the size of the off-the-record economy. He told me that there were no reliable studies, but it was his best guess that the unreported economy could not be less than 20 percent of the GNP. I had lunch that same day with a professor of economics from the University of Naples, to whom I reported my earlier conversation with the minister. The professor assured me that in the south, the off-the-record economy was more in the 40 to 50 percent range. I had no way of checking either estimate, but there was considerable indirect evidence around that the reported unemployment, income, and other indicators did not reflect the facts. The economy was clearly doing much better than the official data suggested.

While the Communists may have helped to hone the politicians' skills, the large industrialists faced a strong challenge—how to deal effectively with organized labor, only part of which was under Communist leadership. It was my impression, from visits in the early 1970s to Fiat and other large employers in the Turin area, that management was very much on its toes because of the relentless pressures that they faced from their workers. In the cozy 1950s and 1960s in the United States, the major corporations found it relatively easy to negotiate with their major unions by agreeing to most of labor's demands and passing on the costs to the consumers; however, this was not the position in which Italian employers found themselves: They faced intense competition both in their domestic and foreign markets and had to keep tight control over their costs.

There are several other aspects of the Italian economy that I had the opportunity to become acquainted with: the extent to which migration from the south to the north, to other parts of Europe, to North and South America, relieved some of the pressure of too many people chasing too few jobs. I also got a little perspective on the extent to which the large public corporations were simultaneously dealing in critical products and services—such as oil, electricity, and transportation—and providing jobs for party hacks. Finally, through my friend Marissa Bellisario, the CEO of Italtel, I realized that part of the skill of a quasi-public-sector manager is to be able to make deals with the government and the trade unions to pare down enterprises that were carrying too many workers.

Although I would be hard-pressed to provide convincing evidence to support my thesis, I have long believed that of the four major European economies, Italy's is the closest to that of the United States because of the vitality of its entrepreneurial class, its disdain for government, and the skill with which many large public corporations are able to profit from their linkages to the government. And there is another parallel: the role of the criminal sector in making things happen. One can't put up a building in New York City without a long list of people who must be taken care of; and the new Rome airport could not be completed until the government recalled a discharged inspector who was the payoff man.

Of the four countries, I know Great Britain the best, but that does not mean that I have a clear understanding of its post-World War II development, including what has been called the "Thatcher revolution." To begin with, one must recall that Britain alone, among the big four, was on the winning side of World War II, even though it had consumed most of its accumulated treasure in the effort. When Attlee replaced Churchill in the election of 1945, the Labor party was in undisputed control of the government for the first time in British history, and it had an extended agenda including, in particular, the reform of the nation's health care and other social services and changing the balance between management and labor in the workplace.

I had repeated opportunities to talk with Aneurin Bevan during the 1946–1948 period, when he was fashioning the National Health Service, and what impressed me at the time, and has impressed me since, was the intensity of his commitment to equity both in access and in treatment. He was badly scarred by his recollections of the gross neglect of the health needs of the South Wales coal miners, among whom he was reared and whom he later represented in Parliament.

But for every Bevan, the reformer, there were surely two or three conservatives in management and among the senior civil servants. I recall my friend, Lord Sieff of Marks and Spencer, telling me of a return visit that he made to the mills in the Midlands, forty years after his first buying mission. He could hardly believe his eyes: nothing had changed over the four decades. He commented that it seemed as if the clock had stood still.

There was additional evidence of behavior deeply rooted in Britain's past on the part of management as well as among the trade unions. In the 1960s I addressed the directors of the European headquarters of a major international oil company located in London. The American vice-president for human resources was being rotated home and had recommended that a British employee be promoted into his position. But the proposal failed because the directors' wives wouldn't accept the candidate's wife. The unsuccessful candidate later became a cabinet minister!

While class differences appear to be much sharper in Europe than in the United States, they are most pervasive, as far as I can judge, in the British Isles, where a person reveals so much about himself, his family, his education, and his career as soon as he opens his mouth. During most of the postwar era, the industrial relations arena gave repeated evidence not only of class differences but of class conflicts. While some, possibly much, of the trouble could be laid at the door of Communist and fellow traveler shop stewards, the explosive labor-relations environment can be understood only by reference to the long-festering class antagonisms. Many workers saw no alternative to strikes, walk-outs, and other forms of workplace disruption because they had concluded that management had no interest in giving them a square deal.

Margaret Thatcher has been given a great deal of credit for bringing about a major change in industrial relations, primarily by having the laws amended in such a way that the freedom of trade unions to act disruptively has been curtailed, and the costs of their acting in defiance of the law have been raised to prohibitive levels; such behavior threatens them with the loss of all of their assets. But the strikes of the spring and summer of 1989 are a reminder that the Thatcher revolution may yet turn out to be partial rather than total. It is not a foregone conclusion that the old hatreds have been put to rest.

Consider the disturbing episodes during the Thatcher era, for example, the destructive behavior at home and abroad of the soccer enthusiasts, primarily from the Midlands, resulting in rampages leading to widespread injuries and deaths. Or consider the growing number of bloody confrontations between natives and immigrant groups in different parts of the country. For a people who line up voluntarily in queues without pushing or shoving, the aforementioned explosions carry special significance. In my long-distance perspective, these outbursts reflect the fact that large numbers of secondary school dropouts, without jobs and with little prospect of obtaining jobs later on, must find and take their pleasures where they can. Thatcher notwithstanding, the United Kingdom must be placed behind Germany, France, and Italy in terms of post-World War II economic development.

Let us look more closely at the changes that were occurring in the labor market, and the opportunities that young people faced in preparing themselves for work and adulthood. The sustained post-World War II economic expansion linked to the reconstruction and catch-up boom created tight labor markets in all of the four major countries, except for the south of Italy. Anybody who was able and willing to work could find a job. This was true not only for men but also for more women, who were increasingly able to find part- or full-time employment. In fact the strong labor market opened opportunities even for immigrants. The British admitted sizable numbers from India and Pakistan as well as from the Caribbean. France had jobs for large numbers of refugees, as well as for increasing numbers of Arabs from North Africa and smaller numbers of blacks from its former West African possessions. West Germany launched active labor recruitment campaigns in Turkey and attracted sizable numbers.

Throughout the 1950s and the 1960s, there was constant finger-pointing by the West European countries at the poor performance of the United States labor market, with its 5 and 6 percent—and occasionally higher—unemployment, compared with unemployment rates of 1 to 2 percent characteristic of most of the advanced economies of Western Europe, large as well as small. I recall helping a Turkish worker on a German-

Dutch express train decide on which station to alight in Holland to report to the employer who was expecting him; the worker knew not one word of any West European language.

None of the countries, with the possible exception of France (which had long offered refuge to large numbers of displaced persons), was comfortable about actively seeking "guest workers"; but facing the reality that without them essential work—such as garbage collection, street cleaning, and restaurant service—would not be adequately performed, they opted for importing labor. And in the case of Germany, many of the imported workers were used to staff the automobile assembly lines, the products from which contributed to the revival of German exports.

Despite the general tightness of their labor markets, the West European countries moved relatively slowly to lower the bars against the employment of women, particularly in the higher levels of the occupational structure. The number of women in the male-dominated professions, in management, and among higher-level technologists and technicians increased slowly. Part of the explanation lies in the rigidity of the educational and training systems, but the larger part of the explanation reflects the concentration and rigidity of the social systems, with their sharp differentials based on gender. In 1979 I chaired a conference in Paris under the joint sponsorship of the German Marshall Fund of the United States and the French Assistant Secretary of Labor for Women's Employment, which revealed the existence of a sizable gap in commitment and execution to lowering barriers facing women employees in the United States and in Western Europe.

This is not to say that discrimination against women has largely disappeared from the U.S. labor market, but only that we are definitely farther down the road. The situation in Sweden is particularly challenging. Sweden is far in the lead when it comes to the proportion of the female population that is employed; but most women in Sweden work less than full-time. There are simply not enough childcare facilities to permit more mothers to work full-time and only the wealthy can afford an au pair. In the mid-1980s my wife and I were the guests in Uppsala of a professor of medicine whose wife was employed as a teacher on the outskirts of Stockholm, about fifty miles from her home. She told us that she had to plan the meal so that she could do much of the cooking several days in advance; she had to use all her connections to find a young woman to help her serve and clean up; and her husband played a large role in this effort before, during, and after dinner.

The Dutch were at the other end of the distribution, with the lowest proportion of women in the labor market. I recall making the point at a Conference on Micro Electronics in Amsterdam in the late 1970s that there was little or no likelihood of the Dutch playing a significant role in the new world of the computer unless they moved quickly and strongly to tap into the female part of their talent pool, which they had substantially neglected. I pointed out that sitting for a half-hour in the lobby of this leading hotel and observing the traffic, the proportion of women to men could not have been more than 1 to 10.

The situation in France with respect to women's employment has several paradoxical aspects. France has long been among the leaders in the proportion of women who work. Moreover, France has a unique support institution, l'école maternelle, which provides full-day care and supervised play for children from about two-and-a-half years of age. Despite this critical resource, which is available throughout large parts of the country, France does not have a significant proportion of its women employees in high-level jobs.

All of the West European countries, large and small, were confronted with pockets of above-average unemployment, usually in coal-mining, steel-manufacturing, and other older industries. Although each of them experimented with a range of policies—including special development policies to accelerate the establishment of new industries (and jobs) to replace those that were being eliminated by changes in technology and/or markets—these areal efforts were for the most part not very successful and involved large outlays per new job.

While the United States also has been faced with depressed areas, such as Appalachia and the mining region of northern Minnesota, it has never seriously pursued a regional development policy. In thinking about this difference in approach, I have been impressed with three factors in the U.S. situation that have no direct counterpart in Western Europe: the weak attachment in this country of people to their regional culture; the willingness of American workers to follow the jobs; and the relatively easy access of relocated workers to new housing, including temporary housing.

A critical question about the post-World War II labor market relates to the extent to which the advanced countries opened up their educational systems to extend and improve the educational and skill qualifications of the younger generations entering the labor force. Almost without exception, youngsters remained in school longer—that is, until their seventeenth or eighteenth year (except in the United Kingdom, where leaving school at sixteen has until recently remained the norm)—and many who were more qualified were admitted to the university, although in almost every case the higher educational systems' resources lagged behind the numbers admitted. In sharp contrast to the United States, most European countries subsidize university students, either fully or to a large extent, for both tuition and living expenses.

I have never been able to relate the changes on their educational fronts to the sustained expansion of the West European countries, at least up to the mid-1970s. The improvements in the lower and higher schooling were not that dramatic, and the additional skills of the new workforce were not that significant. The explosive growth in post-secondary and higher education that characterized the United States during the early decades after World War II had no close parallel in Europe, in part because of the fact that our baby boom came earlier.

In 1975 I delivered an address at an Organization for Economic Cooperation and Development (OECD) Conference in Paris in which I sought to alert the Europeans to the probability that they would soon face a growing youth unemployment problem as a consequence of the much larger numbers of young people that would be entering their labor forces—a forecast that turned out to be very much on the mark. Not only did the numbers of young people entering the labor force increase substantially but the postwar expansion had run its course, and the European economies had to confront the challenge of stagflation.

No longer was there finger-pointing at the United States. Unemployment rates in the United Kingdom, Germany, and France reached and exceeded 10 percent. Moreover, their economies, unlike that of the United States, had almost no new net job creation. I recall an informal meeting in the early 1980s with the premier of France—Raymond Barre, a professional economist—in which we discussed the growth of the service sector in the United States, which had been the engine for our adding 20 million new jobs over the preceding decade. With France's total employment at around 25 million, Barre was unable to fathom the reasons that lay back of this disparate national experience in job creation.

A few more contrasts between "them" and "us." The British are in the most difficult position because of the long-term estrangement between academe and the world of business and its tightly controlled and obsolescent systems of skill training. German industry gets on, except in the natural sciences, with relatively little dependence on its universities, which can best be explained by the strength and depth of its apprenticeship system, which provides the economy with large numbers of highly motivated, capable mechanics and technicians.

It is not clear to me how Italy and France, with their traditional, largely unchanged educational systems but with greatly swollen numbers of university students, have been able to meet the changing requirements of their labor markets. Part of the answer must lie in the strength of instruction in their secondary schools; part must lie in effective on-the-job training.

With the single exception of Sweden, none of the West European countries continued to adhere to the doctrine of full employment after the mid-1970s. The approach was scrapped in favor of such old-fashioned policies as tolerating rising unemployment, the pursuit of balanced budgets, and a constraint in the growth of the public sector. Because of the imbalance between the number of job seekers and the number of jobs, both public and trade union policy sought to speed the retirement of older workers by providing attractive inducements for persons of sixty to leave the labor market, and they further aimed at improving the labor market balance by reducing the number of hours of work per week—a favorite plank of the German trade union movement. On my relatively frequent trips to West Berlin, I have been repeatedly struck with the fact that, despite its heavy dependence on tourists, department stores and many other retail shops are open only one Saturday per month. In the United States we have moved in the opposite direction: many stores are open seven days a week, and an increasing number remain open twenty-four hours a day. Herein lies at least part of the answer to the dichotomy between rapid growth in employment in the United States and no job growth in Germany over the last two decades!

There are all sorts of theories around that seek to explain the differences between the U.S. and West European economies since the early 1970s. I have been loath to buy into any of them. I recall that Arthur Burns, our long-term ambassador to West Germany, shortly before his retirement told me that in his view Germany had "lost its way." There is nothing in its growing trade balances of the last years to suggest that Burns was correct. My own view has been that Germany, as usual, was disinclined to be the first or even the second to move full force to shift its manufacturing from a mechanical to an electronic basis. But shift it did, and very successfully. With strong social services, it has tolerated a high level of unemployment, looking to the demographic downturn in the 1990s to right matters.

In both the United Kingdom and France, government policies aimed at deregulation and privatization have clearly contributed to the establishment of more entrepreneurial economies, and in Britain this trend was accelerated by the government's ability to check the power of the trade unions. That leaves Italy, which as far as I can judge continues in its inimitable fashion to establish and hold all sorts of niches in an expanding European and world economy based on aggressive owner-managers who have learned to survive and prosper no matter how great the confusion and disorder in the public domain.

The interesting problem that remains is not to refine the points of similarity and difference between the United States and the principal countries of Western Europe, no one of which is even a quarter the size of the United States, but rather to ask what will happen in 1992 and the years following if the European Community succeeds in speeding integration of its several economies.

Eastern Europe

The Pluralistic Economy, which I coauthored with Hiestand and Reubens in 1965, called attention to the large and growing importance of the public sector in terms of both income generation and employment. As chair of the National Manpower Advisory Committee, I was unclear as to where the jobs would be coming from to take care of the much-enlarged influxes into the labor market. Our answer to this rhetorical question was the important role of the governmental and nonprofit sectors as job-creating sectors.

The book was ignored in the U.S. academic world, but the State Department sent copies abroad and followed up by asking the East European countries whether they would like me to visit and discuss with them the implications of our analysis for their economies, particularly the critical role of services, which had been given short shrift in Marxian and post-Marxian theory. All of the East European countries except Poland replied enthusiastically, and in the early winter of 1967 my wife and I set out on a two-month study mission to Yugoslavia, Bulgaria, Romania, Hungary, and Czechoslovakia. What follows are some of the highlights of that trip and particularly what struck me as important about the methods—both those they had in common and those that varied—by which these five countries were trying to cope with their many problems.

At the end of our two-month visit and after talking with large numbers of officials, managers, and professors, a number of common factors impressed themselves on me, specifically, the extent to which each of the so-called independent countries had to consider how far it could go to shape its policies without attracting the attention or reaction of the U.S.S.R. The answer appeared to be not very far, not only because a serious misstep could start the Russian tanks moving west (as they had earlier into Budapest and would shortly after our visit into Prague), but particularly because of the extent to which these Eastern-bloc countries were tied to the economy of the U.S.S.R. They depended on their big neighbor for essential raw materials, and the U.S.S.R. also served, directly or indirectly, as a market for their surplus output. The authorities in Moscow often told them to send the specified exports, for which they would credit them, to a third country.

But it would be a mistake to assume that any of the five—even Bulgaria, which had the closest ideological bonds to Moscow—wanted to get any closer to Big Brother than they had to. The U.S.S.R. tried, not once but repeatedly, to develop an Eastern-bloc market in which the satellites would integrate their economies with that of the U.S.S.R., permitting each to achieve a higher level of specialization, but the satellites backed off realizing that they would be better off if they could establish and strengthen their ties to the West with its superior technology and much richer consumer and producer markets. The fact that the "opening to the West" was difficult to accomplish did not diminish their interest in moving in that direction.

It would be a mistake, however, to exaggerate the extent to which the U.S.S.R. was a day-to-day player in the affairs of the satellites. If they did not throw down a challenge to Moscow on the military-diplomatic front, they had considerable freedom to act, under the direction of their respective Communist party organizations. But it appeared to me that the national political chieftains had their hands full dealing with their bureaucracies' squabblings, which were intensified by geographic and ethnic tensions within each of these countries, tensions from which no satellite was free.

These regional pulls and tugs were most acute in Yugoslavia, where the political leaders had opted for a high degree of decentralization, a helpful but not altogether cost-free device because it contributed to a widening, not a narrowing, of the standard of living among the most and least favored provinces. Yugoslavia differed from the other Eastern-bloc countries in the sense that it was not a satellite—at least not within the technical sense of the term—since it had refused to accept political dictation from Moscow. But it differed in other respects as well. It had avoided the collectivization of agriculture, which in most of the other countries approximated 90 percent. And Yugoslavia had also experimented with decentralizing decision-making power to "workers' councils," which were given the authority to decide on relative wage rates and the uses of investment funds.

But these differences aside, Yugoslavia was similar to other Eastern-bloc countries in that it never found a way to avoid the excessive bureaucratization of the public-sector decision-making mechanisms involved in production and distribution, both of which were costly because of the excessive numbers of functionaries and the stifling of personal initiative. Moreover, all of the Eastern countries failed to appreciate the critical importance of a service infrastructure, without which the gains from a higher order of specialization of labor could not be achieved. Similarly, the effective signaling required between what consumers wanted and needed and what producers manufactured and sold was missing.

I recall visiting up-to-date manufacturing plants in Yugoslavia and in Romania where the workforce was busy in classes studying socialist theory because the production line was suspended awaiting the arrival of a critical part or because of some slippage in the delivery of the necessary raw materials. Upon inquiry, I learned that such hiatuses could last anywhere from a number of days to a number of months!

I made special efforts to inform myself about how the workers' councils were functioning but I learned more about the theory of how they were supposed to function than the realities that governed their decision-making processes. In a few enterprises, I was impressed by the hard-headedness of the individual or small group who appeared to be in charge and who had a reasonably clear idea of how to make the "collective" decision-making function. But in most instances, I thought the work councils were floundering under a combination of a flawed mechanism and weak implementation.

Throughout my extended visit to these East European countries I had the opportunity to meet many senior civil servants, professors, and other members of the elite. Although I tried repeatedly to engage them in discussions about their experiences in operating a central or planned economy, they tended to duck such discussions. The only exception were some of the research economists in Hungary, who were eloquent about the theories, if not the realities, of their planned economy.

Unable to learn much through discussion, I had to rely increasingly on what I was able to observe both in general and in the concrete. The weather in Eastern Europe during January and February left a great deal to be desired, in particular because the area relied heavily on peat and soft coal for fuel. The smog was heavy and incessant and must have represented a major health hazard to the population. In Budapest we could not see across the Danube.

On the plus side, the urban population appeared to have clothing adequate to protect them from the coldness and dampness of the winter, although the way they dressed was not attractive. In the preferred hotels, restaurants, theaters, and private homes where we were entertained, there was always adequate heating. But I recall vividly on our first morning in Sofia, with snow and ice on the ground, my shock at seeing a grandmother of around seventy years of age chopping away at the ice with a blunt pick, an activity at which she was busy during the rest of the day. Her job may have helped to keep the unemployment rate down, but it made me more than a little restive about the "workers' paradise" that the Communist enthusiasts talked and wrote about.

Although we were put up at Sofia's finest as guests of the Bulgarian government, my wife, who wanted to stay indoors editing a book of mine, was unable to cajole or bribe the maids on our floor to make up our room until they wanted to—which was sometime late in the afternoon. Admittedly, Americans, even those who were guests of the Bulgarian government, may not have elicited much warmth or respect, but my interpretation was much simpler: There was no effective management or supervision in our premier hotel, with the result that the disgruntled workforce did as little work as they could get away with.

I was scheduled to give an early morning lecture at the university; before the lecture, I had to drink the two schnapps urged upon me by hospitable hosts, the one and only time in my life that I drank before breakfast. It was a friendly audience, but during the discussion period it became clear from several comments and questions that the students and faculty had a picture of Americans as persons who never walked but got into and out of their automobiles. On the spot, I asked for a show of hands as to how many in the audience walked to work, and not one in twenty indicated that they did so. I explained that, with the exception of the years during World War II when I worked in the Pentagon, I had always walked to work and was doing so currently. It was an appropriate rejoinder, but I doubt that anybody believed me.

I learned later during a walk in the woods—the only place that my informant thought we would be safe from being overheard—that the Bulgarians did a lot of hiking on the weekends not only because they liked the out-of-doors but because it was the only place where they were free of surveillance. I learned from my walking companion that, while the Bulgarian government's position followed Moscow's line of breaking off relations with Israel after the Six Day War, the vast majority of the informed populace were strongly pro-Israel, preferring the underdog.

The government officials who had direct responsibility for overseeing our four-day visit to Sofia were the beneficiaries of the Bulgarian equivalent of an American expense account. They saw that we were well taken care of, and it was my distinct impression that they found our visit a boon, since it enabled them to eat at the best restaurants and have preferred seats at the opera.

In the late 1960s, at the time of our visit, it was generally acknowledged that Bulgaria was the closest to the U.S.S.R. of all the Eastern-bloc countries. In fact, some informed persons believed that the Communist faith burned purer in Sofia than in Moscow. But the idealization of Communist doctrine was not sufficiently powerful to attract physicians to the countryside. The government offered all sorts of benefits—a superior house and a promise that after a decade of rural practice, the physician would be eligible for specialized training and would eventually be given a superior position in an urban teaching hospital. There may even have been a cash bonus as an added inducement. But there were very few applicants for this special deal. No physician wanted to go to the boondocks. In Belgrade, I was impressed that many recent medical school graduates assigned to rural areas went underground, worked in the daytime as waiters or at some similar occupation, and worked as physicians without permission at night.

Among the striking sights in Bucharest, Belgrade, and Budapest were mammoth public housing agglomerations, larger than any such concentrations that I was acquainted with in the West. It took relatively little probing to discover that these Communist governments looked with favor on allocating some of these apartments to families that were able to put down a sizable initial payment and to finance a multiyear mortgage. A large number of the apartments were reserved for the Party faithful at ridiculously low rents. The possession of a desirable apartment was a reward that could be matched by few other privileges or benefits.

I had no way of knowing whether the construction was of high quality, whether the apartments were efficiently laid out, or whether the maintenance was satisfactory. But I had no difficulty in concluding, based on nothing more than close-up walk-arounds, that there was nothing inherently impossible about a planned economy doing some production jobs more or less right.

But my wife's and my visits to several department stores, particularly in Bucharest, which still cherished the illusion that it was "la petite Paris," provided proof positive that this planned economy lacked the minimum essentials to meet consumer needs and demands. The merchandise was so shoddy that even the shoppers who were looking for an excuse to spend their money turned away in disgust.

One may legitimately ask what kind of advice I offered these governments that had asked the U.S. Department of State to make me available. It must be recalled that I came as an "expert" on the role of services in a modern economy, a role that meant that I had my work cut out for me, since the Eastern-bloc countries, following Marxian doctrine, looked on services as parasitic activities, nonproductive and non-value creating. Only physical output, intermediate and final, had real value, according to doctrinaire Marxists.

My first effort was to provide them with some background about the role of services in the advanced Western economies, not only in the United States but also in Western Europe. (In the late 1960s Japan was not yet a model with lessons for export.) I did my best to avoid entanglements in doctrine and to stick to the facts that suggested that in all advanced economies services accounted for the majority of all jobs and for half, plus or minus, of all GNP. Here was proof positive that a Communist state could continue to ignore or downplay the role of services only at the risk of sabotaging its own development.

A frequent response to this was that the Communist planners did, of course, recognize the importance of such critical service infrastructures as transportation, power, and telecommunications. That led to the second point on my instructional agenda, which focused in and around the necessity of expanding and improving "producer services." I called attention to a recently published book of ours dealing with producer services. I did not argue with or criticize the inherent limitations of operating a planned economy, including establishing and maintaining a system of regulated prices, but I sought to persuade those with whom I talked about the critical role that services, particularly producer services, had to play in a dynamic industrial economy.

The next lesson on my agenda—and one that I stressed in particular in Budapest, where the government officials and economists whom I met were closer to the thinking in the West—related to the criticality of financial intermediaries to facilitate savings and investments and to broaden the foundations for larger and more diversified foreign trade, as well as to facilitate the redirection of domestic capital.

I acknowledged that there were many reasons that a Communist society would look critically at any suggestions to expand and diversify its financial system, but I emphasized that, for better or worse, banks are service institutions that can contribute a great deal to improving the accumulation and use of scarce capital. Moreover, I pointed out that the Eastern-bloc countries were paying a heavy price for conducting so much of their foreign trade in barter rather than in dollars or marks.

The last point on my agenda related to the fact that many service industries depended on family or small-enterprise units. It was essential, therefore, if the latent capabilities and talent of the population were to be more productively employed—and my critical contention was that effective services were as productive as useful goods—for the planners to loosen their rigid controls over the number of workers that the family firm was permitted to hire.

The touchstone of my presentation was that the only prospect of maintaining, over a longer period, a planned economy that would enjoy a rising standard of living was for the authorities to take immediate steps to encourage the development of the service sector. If Marxian orthodoxy stood in the way of such early accommodation, I could see little prospect for continued economic growth. Admittedly, introducing the flexibilities that the expansion of the service sector would require would make it more difficult for the central planners to stay in full control. But since the latter approach was the road to stagnation, the less-risky path was to encourage the growth of the service sector.

The production-oriented communist planned economies had moved a fair distance—some might argue all of the way—to separate quantity from quality. Khrushchev's boast that he would bury the United States with an ever-larger output of steel never explained what the additional tons of steel would enable the U.S.S.R. to accomplish. In Budapest I was alerted to the fact that some of the more reflective officials had caught on to the dangers of this emphasis on quantity output. The Hungarians had built a larger number of creches and nursery centers for infants and children under three to facilitate their mothers' returning to work shortly after giving birth. But my host, a physician who was serving as mayor, explained to me that the health authorities had discovered that this system was not all that efficient because the large centers facilitated the spread of contagious and infectious diseases, which led to excessive morbidity and mortality. Hence the government had legislated that mothers could have a two-and-a-half-year maternity leave at half-pay, and employers were obliged to reassign them to their former jobs—a commitment easier made than implemented. The mayor also told me of the great pressure on the adult health care system. In some hospitals, two patients often had to share one bed!

The assumption that a major revolution sweeps away all of the past was proved to me to be a vast exaggeration once I made contact with university professors in the Eastern-bloc countries. The structure of the university, the critical role of the ordinarius—the full professor—and the subservient position of everybody else, including students, assistants, and librarians, reminded me of the year I spent in Heidelberg in 1928–29. In fact, as I thought about the two situations, I concluded that Heidelberg before Hitler had modernized its ways to a greater extent than had these Eastern-bloc institutions in the post-World War II era. The Communists have enabled a great many newcomers to make their way up the career ladder, but it was clear that one preexisting ladder had remained in place.

Nowhere was the isolation that characterized most of these Eastern-bloc countries (except Yugoslavia) more oppressive than with respect to those who sought to pursue a scientific career. University libraries, at best, were able to subscribe to only a few journals because subscribing required hard currency, and few if any of their professors had the money or could obtain the permission to participate in conferences held abroad. Academics, cut off from their colleagues, are academics more in name than in fact.

When we arrived in Prague—our last stop—we were informed that our bags had been sent on by error to Paris, but that they would probably be back within forty-eight hours, which in fact turned out to be the case. My wife suggested to the aide from the U.S. embassy who met us on our arrival that she would like to pick up a few replacement items, such as toothbrushes, dental cream, and so on, on the way to the hotel. He pointed out that shopping would be of no avail but that he would be glad to give us the essentials. Clearly Prague was no better with regard to consumer items than the other countries that we had visited.

Our visit to Prague occurred about six months before Alexander Dubcek was toppled and the hardcore group grabbed control, with a military assist from the U.S.S.R. In all of my many trips abroad, Prague was the only place where I was of any interest to the secret police; in Prague I quickly learned to spot them in their small cars following me wherever I went. But my wife upstaged them, at least on the telephone. They called one morning to inquire where I was, and she told them that she hadn't the foggiest notion as to my whereabouts. They then identified themselves as the secret police, as if that would insure them the information they sought. My wife told them that if they were who they said they were, it was their job, not hers, to know where I was and where I might be going!

Despite the secret police, who did nothing more than shadow me throughout the week that we were in Prague, I found the visit to Czechoslovakia to be the high point of our stay in Eastern Europe. In fact, the people with whom I interacted in Prague were not carrying the extra burden of strained relations to all Americans that existed in Budapest because Joseph Cardinal Mindszenty had taken refuge in the U.S. embassy, which greatly strained relations between Hungary and the United States.

Moreover, both Czech industry and Czech intellectuals had at least selective and ongoing contacts with the West, particularly with West Germany. And I was more impressed than I had been in the other

Eastern-bloc countries with the level of competence and sophistication of both management and the working population, which still gave evidence of a long tradition of skill.

But there were other aspects of the Communist regime that gave me cause for pause. I was told by an official who knew what he was talking about that the per capita consumption of concrete was extraordinarily high in Czechoslovakia, apparently because so many who had access to the plants helped themselves illegally to large amounts so that they could speed the building of a house in the country. This spoke to the initiative and entrepreneurial spirit of the population, although it reflected adversely on their respect for state property.

I was also told that in the normal course of events it would take about three months to have one's car repaired; that is, unless one left a sizable tip of cash and cigarettes on the front seat, in which case one could pick up the car at the end of the week.

One evening, at a party comprised primarily of academics, I was informed by the professor of neurosurgery at the university that his wife, who was employed as a hair stylist, earned approximately the same as he did. Moreover when I pressed him about the opportunities for physicians, especially members of medical school faculties, to earn large sums under the table, as I had been informed was the pattern in Bucharest, he told me that that was not the case in Prague, unless one were willing to risk a prison sentence of a year or more. He knew several colleagues who were in prison because they had taken that risk and lost. My informant went on to explain that those in power in Czechoslovakia took a dim view of all intellectuals and were determined to put and hold them in their place.

In 1971 I concluded my chapter on the Eastern bloc in *Manpower for Development* with the following paragraph:

> The East European countries are slowly rediscovering Adam Smith's argument that the market mechanism is efficient and effective, that advantages accrue from the use of material (over moral) incentives, that centralized power has indirect limitations, that gains follow upon individual freedom for decision-making, and finally, that the end of production is consumption. (P. 239)

Twenty years later adaptations were taking place, but at an abysmally slow rate. One assumed that the slowness reflected the fact that two to three generations of people who had lived under a Communist society had been ground down into acceptance and inactivity. And then in 1989 this assumption proved to be false. It will take more than a few years for the countries in Eastern Europe to determine the paths that they intend to follow in the future, but it will not be the path that they have been following.

15

Consulting Abroad: Africa and Asia

I was in Niagara Falls, Canada, in the fall of 1965, lecturing to the Canadian Guidance Association when I received a message to call my friend Alvin Eurich at the Department of State. He wanted to know whether I would be willing to undertake a manpower study of Ethiopia. Washington had promised the emperor, Haile Selassie, that they would provide an American expert. As my friends commented later: what does one give an emperor who has everything? Ginzberg! I asked for a few days to think it over and then answered yes. I would take responsibility for the study and go twice to Ethiopia—at midterm in January 1966 and again in June—if the department would agree that I could collaborate with my friend, Herbert Smith, the director of the Israeli Manpower Authority, who held dual citizenship—U.S. and Israeli—and who was willing to spend six months in Ethiopia. The State Department agreed and in early January 1966 my wife and I were on Ethiopian Airways out of Cairo on our way to Addis Ababa. Neither of us ever forgot the ride from the airport to our hotel: a stark naked man stood in the middle of the road—our first sight of the many mentally ill people who roamed the streets.

Between January 1966 and early 1971 I undertook four consulting assignments for the Department of State—to Africa, Iran, Southeast Asia, and East Asia—in addition to several additional study visits to Israel (which I have written about elsewhere [*My Brother's Keeper*]).

Africa

My trip to Ethiopia alone resulted in a published volume: *Manpower Strategy for Developing Countries: Lessons from Ethiopia*. In addition, I published selective analyses of Iran, Afghanistan, Pakistan, and India, with passing references to Egypt, Nepal, and Sri Lanka. In this chapter I will consider the countries mentioned above and the seven East Asian countries that I visited; they ranged from South Korea and Japan to Indonesia and Thailand.

Smith and I faced formidable hurdles in developing a manpower study of Ethiopia, since it had never undertaken a census and the overwhelming majority, over 90 percent, of the estimated population of about 23 million was rural. During his six-month sojourn, Smith was able to use various estimating devices to get a rough picture of this isolated, benighted, and very poor country, whose ruling dynasty dated from the nineteenth century but whose cultural roots dated from the Queen of Sheba. Mussolini had decided that Ethiopia offered an important early prize on his imperial journey; he had succeeded in establishing military control in the late 1930s and had encouraged the emigration of skilled Italian workmen to help support his troops. One of Emperor Haile Selassie's first decisions in regaining control of his country during World War II was to assure the safety of these Italian workers and thus to encourage them to remain. The emperor realized that they represented a major manpower asset.

In Ethiopia, 90 percent of the population were living in rural areas, many of them unable to use wheels because of the ruggedness of the terrain. More than half the population lived more than a half-day's mule ride to a good-weather road. It is not rare to hear of people walking for seven days from one community to the next.

The illiteracy rate, not surprisingly, was very high—above 90 percent. The literate population was overwhelmingly urban, and it consisted largely of the younger age groups, who had had an opportunity to attend school. The Coptic church operated a modest school system in which pupils were taught to memorize their prayers; a few went on to learn to read and write.

Although the Amharas, who are Coptic Christians, held the dominant positions, the country was probably approaching an equal division between Muslims in the north and Christians in the middle and the south. The emperor spent considerable time traveling around his domain to show the power of the national government and to put some check on his local governors. On one such visit to Gondar, where he visited a U.N.-supported medical technicians' school, the emperor was invited by the Chinese principal to his home for luncheon. The emperor was so impressed with the cuisine that he persuaded the principal to resign his post, relocate to Addis Ababa, and open a Chinese restaurant that I can personally attest was of superior quality.

Some perspective on the conditions that led to the bestial civil war that erupted in the 1970s and the slaughter that continued almost uninterruptedly through 1991 can be gained by my recalling that, when the emperor's horses were taken out for morning exercise, they had the sidewalks for themselves. Pedestrians had to walk in the gutter.

The U.S. government directly and indirectly had sought in various ways to help Ethiopia. TWA had a long-term contract to run Ethiopian Airways and to train the flight and ground crews. On my return visit in June 1966 I flew with a completely Ethiopian crew from Lagos, Nigeria, via Entebbe, Uganda, to Addis Ababa. The Peace Corps had a sizable number of enrollees who were filling many needed positions as teachers. Americans played an important role in staffing the university in Addis, the only one in the country. Oklahoma State University, under a grant from the United States Agency for International Aid (US-AID), had been training agricultural specialists since the early 1950s, but the American faculty lived some distance from the capital in a compound adjacent to their experimental farm, and most of them had relatively little contact with the government bureaucrats and even less with the farm population. Our analysis disclosed that, after more than a decade, only seventy-five of its several hundred graduates were working as farm agents.

The dominant view among development specialists in the mid-1960s was that the best way for an underdeveloped country such as Ethiopia to propel itself forward was for it to seek substantial amounts of foreign aid and to use that aid to speed its industrialization. Our analysis of Ethiopia's present and future prospects led us to question this conventional wisdom We did not see how this rural, illiterate, largely isolated population could possibly be transformed into an industrializing nation by century's end.

Our counterproposals focused on the importance of assisting the dominant rural population to make progress. For instance, we discovered that most migrant farm workers who helped to harvest the coffee crop did not return home with their earnings. Rather, they spent their earnings in riotous boozing and sex because they knew that, given the opportunity, the local military or civil authorities would confiscate their earnings with or without pretext. In the absence of the rule of law, economic progress was likely to be slow or nonexistent.

The farmers and cattle-raising population were illiterate, and they also suffered—as did their animals—from a great number of serious diseases. The difficulties in eradicating these diseases were complicated by the widespread illiteracy. The thrust of our recommendations was that most of the development funds should be used for a combined effort dedicated to raising agricultural productivity via basic schooling, health reforms, improved roads, and agricultural support services. But we recognized as we framed our recommendations that the bureaucrats in Addis Ababa had a different vision, tied to urbanization and industrialization.

I had learned that the emperor was disinclined to read reports in English, and, on the advice of his sophisticated and politically active niece, I persuaded US-AID to invest a few dollars in having our report translated into Amharic. However, I had no feedback on whether the emperor took the time to look at it. But I do know, from the Israeli ambassador, that the emperor appreciated foreigners who learned his language and were able to communicate with him in Amharic.

Toward the end of my first visit, US-AID decided that my wife and I, who had been kept quite busy and confined largely to Addis, should spend a day in the countryside. We readily agreed. Some forty or so miles from the capital, bouncing along in our jeep over a pretty country road, we encountered two sights that were powerful reminders of how far Ethiopia had to go. The first was a landowner-nobleman riding on a horse with his servant running barefoot ahead of him. And shortly thereafter, off slightly to our right, was a family of baboons, with the male in the rear who saw to it that they all passed safely over the crossing. He spotted our car and thumbed his nose at us.

My willingness to accept the invitation of the State Department to undertake the Ethiopian study mission was greatly influenced by my interest in visiting Egypt, both to see what was happening there and also to see how the Egyptians looked at their short- and longer-term relationships with Israel. At the end of my first visit to Addis Ababa, the visit to Cairo became a reality. Through one of my students at Columbia, who was later expelled from the United States on the advice of the FBI, my sponsor was Mohammud Yunnes, deputy prime minister and minister of ports and communications, my student's father-in-law.

Ethiopia was a country with a long past; but Egypt was venerable, possibly the oldest nation-state in the world. If its suburbs with the pyramids are included, there would be no difficulty in identifying about

four millennia of continuous human existence in Cairo, made more vivid
by a visit to its great museum with its many artifacts.

The Cairo airport between midnight and 6 A.M. was one of the busiest
airports in the world: planes from the three intersecting continents
criss-crossed on their paths to the other three outlying continents—North
and South America and Australia.

But not many people were sufficiently intrigued to get off and spend
some days in Egypt, especially if they had once visited its great temples
and tombs. It was not relaxing to visit Cairo, with its overwhelming
numbers of poor people living in abysmally crowded conditions.

But there was much more to Cairo than the poverty-stricken masses.
There were sizable numbers of well-educated professionals and businessmen, junior and senior civil servants, and writers and journalists, as
well as the upper ranks of the military, who kept largely to themselves.
Cairo may have had direct links to the Third World, but it also belonged
to the modern world, in ways quite different from Addis Ababa.

I visited Minister Yunnes in his office and was struck by the turmoil
and noise that pervaded the outer offices, with scores of people vying for
the attention of his staff. But I also observed that the office "worked," in
the sense that many who came to ask favors apparently got what they
sought and left contented. I recalled the West's contemptuous opinion
that the Egyptians would never be able to manage the Suez Canal after
they had unceremoniously nationalized it. Within a few weeks or months,
under Yunnes's leadership, the ships were passing through without
mishap. The city worked; the airport worked; some of the factories that
I visited worked. Admittedly, Cairo wasn't Athens, and it certainly wasn't
Milan or Paris, but it was alive and functioning.

The countryside, as I saw it during my day's outing to the delta in the
company of the minister of agriculture, also worked, with its admixture
of old and new technology. But the linkages to the far-distant past were
still real and vital. When our host, the governor of the province that we
were visiting, sought to impress me with the importance of his area, he
told me with great pleasure and pride that it was the home of the prophet
"Moise" who had been taken from the bulrushes but a few miles distant
from where we were.

In meeting with the middle- and higher-level bureaucrats, I was struck
with how much the best of them resembled the best in Jerusalem; I was
startled by how little attention and energy they directed to the tensions

between the two countries. According to local maps distributed in the leading hotels, there was no country such as Israel. The area between Egypt and Lebanon was simply a blank. But I came to realize that the Egyptians, at least those with whom I had discussions, were preoccupied with their national problems, with how to speed their industrialization, improve their agricultural output, and, particularly, get their birthrate under control. As far as I could judge, they had no good answer for any of these three challenges, but least of all for the last. And Egypt, a quarter-century later, is more vulnerable because of its large population, which in the early 1990s still continues to grow rapidly.

Egypt, like Israel, has been and continues to be a major beneficiary of U.S. aid; it receives about $2 billion per annum. But in Egypt this sum must be spread among more than fifty million persons, while in Israel the beneficiaries number around around four million. Unless governments learn how to make the desert bloom in ways that up to now have exceeded their know-how and capabilities, or unless the rapidly expanding birthrate can be brought under control, the outlook for Egypt is bleak.

On my return visit to Ethiopia in June of 1966, the State Department suggested that I spend two weeks in four West African countries—Senegal, Sierra Leone, Liberia, and Nigeria. Here are a few brief observations of my only exposure to that part of the world.

Dakar, the capital of Senegal, had very much the quality of a French provincial university city. As far as I was able to ascertain, France continued to make large annual grants to Senegal, among other reasons to assure the economic well-being of its large expatriate population, who continued to dominate the higher reaches of the economy—senior civil servants, the university, the professions. Furthermore, the Quai d'Orsay appeared to view these large subsidies as an investment for the future. France was no longer in "possession" of its colony, but for all practical purposes it remained the key guiding force.

One way that it sought to remain in effective control was to continue to monopolize the key professional and technical jobs. When a French company won a contract to build a road or some other piece of infrastructure, it brought all of the necessary expertise from home, and it took care not to train the locals whom it hired, at least not beyond first-order skills.

To an outsider like myself, it was questionable whether France, as a collective entity, was getting even a modest rate of return on its sizable annual investment, but there is no question that the substantial subsidies provided by Paris made life very comfortable for the expatriates who lived and worked in Dakar. It was difficult to see how Senegal could survive and prosper without the continuing good will of metropolitan France. The peanut crop was hardly a foundation on which to build a modern state.

The British presence in Freetown, the capital of Sierra Leone, was distinctly less visible than that of the French in Dakar, although directly and indirectly London still exercised some influence over its former dependency, whose economy was built on the diamond-mining industry. There had been not one but several political coups over the years since the former colony had gained its independence, and politics seemed to be the major arena for the engagement of the energies and talents of the leadership and those who aspired to power.

It was not easy for an outsider to recognize how the people in Sierra Leone, who numbered between three and four million, differed from their neighbors to the north, south, and east. The nagging question that remained was whether such differences created the basis of a national state and could possibly justify the sizable overhead costs connected with national sovereignty. A number of the Western countries had aid projects under way—in health, education, industrialization—but the effort that caught my attention was a U.N. agricultural project in the countryside. The project was run by Taiwanese farmers, who were experimenting with the introduction of new crops and crop-improving techniques. They were making good progress, but my inquiries led me to conclude that only a few of the locals were interested in taking advantage of the demonstration.

Of all of my foreign consulting work, Sierra Leone stands out in my memory because of the prime minister's unsubtle attempt to explore a deal with me: He was scheduled to visit Washington and wanted help in persuading the president to provide him with additional aid, including, if I remember correctly, a couple of passenger planes. He made it clear to me that if I helped, my assistance would not be overlooked. Aside from mentioning this proposal to our ambassador, I let the offer die.

Liberia is the one country on the West African coast with which the United States has had an ongoing relationship, not for a few years or decades, but for more than a century and a half, since it was the country that freed American Negroes had selected for possible resettlement. Few Americans remember, if they ever knew, that some of our greatest political leaders, including Henry Clay and Abraham Lincoln, favored the voluntary relocation of freed U.S. slaves to Africa, specifically to Liberia.

Although Senegal and Sierra Leone left me unenthusiastic about the future of West Africa, Liberia was truly depressing because, even with long-term American interest and benevolence, it was hard to identify any constructive core around which development was likely to occur. Once again, the major energies of the so-called educated minority were focused on gaining and holding political power, since control enabled them to distribute jobs and foreign aid to their supporters and allies. Most of the two million or so population are members of tribes that practice a primitive agriculture and that have little or no contact with the forces of modernization, pursuing religious practices involving voodoo and occasional human sacrifice.

The Goodyear Tire and Rubber Company, which many years previously had obtained a major rubber concession in Liberia, resorted to employment practices that were only one or two stages removed from slavery, in that the local authorities helped it to recruit the laborers it needed to work the plantations. Admittedly the company provided its workforce with benefits that exceeded what they had previously known, but it also held many of them under duress.

The long-term special relationship between Washington and Moravia, the capital, had little to show in the way of benefits to the general population. There was little activity and less development. One could argue that Washington had not extended sufficient amounts of aid or had not exercised due diligence about the uses to which the aid was put. But the less-strained explanation would be that Liberia never had the wherewithal for nationhood and that development would at best be very slow.

On the trip from Moravia to Lagos, the plane stopped at Accra, Ghana, where it was boarded by a soldier who pointed his machine gun at the passengers and told us to stay in our seats; no one challenged the order. The soldier's presence reflected some recent coup, which explained why the original State Department plan to have me spend some time in Ghana had fallen through. Even without any first-hand observations of the capital and the countryside, here was one more piece of evidence of the turmoil and trouble that appeared to be characteristic of most of the West African countries.

Nigeria was something else. As soon as we put down at the Lagos airport, and surely by the time we had settled in at the hotel, it was clear that we were in the midst of a large number of energetic business people who were actively engaged in nation-building and economic development. Two things were striking. First, the important role that women played as traders; and second, the extent to which Lagos, in a relatively few years, had grown into a metropolis of many millions, with all of the problems of an "overextended" metropolis in which the public authorities were lagging far behind in the construction and maintenance of a minimum infrastructure: roads, water, sewage disposal, housing, and schools.

Visits to key governmental agencies and discussions with key officials revealed both assets and liabilities. Nigeria was big and relatively rich, with its oil industry still in an early stage of development. The British had trained and left in place a considerable number of well-educated, competent bureaucrats. But they were not in control. A small number of senior military officers held most of the executive power. But theirs was not an easy task, for Nigeria is an amalgam of disparate tribes and religions, each with strong regional roots. The bloody and prolonged civil war that broke out in the 1960s between Biafra and the national government reflected the unsolved tensions between the center and the provinces.

Meetings and conferences with university professors and their students revealed another source of Nigeria's potential strengths, for such interchanges revealed that the British, before their withdrawal, had laid the groundwork for at least some selectively strong educational institutions. But I questioned whether oil reserves, a trained bureaucracy, and some strong educational institutions were sufficient to the task at hand. Nigeria appeared to me to face major hurdles in melding its discrete groups into a unified nation. The explosive growth of Lagos was a warning of the strains between countryside and city; there was no evidence that the trained bureaucrats could assure that national and foreign capital would be productively invested in the face of the power of the military and civilian oligarchy. And to add to these difficult problems was the rapid and hard-to-constrain growth in the population. Even before the costly and destructive civil war erupted, the impediments to nation-building and economic development were easily recognizable, and the subsequent quarter-century has shown their ability to slow Nigeria's progress.

We ought not to be surprised. It required centuries for the countries of Western Europe to become effective nation-states. How could one possibly expect Africa, the home of tribal groups, to do so within a quarter- or a half-century? The optimistic expectations of local leaders and foreign observers were ill-guided and extreme. History can be hurried along, but it cannot be circumvented. Nigeria remains the test case in national development in West Africa, but it needs considerably more time to prove—or disprove—its potential. And if it eventually succeeds, its size and weight will be felt far beyond its borders.

My two encounters with Africa, in the east and the west, left me with two dominant convictions: neither survival measured in terms of millennia, as in Ethiopia and Egypt, nor decolonization, as in the four West African countries—Senegal, Sierra Leone, Liberia, and Nigeria—could assure the national stability and the institutional bases for economic progress and social development.

Iran

Only an occasional scholar is likely to remember that Iran was one of the first areas of confrontation between the United States and the U.S.S.R. at the outset of the Cold War. Shortly after the end of World War II, the United States assumed a sufficiently bellicose position to get the U.S.S.R. to withdraw its troops from Iran. Later on, the CIA played a role in removing Mossadegh and returning the shah to his throne. And from that point on, the United States focused a great amount of attention and expertise on Iran, convinced that it was the key to restraining the U.S.S.R.'s movements to the south, as well as helping to stabilize the unstable Middle East.

I first visited Iran in January 1969 on the first leg of a five-nation tour that also included Afghanistan, Pakistan, Sri Lanka, and India. My second visit was two years later. The State Department asked me to concentrate on the role of manpower in economic development. Most of my time was spent in Teheran, but I spent a couple of days at the University of Shiraz and visited the ruins at Persepolis. Teheran gave every evidence of being a boom city. It was clear from the auto traffic and the stores and in casual conversations that a great many people were making money, and that many, both Iranians and foreigners, were making lots of money.

It was also clear relatively early on that, while the shah was engaged in all sorts of reform activities in the countryside, in urban centers, and in the ports, he was determined to keep a tight rein on political power, which he had no intention of sharing with anyone else. In talking with several of his cabinet ministers, I learned that they were often rotated after a very short tour of duty, six months or so, on the theory that if they remained in place for a longer period of time they might develop a constituency and thereby become a power center. The insecurities reflected in such a rotational system of governance alerted me to one of many problems that the shah had to solve.

Another surfaced when I visited the University of Shiraz—the shah's university—which I found more or less shut-down because of a strike among the students over the opposition of the Muslim Orthodox to "mixed" dancing. There was something discordant about the rapid reform program under government aegis in Teheran, on the one hand, and the strength of religion and traditional culture in Shiraz, on the other. I also learned from several of the professors at the university that they were unable to teach courses on recent economic developments in Iran because the government considered most data confidential. It deliberately sought to discourage objective analysis and open discussion. Once again, I could not figure out how such a practice could be made to conform with a national agenda of rapid reforms.

But my most serious questions arose as a result of several group discussions that I held with upper-class professional, managerial, and technical personnel in Teheran, who conveyed to me directly and indirectly their personal dissatisfaction and frustration with the regime in all regards, except the opportunities that it offered them to make money. Admittedly, making money, especially lots of money, had much to commend it; but what was the point if a man was not free to chart his future; if he had to watch what he said to his friends and neighbors; if he was unable to play any role in shaping the society in which his children were to live? A few probes revealed that Iran was losing a large number of its ablest people, who welcomed a chance to travel abroad in the hope of relocating themselves. When they succeeded, as many did, they turned their backs on generous inducements to return.

In my debriefing notes to the Department of State I made the following observations and predictions about Iran:

1. It had an effective government.

2. It had developed rapidly, both socially and economically.

3. It was basically pro-West in orientation.

4. It was a key partner in the regional alliance with Pakistan and Turkey.

5. It would continue to make sound progress on all fronts.

But in the next paragraph I warned that the foregoing were reasonable only if satisfactory answers could be found to the following questions:

1. Would the shah be able to resolve, in a peaceful and constructive manner, the substantial tensions existing between the intellectuals and their allies, who were outside the political decision-making process, and the few people who at the time helped him run the country? (I thought possibly not.)

2. If the shah were to die in the near future, would the regency, even with army backing, be able to rule effectively? (I thought probably not.)

3. Investments were being made—at the rate of about $1 billion annually—but the prospects for improvements in agriculture and transportation within a decade were not clear. Unless these occurred, what was the outlook for continuing development? (Poor, in my opinion.)

4. Was there any sound basis, except in a few regards, for significant regional collaboration among Iran, Turkey, and Pakistan? (No.)

In conversations with some of our senior diplomats and military advisory group, I found all of them, without exception, convinced that the shah was the best thing that ever happened for the foreign policy of the United States. But I ended my first and second visits to Iran deeply unsettled because I distrusted the admixture of large-scale money-making, tight controls by the secret police, alienation of the intellectuals and the middle class, and resistance by traditionalists as an unsuitable combination for the transformation of a broadened oligarchy into a modern progressive democracy.

Southeast Asia

Afghanistan

The morning we arrived in Kabul we learned that there had been a ground accident at the airport that knocked most of the army's planes out of commission, an incident that alerted me to the early stage of the economy's industrialization. Another recollection: There was no hotel in the capital suitable for caring for Westerners; my wife and I were put up at a U.S. Air Force base.

There was a considerable amount of stirring in and around the governmental offices as a result of the king's efforts to open a window to modernization without, of course, sharing any significant amount of his power with the hitherto excluded groups who wanted a role in decision making. The principal engine of change was the competition between the U.S.S.R., Afghanistan's northern and much-interested neighbor, and the United States, some ten thousand miles distant, which was concerned with this quasi-nomadic country if for no other reason than to check the Soviets.

I was startled to find my friend Robert R. Nathan, a consulting economist from Washington, D.C., ensconced with several members of his staff in a serious effort to help the government put a planning mechanism in place. The U.S.S.R. had taken the lead in building some important new roads, and the United States was responding with grant funds to match them. In discussions with our ambassador it became clear that, but for the Soviet presence, we would not be involved in this primitive landlocked country where relatively little had changed in centuries, except that guns had become a staple. My wife wrote home that if Genghis Khan and his Mongol hordes should revisit Kabul, they would feel right at home; nothing had changed.

But of course that was not altogether true. More students were attending school, and the university that I visited and where I lectured had experienced an increase in enrollment as a result of more students having graduated from secondary school. At the time of my visit, there was some minor trouble brewing because the students who were on complete government stipend—tuition plus living expenses plus clothing—were agitating for *colored* toilet paper!

On a visit to a large market town, not far distant from Kabul, I was startled when, at a given signal, hundreds, possibly thousands, of men suddenly dropped to their knees on their prayer mats and intoned their prayers; they soon returned to their haggling and buying.

I had no prevision of the tragedy that was to befall Afghanistan once the existing political structure gave way under the combined blows of local Communists and Moscow. But I sensed that little good was likely to come to the locals from all the interest, attention, and help that their nation was receiving from the world's two greatest military powers. To add to the uncertainty was the fact that the king had begun to modify the political structure, although not to the point of being willing to bring the excluded tribes into the decision-making process.

My debriefing notes to the U.S. State Department concluded:

1. Afghanistan was at the moment in a hiatus with regard to both its political and economic development. The country had recently begun to move, but it was not clear whether it would be able to continue its momentum.

2. The extent of U.S. interest in Afghanistan was not altogether clear, nor was it clear what the U.S. interest should be, nor what the limits were of our power to influence developments, since the U.S.S.R., which borders the country, was heavily involved in the military and economic spheres in Afghanistan.

Pakistan

After several days of consultation with the civil servants in Rawalpindi and Islamabad, I had to keep tight rein on my emotions not to write them off as the most arrogant, opinionated, supercilious group of government officials to whom I had ever been exposed. Admittedly, my visit came during a stressful period. The long-term military dictator, Ahga Khan, had maneuvered himself into a corner by mishandling a series of conflicts with university students, which foreshadowed a coming political crisis that made many officials anxious to the point of rudeness.

The British had left in place a high-quality senior civil service, but, with independence, Pakistan had had to enlarge its bureaucracy by several orders of magnitude. Many of the newcomers took on the airs and attitudes of the senior staff. But furthermore, the bureaucracy, as far as I was able to judge, saw itself as a third center of power and influence in addition to two existing centers of power: one in the military, the other in the large landowners, who also owned many of the principal manufacturing firms.

I recognized that some of the chill in the relations of the governmental officials toward me reflected the hostility that the Pakistanis still felt as a result of the U.S. position during the earlier troubles in Kashmir, when we had thrown our weight behind India's claims and against the Pakistanis. Another source of difficulty may have been my probing about what was going on in east Pakistan; I had early on developed the impression that autonomy or secession was the most likely near-term development. Neither prospect was at the moment acceptable to the leadership in west Pakistan, which continued to treat its eastern province as an exploitable dependency.

Once we left the seat of government and moved to Karachi, my view of Pakistan, its achievements, and its potential became considerably more favorable. Karachi was then a bustling metropolis of three million. It had been established by Muslim emigrants fleeing from India at the time of the separation, less than two decades earlier. It was impressive, indeed, to see what the newcomers had been able to accomplish, primarily as a result of their initiative and hard work. Major metropolitan centers usually develop only through accumulating capital and infrastructure over long periods of time, but Karachi was literally transformed from swamplands into a major urban center in less than two decades.

My days in Karachi also helped to put two other aspects of Pakistan's problems into sharper perspective. The extent and degree of regional differences within west Pakistan came into sharper relief; and I realized the necessity to contain the separatist inclinations of the different groups, which, aside from their religion, shared little in terms of a common past or a vision of the future. Without a strong military with an overriding sense of national destiny, the artificially constructed country would be likely to break apart. But it also became clear to me that the cost of a powerful military was high both in terms of its preemption of economic resources and of its limitations on individual and commercial freedom. Moreover, the sheer numbers and economic vitality of the people in Karachi, as well as their interactions with foreign visitors and business- men to whom they were exposed, inevitably introduced additional stresses on an already heavily stressed society that was trying to find its place among such major powers as the U.S.S.R., China, and India.

The best summary of what I had learned during my brief stay in the country is contained in the following letter to the Chairman of the National Commission on Manpower and Education:

February 28, 1969

Mr. G. Ahmed, H.Q.A.
Chairman
National Commission on
 Manpower and Education
43 North Pechs
Karachi, Pakistan

Dear Mr. Ahmed:

Here are the brief notes on your Commission's work which I promised to send along. As I see it, the primary task of the Commission is to identify a relatively few critical factors which help to determine the development and utilization of the nation's human resources and to suggest the directions for future policy.

1.   The country's educational effort is askew. It has been strained for a long time. Unless serious and sustained efforts are made to broaden elementary education, to redirect secondary education so that most of it becomes terminal, and to raise the standards of higher education Pakistan will produce more and more certificate and degree holders who know little and can do little. Teachers must be paid a living wage; they must be given more scope for initiative; emphasis must be on analysis not rote learning; and the stranglehold of a few universities through external examinations must be broken. None of these steps can be taken easily. But a major commitment must be made to bring such fundamental reforms about, or other recommendations will prove of little avail.

2.   While the Civil Service tradition has much to commend it the senior civil servants have too much direction over the country. Their conviction that they know best and their corresponding disdain for intellectuals and technical persons prevents normal progress. Moreover, their salary structure is probably considerably in excess of their productivity since a premium is placed on their avoiding errors and delaying decisions. The gap between the salaries paid for white and blue collar work should be narrowed and the government should take the lead in the public and quasi-public sector to offer opportunities and careers to people which carry salaries based more on performance than on certificates and seniority.

3.   The planners failed to pay adequate attention to the interrelations between investment and manpower. Hundreds of millions of dollars for new technical investments and not even a few thousand dollars for technical training! Similarly, there is no mechanism for assessing the manpower implications of alternative tariff, tax and related policies. To subsidize the sale of imported tractors when Pakistan has an inadequate growth of jobs is questionable policy. Manpower policy will fail unless it becomes an integral part of economic policy.

4.   Although much is said about the country's openness to economic development through the private sector, including the encouragement of foreign enterprise, my sense is that many short-sighted bureaucrats are opposed to this policy and seek to thwart it. They should be pressed to avoid such sabotage since there is little prospect of rapid industrial growth without foreign investment. Moreover, competent industrial management and a high level of engineering skill can be developed only with the help of international firms. I would encourage the development agencies to require, as a price of letting a foreign firm come in, a commitment to undertake substantial training.

5.   With regard to skilled and technical training, a major effort should be made to use large enterprises, public, quasi-public, and private, as training sites and to use their personnel as trainers. There are different kinds of incentives which can be offered to the enterprises to make this more palatable.

6. Pakistan has had a wonderful break in the last several years as a result of the agricultural revolution. This should be followed up. Many new agro-business enterprises should now become viable. Government should encourage the private sector to exploit these opportunities and restrict itself to supportive actions, such as helping to develop more roads, storage capacity, training programs for farm management, etc.

I have been impressed indeed by much of what Pakistan has been able to accomplish within a bare twenty-two years. But I am unable to ignore the fact that there can be *no* satisfactory answers to the manpower problems that loom ahead. There will be more entrants into the labor force than jobs; there will be serious imbalances between skills required and skills available; the brain drain will continue—in fact, it may get worse.

I think it is important for your Commission to delineate the major areas where changes are urgently required—in the educational system, the Civil Service, training mechanisms, the encouragement of private foreign investors, agro-business. If you succeed you will have done a great deal—especially if you can get the political muscle to follow through.

You asked me for my frank views. I have put them down as bluntly as possible. Of course, if I had had the opportunity to stay longer in your country and to learn more I would be less certain about the directions that I have sketched above.

I will, of course, be pleased to reply to any inquiries which you have.

Sincerely,

Eli Ginzberg

Sri Lanka

The only way that I could keep my strenuous schedule was to travel from Karachi to Colombo by Aeroflot, a decision that the State Department accepted reluctantly. We checked into the Karachi airport at around 10:30 P.M. for a flight scheduled to leave at 1 A.M. Shortly before departure time we learned that the plane would be late—how late nobody could say. After several hours of waiting around, the ticket agent suggested that we go to the airport motel, where he would contact us if, as, and when the plane arrived. He explained that the Russians didn't communicate until about thirty minutes before arrival time. We waited for two days! I was sure that there would be compensations when the plane took off, such as caviar and champagne, but no such luck. The unattractive Russian hostess served us an unattractive snack and then put out the lights. But the plane got us to Colombo.

There was a lot that didn't seem to be right in Sri Lanka. The loading and unloading in the Colombo harbor was horrendously inefficient, which added a substantial cost to all imported items. I noted that tens of thousands of people made their homes on the street, my first exposure to such a practice. I met with a leading member of the legislature, who was a Trotskyite whose views were as piquant as they seemed to me to be irrelevant. What was left of the earlier British presence was less conspicuous than in Pakistan or, as I later discovered, in India.

The visit to the University of Kandy was an aesthetic delight, but it left much to be desired in terms of intellectual stimulation or in discovering how it was making a significant contribution to meet the nation's manpower requirements. A visit to a large tea plantation alerted me to potential trouble with the exploited Tamil labor force; I also saw there the substantial slippage between the producers and the changing marketplace. Even though tea was the country's principal export crop, the plantation owners did not appear to be properly knowledgeable about the changing market demands for tea.

My letter to Ambassador Andrew V. Corry summarized what I had learned:

March 17, 1969

Ambassador Andrew V. Corry
Embassy of the United States
 of America
Colombo, Ceylon

Dear Ambassador Corry:

You asked me to send you a few notes on aspects of employment and youth that might be helpful in your conversations with the Government of Ceylon. I am sorry that it has taken me until now to get them in order but the weeks after our return were hectic because of the start of the new semester at Columbia, debriefing in Washington, and other duties and activities.

Here are a few brief points which may be of use.

1.   With respect to increasing the opportunities for employment in Ceylon, I believe that the most favorable prospects are in:

a)   The development of agro-business in conjunction with the green revolution that is getting under way. Expansion can be speeded by favorable governmental policies aimed at loosening controls and undertaking supportive action, such as easing credit to small businessmen, etc.

b)   More processing and packaging of tea for special markets abroad would be a highly desirable move not only because of its potential contribution to employment, but also because of the potential increases in profitability.

c)   One of the comparative advantages of Ceylon should result from increased tourism which will be greater as we move into the supersonic. However, to be in an improved position by the early '70's action must be taken now. Since hotel and related activities are labor-intensive, this lead should be thoroughly explored.

d)   Although it takes about seven years to reap a yield from cashew trees, land and labor are available for this crop. With a strong international demand for these nuts, special efforts should be made to speed the exploitation of this high earner.

e)   Since both capital and competence are in relatively short supply in Ceylon, it is advisable to seek out possible partners, such as the Japanese, who might be able and willing to play a constructive role in developing processing industries in Ceylon based on its raw materials. I do not know the specific potentials, but this is a facet of development that should be explored.

f)   In conjunction with developing a more rapid increase in tourism, it would be desirable to expand and improve the production of novelties. We saw many products in wood, ivory, etc. that were well made and relatively inexpensive. Much more might be done. Here, too, it might be advisable to seek foreign help from the start to facilitate penetration of foreign markets.

g)   My wife was impressed by—and bought—some batik. She said it was of good quality and relatively inexpensive. Here too there may be room for sizable expansion—but again, some foreign help to facilitate sales abroad might be desirable.

h)   Since Ceylon has natural rubber I wonder whether adequate studies have been made of the potentialities of processing it for purposes other than tires. There may be some specialty products that could be manufactured to advantage close to the source of supply.

i)   In addition to looking for new projects that might add to income and employment, since Ceylon is an island it is essential to improve the Colombo port which from my short study suggests that its inefficiency is taking a horrendous toll. Unless it is modernized and made to operate more efficiently, it will continue to handicap all efforts at development.

2.   With regard to youth projects in the U.S. that might contain lessons for Ceylon, I have the following few suggestions:

a)   It might be desirable for a Ceylonese official to visit the U.S. and to explore with various nonprofit groups, such as the American Friends' Field Service, the types of youth projects which they have under way, both at home and abroad.

Perhaps the Department of Health, Education and Welfare or the Department of Labor could take the initiative in steering such a visitor so that he could make effective use of his time.

b) He might acquaint himself with the history of the Civilian Conservation Corps. It might be possible to get a report on the C.C.C. into his hands before he reaches the U.S.

c) Through the Department of Agriculture, he might get in touch with the 4H Clubs in high schools in different parts of the country to learn how they stimulate interest among students in improved farming.

d) The visitor would also want to become acquainted with different types of skill development centers for out-of-school youth and adults. He could be steered by HEW and Labor to the best of these.

e) While we have not been doing as much as we should, we are expanding work/study programs and he could learn about the potentialities of these through the U.S. Office of Education.

f) Because of earlier contacts between Israel and Ceylon with respect to problems of youth, it might be a good idea for the visitor to stop off in Israel on his way to or from the U.S., to have a closer look at their various agricultural and related experiments.

I hope these notes will be of some help to you. If you would like to pursue any of them further, please do not hesitate to write to me.

Ruth joins me in sending warm regards.

Sincerely,

Eli Ginzberg

India

Chester Bowles, the U.S. ambassador to India, suggested that I not travel directly from Colombo to New Delhi but rather come to the capital after seeing some of the major Indian cities. My itinerary took me to Madras, Bangalore, and Bombay before I arrived in New Delhi. I found much merit in Bowles's suggestion because I came to the capital with at least some preliminary understanding of the scale, scope, and variety that characterized the subcontinent. And again, before my first visit to India came to an end, I followed another of Bowles's suggestions and canceled a trip to the Taj Mahal in order to see first-hand how the green revolution was progressing in the Punjab.

Two years later, I made a second, more extended trip to India, this time under the auspices of the Ford Foundation. This trip was heavily focused on the eastern provinces, including West Bengal (Calcutta) and the backward and very poor province of Orissa, with its capital in Bhubaneswar.

My very first days in Madras alerted me to the need to adopt a broad vision if I sought to arrive at a balanced judgment of what was going on. Many people were obviously very poor, no one had excess flesh, and the men wore loin cloths, nothing more. But inquiry disclosed that Madras had been growing rapidly in population and economic activity, and, low as the standard of living was, it was dramatically better than it had been five and surely ten years earlier. Finding a baseline from an earlier date kept me from being overly discouraged by the negative aspects of the current situation. Moreover, looking backward also provided a clue or two as to the rate at which improvements were likely to be introduced in the near or middle term.

I was early made aware that most Indians had to look to themselves and their extended families to survive, since neither the national nor the provincial governments had the resources to alter their circumstances, surely not in the near term. Two other early impressions: it was clear that many Indians had some affinity for business and industry—I visited an impressive industrial park—and it soon became clear that many Indians, especially among the urban population, were eager to pursue an education, with many of them progressing all the way to the university and to earning a degree. A willingness to work hard, a flair for business, and a commitment to education are not marginal resources when it comes to economic development.

Why, then, were so many Indians and even more foreigners despondent about India's outlook, especially about any prospect for substantial improvement in the years immediately ahead? I early recognized, as a result of my many meetings and conferences with government officials, businessmen, and the world of the university, a number of serious liabilities. With few exceptions, the government planners, high up and lower down, had bought into the following strategy: India needed to make large-scale investments in heavy industry to provide the foundations for an industrializing economy, but they did not consider where they were going to get the managerial and technical skills required to run the big companies and complex plants; furthermore, they did not estimate whether the market would be in a position to absorb the output if and when the new plants reached their operating capacity.

Nehru's championship of China's planned economy had put down deep roots, and many of the senior civil servants were products of the London School of Economics in its "planning" heyday, before it was captured by the market theorists. Hence, the bureaucracy had a pronounced anti-enterprise orientation, particularly toward foreign enterprises. True, the foreign oil companies had taken the government for a ride, and other firms had abused the freedom they had been granted and were making large profits. But these and other untoward experiences did not justify, in my view, the antienterprise, antiforeign orientation of Indian development policy.

Another cause for my concern was the continuing very rapid population growth—150 million people added in the two decades since independence—with little prospect of checking even-larger increases in the future, despite a much-talked-about and even moderately financed "family planning" effort. As far as I was able to ascertain, most of the family planning staff were sitting at desks in urban centers rather than propagandizing and providing instruction and preventive services in the countryside, in the 550,000 villages that were home to three-quarters or more of India's more than half-billion population.

There were many things askew in the critically important agricultural sector—inadequate fertilizer; limited storage capacity; flaws in the transportation system and the laws of ownership and tenancy; crop losses to birds and rodents; and, most serious of all, the manipulation of farm prices in favor of the urban consumer. But as my visit to the Punjab made clear, the green revolution was under way and there was a good prospect—that soon turned into a reality—that India would in the future be freed from the scourge of periodic famines and would be able to feed even a rapidly growing number of consumers. What few optimists contemplated, but which also came to pass within a decade or so, was that India would become an exporter of selected agricultural produce.

The two areas affecting the well-being of the population on which the state and the national governments had impacted directly were in the domain of public health—the large-scale eradication of malaria and the reduction of many contagious and infectious childhood diseases—and in the much broader opportunity of the population to attend school, even at the university level. But as is so frequently the case, these significant gains were not without concurrent and consequent costs. The facts that India will probably have a population of a billion by century's end and that many of the educated could not find suitable jobs led to a considerable brain drain. But most recently, history has taken still another turn. Because of its sizable underutilized supply of talented graduates, India is becoming an increasingly important center of software writing and production, with links to the major computer companies in the West.

One has to see Calcutta to appreciate the resilience of India and Indians. When I visited in 1971, it was estimated that no fewer than a quarter-of-a-million persons were living on the street, a figure that overwhelmed me, especially since the phenomenon of the "homeless" in the United States was still to come. But I recall that I was more uneasy in visiting the Tremont section of the Bronx in New York City, where the locals passed each other in silence, each with his or her attack dog on a leash, than I was in confronting the street people in Calcutta, who clearly were part and parcel of a system of mutual support. True, on our auto trip to Orissa and Puri-on-the-Sea we had to get through the outskirts of Calcutta before 5:30 A.M. or the roads would have been impassable, but that was an accommodation that travelers had learned to make.

Another accommodation that my wife failed to make on the six-hour auto trip to Puri was her inability to remember that there would be no gas station with a sign "Clean Rest Rooms." The rest of us, remembering that we were in India, not in the United States, took to the woods when the car stopped.

Indian democracy had demonstrated great flexibility during the first three decades of the nation's existence. India had been in two wars, one with Pakistan, the other with China, neither of which could be defined as more than a standoff. The subcontinent was characterized by a great number of distinct ethnic, racial, and religious groupings, some of which had the stigmata of low and outsider status and were subject to bullying and oppression by their stronger neighbors. While the Centre government had to intervene on occasion and supersede state and local law, this was the exception, used sparingly and only in crisis situations. Although many Indians severely criticized the manner in which the Congress party and the Centre government used its allocational powers over tax revenues and foreign grants and loans to enter into favorable political alliances with some of the states—and not others—my reading of the record is that the Centre government succeeded in making India's fragile democracy work as well as could have been expected in this early, tumultuous period, so that it could be strengthened and improved in the future.

I had the opportunity to meet with the aspirant prime minister of West Bengal, Jyoti Basu, who was an avid left-winger and a severe critic of Indira Gandhi and her Congress party. The fact that this outsider had made it to the top and served as chief minister of West Bengal from 1979 to the present reflected not only his own strengths but also the flexibility of Indian political democracy.

At the beginning of the 1970s, there was widespread criticism of the government from many quarters of academe for its continuing failure to provide adequate work and income for all Indians. While the specialists differed as to the numbers, the majority agreed that perhaps as many as 30 to 40 percent of the population were not eating enough and that sizable numbers lacked such essentials as access to running water and minimal contacts with the health care sector.

On the basis of reviewing their written critiques and from personal discussions with some of the critics, I was willing to accept the validity of their findings. But I stopped short of placing all or even most of the blame on the government. I did not see how different approaches to land reform, agricultural support systems, work-creation projects, and other favorite intervention devices of the critics would have enabled the bottom third of the rural and urban populations to have secured the quantity and quality of work and income that would have brought them above the poverty line. In my view, India had done quite well in adding 180 million people to its 380 million base—just under 50 percent—and in having the standard of living rise even a little for most people, and quite a lot for the fortunate minority.

There were many Indians and many friends of India who believed that had Nehru's advice been followed of using Mao's China as a model, India would have been much further ahead. But that was not his daughter's choice, and history appears to be proving that she had the better judgment. Admittedly, the Centre government—and the states—had pursued a great many questionable and wrong policies, from overinvesting in large capital-intensive projects to expanding the educational system without regard to the availability of competent teachers. And, as is true in all governments, the Congress party tended to take care of their supporters and placed obstacles in the paths of their opponents. Even without elaborating on this much-abbreviated summary, the fact remains that democracy in India was not only alive in 1971 but was even more alive in 1991, and the standard of living of the population continues to improve, modestly but not inconsequentially.

East Asia

I recall that in planning my trip to the Far East in the winter of 1967 my friend Sam Berger, at the time deputy undersecretary for the Far East in the Department of State, persuaded me to scratch the Philippines from my itinerary in favor of South Korea on the ground that the former was going nowhere and the latter was about to take off. And Berger, who later served as ambassador to South Korea, contributed greatly to making his prophesy come true.

The thrust of this section will be to call attention to selected dimensions of the role of human resources in economic development that impressed me at the time and about which I have had an opportunity to reflect on during the subsequent quarter-century.

I was reasonably certain even before taking off on this trip to the Pacific basin countries and to East Asia that Anglo-American economists for the most part had underestimated the combined roles of nationhood and the military in economic development. I decided to pay close attention to the interactions among government, the military, and the economy. In South Korea, I was impressed with the role that the military had come to play in the nation's leadership structure and the contribution that it had made to the establishment and maintenance of public order and national morale, even at the price of delays in the participation of the citizenry in the political process, a source of tension and periodic disorders from that day to this.

The more positive elements in the contribution of the military to the development of South Korea must include the following. Despite centuries of shared experiences, the people of South Korea were welded into a nation by virtue of the military challenge from North Korea in the bloody conflict of 1950–1953, which left its mark on almost every family south of the border. The war greatly accelerated the process of nation-building.

Moreover, the war created opportunities for some of the senior military to prepare themselves for top leadership roles in the government, once the corrupt regime of Syngman Rhee was ousted in 1960. Since hostilities with North Korea ended with an armistice, not a treaty of peace, South Korea has remained in an active defense posture from that day to this, with compulsory military service still in force, which has contributed to skill acquisition by both recruits and the regulars. The continued presence of large U.S. forces and the interaction between them and the South Korean military establishment has also contributed to speeding the acquisition of organizational and technical know-how by the locals. And considerable numbers of South Korean officers were sent for tours of duty at U.S. military academies.

There were additional not-well-recognized but important ways in which the military contributed to the quickening of the economic development of South Korea. The presence of the large contingent of U.S. troops led to a quickening of the local economy. Furthermore, the United States' long, expensive engagement in Vietnam created a range of opportunities for South Korea to assist in building military bases in South Vietnam, to export selected materials, and even to supply small military contingents.

To some extent the tale recounted above had some parallels in the economic development of Thailand, where the military oligarchy had been in control, despite repeated coups, since the 1930s and where the United States came to play an important role in making financial assistance and sizable troop reinforcements available as we sought to strengthen the Thais against Chinese pressure from the north. A major military road that the U.S. Engineers planned and helped to construct opened up major new areas for agricultural production and facilitated the export of diverse Thai agricultural products, which helped to speed the nation's development.

The country where the military had a more equivocal influence and impact on economic development was Indonesia. Sukarno overreached himself in seeking to make himself a leader of a third bloc that led him into close dealings with Peking and with local Communists in the archipelago. This alliance resulted in an abortive coup in which most of the general staff were murdered. According to the estimates of the U.S. Department of State, more than 200,000 civilians also lost their lives, as a result of the combined effects of the food shortage and the Communist uprising. However, my informant in Jakarta, a senior medical corps officer, put the casualty numbers at close to 1.5 million and offered the following in elaboration.

When he had been instructed some years earlier to clean up malaria, he had asked his superiors how the people he saved would be fed, but he was told that was not his concern. He followed his directive, and many who would have died survived. But the Indonesian economy became increasingly strained as Sukarno used more and more of the national output for his grandiose schemes, finally reaching the point where recent in-migrants to the cities from the farms were no longer getting remittances from home and had to return there in order to eat and survive. But the numbers struggling to share the available food exceeded the available stock, which led to the intensive internecine warfare in which so many lost their lives.

But even in the face of this debacle, it was Suharto, another general of the mainline military, who pulled the new nation back from the abyss and who has helped to propel it in a more favorable direction. Admittedly, for a long time the army has been forced to support itself in large measure by one or another form of squeeze, but it has helped to balance the books by providing the nation with the minimum stability it needs and must have.

The great tragedy of U.S. involvement in South Vietnam was Washington's miscalculation about the efficiency and integrity of the South Vietnamese military, which it saw initially—and for too long—as patriots and reformers. In fact, the military leaders eventually demonstrated that they were primarily oligarchs determined to maintain themselves and their relatives in power and wealth while the United States spent its treasure and its manpower in fighting the Viet Cong.

All of the East Asian countries except Japan and Thailand had been under the domination of a foreign power, not for a few decades, but for long periods of time. The colonial powers had permitted only a small number of nationals to acquire education and skill or to occupy responsible positions in the public or private sector. In Malaysia and Indonesia, many Chinese had been recruited by the colonial powers to occupy the middle arena between themselves and the indigenous masses. Singapore was the exception, for here the Chinese were in the majority, accounting for some 70 percent of the total population. But the independence of Singapore came about in 1965, when Malaysia, fearing that the Singapore Chinese would join with the Chinese in Malaysia and block the advance of the Malay majority, expelled Singapore from the Federation.

In light of their exclusion from higher education and managerial positions, the Malaysians had little option but to allow several thousand British expatriates to continue to hold key positions. The Indonesians, after obtaining their independence, invited the Dutch back, since they recognized that they did not have the trained manpower they needed to manage the key sections of their economy. However, when the Dutch balked at hiring and training Indonesians even for middle-management positions, they were shown the gate a second time, in 1958. Indonesia realized that it had to take control of its own future.

In Thailand, South Korea, and Singapore, the government leaders decided that they could accelerate their efforts at speeding development by adopting a welcoming policy toward foreign entrepreneurs and enterprises that were willing to come in with funds and technology and help to train and employ local labor.

The desire for national independence was closely linked to the drive for educational opportunity, since the colonial process had blocked these nations in pursuing either goal. Small wonder, therefore, that all the new governments expanded schooling for the whole population, rural as well as urban, for girls as well as for boys, and at all levels—elementary, secondary, and higher education. South Korea took the lead and so broadened and deepened its educational opportunities that many college graduates had to emigrate abroad to find suitable jobs or jobs where their earnings would assure greater career opportunities for their children.

Improvements in public health, in family planning (at least among the urban population), in expanded roles for women, and in the movement of population off the farm into the city—all these contributed to speeding the pace of modernization and economic development. True, the term "modernization" has to be used with caution when one realizes that the same stream in Jakarta was used for washing, cooking water, and sewage disposal, but Jakarta at the time was perhaps the fastest growing large city in the entire Far East.

If one divides the post-World War II period into two equal segments of twenty-two years each (1945–1967 and 1968–1990), one cannot fail to be impressed with how far these former colonial possessions moved toward nationhood and reconstruction during the first period, and the spectacular success that some of them enjoyed in speeding their economic development during the second period. The acronym "NICs" for Newly Industrializing Countries—South Korea, Taiwan, Singapore, and Hong Kong—made its appearance only in the last decade.

It would take us too far afield to trace the multiplicity of interacting forces that contributed to this late-twentieth-century economic miracle, but we can call attention briefly to a few of the formative influences. As early as 1967, the Chairman of SONY alerted me to the fact that he was moving his more labor-intensive manufacturing offshore. When my friends at the Ford Foundation and I visited Phillips at Eindhoven in the Netherlands in the late 1970s, we were unable to meet with one of the key executives because he was in the Far East expanding existing electrical manufacturing plants and establishing new ones. And many U.S. manufacturing enterprises also moved across the Pacific.

The spectacular achievements of the Japanese economy, with its ever-greater penetration of the U.S. and other foreign markets, provided a model for the NICs, which they studied and from which they learned a great deal.

The third and possibly the most important contribution to the NIC's spectacular success was U.S. trade policy, which created special opportunities for these countries to export a wide array of consumer and, later, selected producer goods, to the United States. In sum, foreign manufacturers found the Far East a preferred place to establish branch factories; the governmental and business leaders of the NICs worked hard to take advantage of the free trade trends and had the benefit of learning a great deal from studying the Japanese model. And the American consumer was the beneficiary of a wide array of quality goods at attractive prices, which led them to support our open door policy. While the U.S. government resorted to informal controls on selected imports, such as textiles, it nonetheless permitted ever-more merchandise to enter from East Asia.

The spectacular economic success of Japan and the NICs is due in some measure to the farsightedness of U.S. policies in the post-World War II era, policies that reflected an admixture of self-interest and benevolence, the appropriate combination for a great power. Clearly our power has been somewhat diminished of late, as the nations of both Western Europe and East Asia have strengthened themselves. The challenge that the United States faces in the 1990s is to help shape new policies for the global economy in which the leading powers seek the right combination of self-interest and benevolence to contribute to the continuing well-being of all peoples.

16

U.S. Corporations

My initial exposure to American corporations, as noted earlier, came in my postdoctorate fellowship year, 1933–34, which I spent in field studies of many large industrial enterprises. It was a good year for a novice, especially one with appropriate introductions, to get a view of what had happened to these corporations during their three years of buffeting during the most devastating depression in the nation's history, when all of the indices moved down—the GNP declined, unemployment rose horrendously, manufacturing output dropped drastically, sales shrank, the agricultural sector collapsed, new building substantially stopped—and other evidence indicated an economy spiraling out of control, moving rapidly towards disintegration.

In the face of so much concentrated trouble during the preceding three years, and with varying degrees of cautious optimism that the New Deal had begun to move the economy toward renewed expansion, many senior executives and middle managers were willing to spend time talking frankly with a young economist intent on exploring what had happened, why it had happened, and how their firm had responded to its recent trial of fire.

While it took me the better part of four years (1934–1938) to assess and integrate what I had learned during my *Wanderjahr* (see *The Illusion of Economic Stability*), I had a more direct and intimate knowledge of U.S. corporate enterprise in the mid-1930s than at any subsequent period in the past half-century.

I will identify below a few of the lasting impressions that I carried away from my first—and most concentrated—exposure to the corporate sector. While some companies withstood the Depression better than others, not one of the large number that I visited had avoided a drop in sales and much-reduced if not negative profits. The universality of such negative results left me with a critical view of corporate management: If the test of leadership is how well an organization performs in adversity, then top American managers did not warrant a high mark, because not a single company on my list had come through without major difficulties or trauma.

A few illustrations: In talking back-to-back with two vice-presidents of GE, I discovered that the first was scouring the marketplace for copper supplies to respond to the recent turnaround in demand, while his colleague a few doors away complained to me that he had such a large inventory of copper on hand at the beginning of the downturn in 1930 that he had not yet been able to work it down to a proper level, three years later.

The CEO of Goodyear explained that in 1929 his company had repeated an error that it had made earlier in 1921, that is, it brought a large new plant on line just as the economy was moving from a tight market to a loose market, except that in the more recent instance the Depression was much more intense and had lasted much longer.

U.S. Steel Corporation, recognizing that its cost structure was seriously awry, took some cost-saving actions in early 1930 to reduce its administrative expenditures, but it was not until three years later that the Pittsburgh directives were first being implemented at Birmingham, Alabama, the headquarters of its principal southern subsidiary.

My visit to U.S. Steel in Pittsburgh in the fall of 1933 coincided with the onset of trade union organizing efforts; management responded by electrifying the fences around its plants. True, the vice-president of industrial relations responsible for this action did not remain long in his job.

At International Harvester in Chicago, I heard about the trials of a company whose sales of major products aimed at U.S. farmers had all but evaporated over the three Depression years. Hundreds of thousands of farmers who had lost their properties were forced to join the trek of the displaced to the West. International Harvester had experimented with pricing its tractors and other farm equipment at below-marginal costs—that is, below the direct costs of materials and labor required to produce the product—but it found that not even this pricing strategy was able to reverse the decline in sales.

On the positive side, each of these leading companies, although they had experienced three damaging years, had come through more or less intact and had a renewed opportunity to prove themselves once again in a less-bruising economy. But my assessment was less favorable: I concluded that if the test of a leader is how well he does, not when things are booming and profits are easy, but in periods of adversity, then there were no accolades for most corporate executives. True, my visits to Proctor and Gamble, Sears Roebuck, and Kodak, among others, suggested that the consumer product companies had been less pressed than the industrial giants, but even they had few success stories to report.

Mr. Justice Brandeis, whom I had visited early in my field trips, had requested that I report back after I had completed my studies to tell him what I had found. I did so in one sentence: There was little to fear from these behemoths; with time their own gross inefficiencies would probably cause them to self-destruct. The justice accepted my assessment, but only after making an addendum: He considered the large company a menace because of the many firms that it would injure and destroy on its way to its own self-destruction. I came away from my first extended exposure to large-scale corporate enterprises with no exaggerated view of their efficiency or even survivability.

Gardner Means, of Berle and Means fame, searching for a retrospective interpretation of the Great Depression, placed in the late 1930s much of the blame on what he called "administered prices," a theory that an oligopolistic enterprise could, in the face of declining market demand, keep its prices up, thereby making the macro situation worse although it might help the individual firm to maintain its profitability. The Temporary National Economic Commission (TNEC), a congressional body investigating the poor performance of the U.S. economy, directed much attention to this explanatory principle of "administered prices" and elicited some, if far from universal, support from the leaders of the economic profession about what had gone wrong. I never bought into this theory, among other reasons because I had found little or no support for it in my earlier field studies.

The TNEC was pushed into the background as the United States came closer to mobilizing for war. The major issue that mobilization brought to the front was an argument about the new production goals that Washington should set. There was an intensive argument among the leadership groups in Washington—the military, the economists on the staff of the War Production Board (WPB), and the engaged industrialists. Fortunately, Robert R. Nathan of WPB convinced the White House that the U.S. had large amounts of idle capacity, of both equipment and people, and that the president was on safe ground in setting such an ambitious goal as the production of twenty-five thousand planes. Once again, as in the nation's earlier experience with the National Recovery Administration (NRA), I was unimpressed with business leadership's ability to point the way to new public policies.

But American industry's record during and after the war was impressive. Once President Roosevelt set the ambitious production goals, they were met and exceeded. And when the war began to near its end and many academics and businessmen feared the spectre of mass unemployment returning with mass demobilization, Paul Hoffman and his associates on the Committee for Economic Development (CED) urged their fellow industrialists to start planning immediately for reconversion to a peacetime economy, a message that made a significant contribution to the smoothness of the reconversion process.

I learned two other lessons from the war years. The first related to IBM's finely honed selling skills. One of my earliest assignments in the Pentagon had been to explore the army's capabilities to deal effectively with a vastly expanded troop strength of around 8 million, up from 250,000 in peacetime. I discovered that the IBM salesforce had been able to lease a great number of card-sorting machines to the army on the premise and with the promise that, once critical data were entered on punch cards, the machines, at the push of a button, would be able to come up with all sorts of useful tabulations that would enable the respective staff agencies to get the answers they needed to deploy and redeploy their manpower more effectively. A nice idea and one that led to millions of dollars of rentals per month for IBM, but more theory than reality as far as the army was concerned. I recommended the cancellation of most of these rental agreements, not because the army didn't need help but because the help it needed could not be obtained from these machines. In retrospect, I recognize an early version of an ongoing conflict that has dogged the steps not only of IBM's customers but of the customers of all computer companies. Customers often acquire new technology on the pitches of facile salesmen only to find that their desired solutions remain a long-term goal, not a realizable short-term reality.

A large number of American businessmen, especially from the higher ranks of industry and finance, filled important civilian and military positions during the course of World War II, and a high proportion of them came to know first-hand and to admire two facets of military organization and training. The first was the development and use of staff personnel to assist in developing strategy, implementing it, and when necessary, making corrections in midstream. Further, many civilian executives, in or out of uniform, learned about the military's systematic use of intermediate and advanced schools for both tactical and strategic instruction. Promising officers were assigned to these schools on their way into the higher ranks, for periods of months or a year, to add to their knowledge and skills. The top-heavy staff structures that came to characterize most large American corporations in the post-World War II era and the admiration of many of these corporations for management-development courses and programs were rooted in executives' largely uncritical reactions to these wartime experiences.

The principal thrust of this chapter is a selected account of my interactions with various U.S. corporations during the nearly fifty years that has passed since the end of World War II. As will soon become clear, I had a great variety of differing relations to a large number of major corporations, enough to develop some strong views but not enough that I can claim a high order of expertise.

In the 1950s, I played an ongoing role in a special training program that DuPont was conducting aimed at converting selected bench researchers into general managers. It was a carefully designed and executed program, with each cycle hosting one lecturer a day for twelve days, held at a luxurious country club in New Jersey. My recollection is that close to twelve hundred young researchers were put through the program. Presumably the program was considered a success because it survived for most of the decade. I was impressed by two facets: First, none of the staff ever sought to influence either the style or content of my presentations, and I assume this was true also for my fellow presenters. And second, as good teachers, we used shock tactics from time to time to more fully engage the attention and participation of the group.

As is so frequently the case in the classroom, including the corporate classroom, teachers often learn a good deal from students. My students helped me to see the top-heavy bureaucratic system that governed the allocation of corporate research funds, which at that time amounted to $100 to $150 million per year. I once defined the R&D process in DuPont as seven signatures on the way up seeking approval for the project, and seven signatures on the way down setting out control and reporting mechanisms. The only critical items that received short shrift were the capabilities of the directors of the laboratories and the bench scientists who were designated to carry out the projects. On that front, I was informed that many (although by no means all) of the research directors were no longer at the cutting edge of their fields, and that the managers above them frequently interfered with the scientific work that was underway as they repeatedly took new readings of the market. Many more investigations were started than completed. I remember pointing out to one of the groups that DuPont in the 1950s would never have allowed Wallace H. Carothers the time and resources he required to bring nylon to the marketplace in the 1930s.

Together with one other long-term presenter I was asked to meet with five or six senior DuPont executives, including several who were members of the executive committee, which at that time was the equivalent of the board of directors. The agenda for the meeting was focused around the seminar sessions in which we had long participated, as well as related human resources issues. I don't recall that we identified, much less resolved, any important issues that morning, but what struck me at the time, and since, is that at no time during the three-hour session did any DuPonter talk unless his superior had first spoken, or had indicated that he would pass. This was hierarchy with a capital H!

Several other recollections of my ongoing relations with DuPont: I suggested several times that it would be good for the recruiting and retention of key scientific personnel if the company stopped interposing objections to those who received and welcomed an offer to serve as an adjunct professor at one of the universities in the area. Current policy frowned on such practice on the ground that it might jeopardize proprietary knowledge and otherwise unsettle corporate routines.

Since DuPont at the time had only an internal board of directors, I recommended that it consider inviting outsiders from time to time, outsiders who did not necessarily share the executive committee's outlook, for a free-wheeling discussion, and I suggested that John Kenneth Galbraith, among others, might be a good luncheon speaker. The proposal died aborning.

At one point the senior executives recognized that research was not getting the attention it required or deserved because, in DuPont's highly decentralized structure, departmental managers realized that they had only about five years to demonstrate their proficiency, and most research took longer to pay off. The company therefore established a company-wide research office that levied a research charge on each of the departments. Edward Gee—a former scientist for the federal government—headed the research office before he left to become the CEO of International Paper. It was Gee who asked me to help him put together a special symposium to be attended by the 100 or 150 senior managers. I persuaded two Nobel-Prize-winning scientists to make a presentation; I also suggested a leading social scientist; I took responsibility for the "human resources" presentation; and DuPont asked its long-term foreign trade consultants to present their assessment of the changing global market. The presentations took place about three to four weeks apart and preempted most of the morning. In the afternoon, the speaker met with those in the audience who were most interested in probing more deeply into the issues that he had earlier raised.

DuPont published a volume containing the five presentations strictly for internal use. It is my impression that even inside the company the book had only limited distribution. What I recall most clearly from the afternoon's interchange after my presentation were the favorable responses of the group to many of my recommendations, even the far-out ones. Nonetheless, the executives told me that even the most modest of my proposals would not be seriously considered because the company was doing quite well, and it had long followed the adage "if it ain't broke, don't fix it."

In the 1950s I also became closely associated with Ewing Reilley, a senior partner of McKinsey and Company. At my suggestion, McKinsey underwrote several projects at the Graduate School of Business at Columbia. The first was the funding of a Round Table on Executive Potential and Performance that included the CEOs or executive vice-presidents of some of the nation's most prestigious companies with headquarters in the New York area: National City Bank (Citicorp), Standard Oil of N.J. (Exxon), American Can, National Biscuit, General Foods, Mutual Life Insurance, General Dynamics, Bloomingdale's, Consolidated Edison, and General Electric. In addition, I included several from outside the corporate world to provide some counterpoise and challenge—the president of the Rockefeller Institute, a Catholic priest, a psychiatrist, a former presidential advisor, and the secretary-general of the Guggenheim Foundation. Reilley and Marvin Bower, the managing partner of McKinsey, also participated.

There were eight discussion meetings, which I chaired, and the commitment was made at the outset that the discussions would be off the record, although my associate would take notes. If at the end we had anything worth publishing, there would be no specific attributions. The attendance was good—most of the attendees were present at most of the meetings, and some attended all.

I was able to shape the dinner discussions into a book entitled *What Makes an Executive?*, which dealt sequentially with the development, education, identification, evaluation, and career stages of executives in different corporate settings and different business environments. The strength of the volume was its first-hand quality, but it would be an exaggeration to claim that many new powerful insights into executive potential and performance surfaced.

The related project that the McKinsey Foundation for Management Research decided to fund was a proposal that I had worked out with Reilley: The Graduate School of Business at Columbia would invite outstanding leaders in different sectors of society who had recently retired from key positions to reflect on their experiences and to analyze some of their more important successes and failures. We selected General George C. Marshall as the first lecturer and Alfred F. Sloan as the second. Unfortunately, General Marshall's health deteriorated so rapidly that we could not issue the invitation, and explorations about Mr. Sloan's availability disclosed that he had recently signed a contract with Time-Life that prevented him from accepting the Business School's invitation. Dean Courtney C. Brown, with the McKinsey grant in hand, got restive and altered the approach by inviting a succession of CEOs of America's premier corporations. The first was Ralph Cordiner of General Electric; he was followed over the years by the heads of DuPont, U.S. Steel, Chase Manhattan Bank, AT&T, and many others. Each speaker gave three lectures, which were later published by McGraw-Hill.

The dean also arranged a dinner party after one of the three lectures at which the speaker and guests could engage in further exploration of points that the lecturer had raised in his formal presentation. I attended all of the early lectures and many of the dinner meetings but came away depressed with the quality of the presentations. Even the most talented and incisive CEO would have been hard-pressed to say much of interest after his script had been gone over carefully by members of his legal department, members of his public relations department, and other members of his staff, each of whom had the responsibility of seeing to it that the CEO said nothing that could possibly be used against the corporation or against himself.

Some years into this program I scanned the published volumes and concluded that if they were being studied in Moscow for clues to the hidden strengths of major corporations in the United States, they represented an outstanding contribution to disinformation. There was not a single clue, as far as I could discern, to what made many of our large corporations leaders in innovation, production, and distribution.

Frederick R. Kappel, the CEO of AT&T, made a statement during the course of one of his lectures that caught my attention, and I wrote him a note suggesting that I would welcome the opportunity to pursue the subject further. He wrote back to say that he would welcome my visit and would take steps to arrange it. I was pleasantly surprised when I arrived to find that his office was not filled with staff experts who were going to give me the word. Rather, Kappel and I had a pleasant forty-five-minute discussion, from which I gained a clearer perception of what he had alluded to all too briefly in his formal presentation.

In the 1960s I did considerable lecturing to the middle and higher management of Western Electric, until its instructional center was relocated to the Princeton area, which involved too much traveling time for me. I also lectured to the Asbury Park division of AT&T, which provided selected managers with a ten-month exposure to reading and discussing the "Great Books." This was an investment that I questioned when I first heard about it, and my exposures to the students did not allay my doubts. There was nothing bad about offering middle managers the opportunity to read and think about key ideas, but I questioned the relevance of the reading list for sharpening their skills. I also participated as an outside lecturer at an AT&T management summer program on the Dartmouth College campus that was less ambitious both as to time and coverage, but once again I was restive about its functional contribution to improving the skills of middle managers.

It seemed to me at the time, and even more so in retrospect, that management training programs grew in popularity in no small measure because of the powerful impetus to do what others do, a widespread tendency in the corporate, as in other, sectors of our society. The Bell system, because of its "monopolistic" control of its industry, had little or no trouble adding these management educational programs into its cost structures, but most other companies had to justify their outlays on some other basis. My impression is that many managers considered attendance at such programs an attractive fringe benefit because, among other reasons, their attendance pointed to the likelihood that they were in line for early promotion.

General Electric Company went in for management training in a big way. It established a major instructional center at Crotonville, New York. Harold Smiddy, vice-president for organizational management, who was a key associate of Ralph Cordiner in the early decentralization of the company, held the view that all executives identified for promotion into top management positions should be pulled out of line responsibilities for an eighteen-month stretch and sent back to school, on the ground that what they had learned twenty years earlier had become largely obsolescent, and they needed to become intimately acquainted with new theories and techniques that had not been part of their original educational exposure. Since the eighteen-month educational refresher program was not practical, GE provided a large number of alternative educational opportunities and made them broadly available to different levels of management.

I did a considerable amount of lecturing at Crotonville, and I recall specifically an incident one afternoon when my presentation led to an outburst by an old-timer, a vice-president of manufacturing, who stood up and shouted that he would not sit by silently while GE was being maligned. I had spent the morning in the Pentagon and had made the observation that, as far as I could see, there was not all that much difference between the public and private sectors. Large organizations in both sectors were inevitably weighed down by bureaucratic rules and regulations, without which their large staffs could not function, even at low effectiveness. The most interesting byplay during this outburst were the multiple signs from the audience that they considered the old man's interruption misplaced, which indicated that they agreed with the tenor of my observation.

The passage of the Civil Rights Act in 1964 set the stage for a much-heightened concern on the part of selected CEOs with affirmative action plans directed at broadening opportunities for both blacks and women. I ran a number of conferences at Arden House under the auspices of the Graduate School of Business that explored these issues. For the most part, I was impressed with the senior business executives who attended these conferences. It seemed to me that they were as open, possibly more open, to enlarging employment opportunities for groups that had experienced severe discrimination than were most other sectors of our society with which I was acquainted, such as universities, government bureaucracies, trade unions, and others that presumptively should have been in the foreground of lowering the bars, but that in point of fact tended to stall and delay because of opposition, expressed and latent, from within their organizations.

In an Arden House conference in the early 1970s on the theme of *Corporate Lib: Women's Challenge to Management*, a striking event occurred as the group was moving into formulating its recommendations. Several of the black women participants asked for a recess, during which they telephoned for advice and guidance from their black male colleagues. They wanted to be sure not to support any policies or programs that would make it more difficult for black males to advance by focusing undue attention on lowering discrimination based on gender.

Another recollection from that conference: A former senior IBM executive, who in the interim had become the head of a liberal college for sophisticated young women, reminded his audience that they might be knocking at a door which, if opened, could lead many to disappointment. He sketched many drawbacks of corporate culture—the top-heavy bureaucracy; the narrow assignments; the innate conservatism when it came to new ideas and new methods of operation; the dog-eat-dog pursuit of the good positions; and other negatives. It was my impression that most of the women activists in the audience felt that his presentation was an unsubtle defense of current discrimination against women in management, but to my ears much of what he said made sense.

Over the years I have had periodic assignments for Pepsico, which from all of my encounters appears to be a well-led, tightly directed firm that pushes its managers very hard but rewards them with frequent promotions and other benefits for effective performance. Early on, the top command adopted a plan to move black men and women up the managerial hierarchy, but some ten years down the road it realized that despite its encouragement not many, in fact very few, had made it even as far up the ladder as the lower ranks of the senior group.

My colleague, Anna Dutka, and I undertook to explore what had happened at Pepsico and at other leading corporations that had committed themselves to facilitating the upward mobility of both blacks and women.

As far as we were able to ascertain, no corporation had had a spectacular success in moving a large number of either blacks or women through middle management into higher management, and surely not into the top ranks. The simple answer was that not enough time had passed, a prerequisite for newcomers to move toward the top, and this answer had merit. Another answer pointed to such facts as that the better positions were hotly contested, and many able white men were strong competitors, often winning out over black men or women who were late starters.

Not enough attention was paid to the disinclination of many able women to accept assignments that required a lot of traveling or that necessitated a change in residence, decisions that often conflicted with their spouses' careers and their own family responsibilities.

All of the above had some validity, but when we reached the end of our analysis we concluded that two factors not yet identified dominated. While top management made favorable statements about its desires and goals, it seldom linked achievements in minority employment to the evaluation of line managers, making such progress a key factor in their bonus payments and promotions. In the absence of such linkages, line managers decided that the increased participation of minorities and women in higher management was not really a serious goal for the senior leadership.

One other principal finding was that the very scarcity of blacks and career women had negative consequences. It is very difficult for one or two outsiders to make their way up the managerial ladder. There is a lot of subtle and not-so-subtle social discrimination in corporate life—who visits whom in off hours; who make up the foursome on the golf course; who joins whom on a recreational trip. It does not require overt prejudice by the dominant group of white males to keep an isolated black or career woman from joining them, and unless one is in the in-group one is likely to lack critical knowledge and information. We concluded that a really serious effort by top management to break the inherited exclusionary pattern would require a major effort at recruitment that would bring sizable numbers of the hitherto excluded groups into the organization; special training, counseling, mentoring, and career assignments must be in place to assist them up the ladder; and top managers must periodically explain to staff and line managers the specific personnel goals that they are expected to meet and make specific suggestions that can help them.

There were many objections among corporate executives to the strong-armed measures resorted to by the federal regulatory agencies and the courts that forced AT&T to meet a set of numerical goals in both hiring and promotion practices after its earlier efforts at employment reforms had been found lacking. At the time of these decisions, and later looking back on the intervening events, I am satisfied that the external pressure on AT&T was an essential step in speeding its progress on the antidiscrimination front. And it was just that pressure that was largely missing in many corporations.

From the early 1950s until today, the Graduate School of Business at Columbia offers a large number of general and specialized management programs, of which the four-week (originally six-week) residential program for senior managers is the centerpiece. For the better part of three decades, I gave the key lecture on "human resources" to successive classes in this program. My presentation was usually scheduled late in the afternoon after the "tougher courses" in accounting, finance, and statistics were out of the way and before the small group sessions met to prepare their cases for the next morning.

I carried away a number of impressions from this long and continuing exposure. When I first began to lecture in the early 1950s, there were at best two, three, or four out of the sixty to seventy corporations represented who had recognized human resources as a critical facet of their operations and had reorganized the function accordingly. Three decades later, according to my informal class surveys, there are still only a small number, five or so, in which the human resources function was viewed as a critical activity on the same level as strategic planning, finance, and marketing. In reflecting on this modest accommodation in fact, if not in words, it struck me that most chief executives, having demonstrated to themselves and to others that they had the talent and the competence to rise to the top, concluded that they did not need to rely heavily on human resources specialists—they could, and would, make the key personnel decisions themselves.

Let me quickly add that such a conclusion does not necessarily reflect an exaggerated opinion of their own worth. It also represents an implicit critique of the shortcomings of their human resources staff. As Stephen J. Drotter, a human resources executive with prior experience in General Electric, INA, Cigna, Chase Manhattan, and, more recently, as the head of his own consulting firm, has made clear in a chapter of a book that I edited in the late 1980s, *Executive Talent*, there are a great many persisting weaknesses in many if not all corporate human resources staffs.

New York City has been a contrast of business strengths and weaknesses since the beginning of its history in the seventeenth century, with periodic economic crises forcing the optimist to stop in his tracks and reconsider. The period from 1965 to 1975 was another such period of uncertainty, which turned into a severe recession, topped by the financial crisis of 1975 when the city was on the verge of bankruptcy. The signal that serious trouble was brewing was the out-migration of scores of corporate headquarters. General Foods went to White Plains; IBM relocated to Armonk; GE to Fairfield, Connecticut; Johns Manville to the outskirts of Denver; Union Carbide to Danbury, Connecticut and a great many others to nearby suburbs or to distant cities in the Midwest, the South, and the Southwest.

With manufacturing in relative decline, with the inevitable reflection of the shift of the U.S. economy from goods to service production, and with urban locations increasingly unsuitable for modern manufacturing plants, private sector employment was in jeopardy, particularly as the administrative headquarters of many of the nation's largest corporations left New York City. But a paradox caught my eye. The prime office buildings remained well-tenanted even after 38 major corporate headquarters had relocated out of the city. The unanswered question was, Who were the new tenants occupying the recently vacated space?

Under a grant from the Rockefeller Brothers Fund, my associate, Professor Matthew Drennan, and I, with the assistance of an advisory committee chaired by John R. White, a senior real estate advisor to the Rockefeller Brothers, prepared a report in 1977 on *The Corporate Headquarters Complex in New York City.*

We discovered that the new tenants were bankers, lawyers, accountants, marketing and advertising specialists, communications firms, management consulting organizations, and a whole array of other "business services." We also discovered that most of the headquarters that had moved out of the city and had relocated in nearby suburbs remained dependent on the city's business services for critical inputs. Moreover, our analysis disclosed that those who had remained in the city had enjoyed a more satisfactory record with respect to export sales than those that had relocated, a forerunner of globalization that was likely to redound to the city's advantage.

Admittedly, the city was a difficult environment in which to work, and an even more difficult environment to live in if one did not have a large income and/or if one wanted easy access to good public schools or to golf courses. But in a world in which technology and markets continue to undergo accelerated changes, it seemed questionable for major headquarters to take themselves away from the center of the action. One example: There are more important deals consummated at breakfast at the Regency Hotel on any one working day than there are in the whole of Denver, not to mention Danbury, in an entire year.

There is a corporate hubris that believes that everything that the senior staff of a major corporation needs to know can be obtained by their interaction with one another in the bucolic environment of Westchester or Fairfield County. I can still recapture the feeling of isolation that I experienced in walking along the deck of the GE headquarters after a company luncheon. Although the real estate experts on our advisory committee were not looking forward to an early revival of commercial building in Manhattan, they bought into the basic conclusion that we had encapsulated in an earlier title of ours, *New York Is Very Much Alive* (1973).

During the summer of 1976 while we were at our Martha's Vineyard house, where I do most of my serious writing, I received a telephone call from a staffer at Celanese who referred to a report in that morning's *New York Times* about some comments I had made about human resources and who said that his boss wanted to talk to me. Homer S. Klock got on and suggested that he would like to talk with me as soon as possible because I might be able to help him think through some scientific and engineering personnel issues of concern to the Chemical Group of Celanese, for whose human resources policies he had responsibility. I indicated that I seldom took on such consulting assignments, but that I would stop by on my next visit to the city. I had a good discussion with Klock and his assistant, David Lacey, and agreed to give the assignment a try, emphasizing however that I would have to visit a number of plants so that I could look at the issues from the perspective of the field as well as of the headquarters.

Some weeks later, with Lacey as my guide, I visited a number of Celanese plants in Ohio and Texas, where I had an opportunity to talk with the local management about a number of human resources issues, including recruitment and retention of research chemists, the interactions between the research personnel and plant operations, and the difficulties of developing and retraining a group of skilled technicians. I recall that one specialist in a Texas plant—just turned thirty and about to be married—planned to take off with his bride for a sail around the world, proof positive that he did not plan to delay gratifications until retirement.

I knew little if anything about the chemical industry when we started off on our field trip, and even after visiting four or five plants and talking with a great many people I had at best only a clue to the problems requiring attention. The few that surfaced included the difficulties of structuring R&D activities so that the bench scientists would sooner or later be able to contribute something new and worthwhile in the form of new products or improved processes; the difficulty that Celanese faced in attracting strong research directors; the slippage and friction between higher headquarters and the field, with the plants struggling to establish and maintain their autonomy; and the lack of significant linkages between the research staff and nearby academic institutions.

As plans were made for me to undertake a second foray into the field, the entire headquarters of the chemical group was disbanded. My friends Klock and Lacey left the company, and I worked out an early settlement of the only retainer relationship that I had ever entered into, having learned only a little and having probably contributed even less.

In the late 1970s, I had a phone call at Columbia from a Citicorp staffer to the effect that Mr. Vojta wanted me to attend a conference on New York City that he was scheduling for some months hence. I asked who Mr. Vojta was—a question that clearly caused surprise—and I was told that he was an executive vice-president of the bank, but this still left me without adequate information. However, we arranged to meet and the mystery was cleared up. George Vojta was in charge of strategic planning for Citicorp, and one of his assignments was to assess whether the bank should remain headquartered in New York City. He had read a presentation that I had made for Salomon Brothers in the early 1970s that carried the title: "New York *Does* Have a Future." Hence his interest in having me attend his forthcoming conference.

As a result of further interchanges with Vojta and with one of his principal staff assistants, it became clear that our interests at the Conservation Project in the rapidly growing but little-studied and less-understood "service sector" of the economy and the interests of Citicorp, at least as represented by Vojta, overlapped at many points. It was not long before Citicorp made several liberal grants to Columbia to have us step up our investigations into the service economy, which resulted in a number of articles and books, the most important of which was Stanback's *Services: The New Economy* (1981).

Among the interesting by-plays of this arrangement was our perception of the complex relationships and stress points within the bank, which were increasing steadily because of the CEO, Walter Wriston's, approaching retirement and his failure, up to this time, to have designated a choice among the contenders for his position. Another source of tension, not totally unconnected with the succession issue—Vojta was an outside candidate—was the skeptical (not to say negative) attitudes of the bank's Economics Department (later liquidated) towards Vojta's interest in "services."

Still another point creating tension was the delayed profitability of the large investments that Wriston, in association with John Reed (his eventual successor), had made in consumer banking, which were being financed heavily by profits from Citicorp's activities abroad. I remember a visit to a Citicorp office in Milan in which the local management team severely criticized the bank's New York leadership for investing such huge sums over so many years in the United States, with so little in the way of results—at least up to that point in time.

Our second year's close engagement with Citicorp was a stimulating experience, not only for me, but also for my senior associates, who were actively involved with the various members of the bank's staff. One of the most interesting by-products of this relationship was my arranging a series of seminars between senior Citicorp staff and some of the country's leading economists, including Simon Kuznets, aimed at developing an in-depth dialogue about the growing importance of services in the U.S. economy and the implications of this trend for the country as a whole and banking and Citicorp in particular.

This engagement between the Conservation Project and Citicorp came to an end almost as suddenly as it had been initiated. Wriston set his retirement date; Vojta, knowing that he was not getting the nod, decided to leave the bank; and the contractual relations between Citicorp and the Conservation Project were terminated. But my friendship with Vojta continued, and in 1985 we collaborated in writing *Beyond Human Scale: The Large Corporation at Risk*, which set forth our views of the post-World War II development of the U.S. economy and focused primarily on how size inhibited the effective deployment of most corporations' human resources.

In reflecting on this short if intensive exposure to the world of banking in the late 1970s and early 1980s, I am impressed that the revolution in financial markets that was about to burst upon the advanced money centers—New York, London, Tokyo—was still hidden from view. The computer had been around for the better part of three decades but the impact of computerization on banking—which literally transformed the industry—was delayed until the middle 1980s.

New York Senator Daniel Moynihan, arriving one day at LaGuardia Airport from Washington, communicated to the press that the Japanese were taking jobs away from New Yorkers because of their growing presence in the city's economy. Within a few hours of that comment, my colleague, William Newman, had been asked by the Japanese to recommend an urbanologist who was well acquainted with the New York City labor market. Newman asked whether I would talk to the staff at the Japanese Consulate, and I said I would.

Once the Japanese officials agreed to make all the necessary contacts and introductions to the key Japanese firms and banks in New York City, my associate Charles Brecher and I set about interviewing them to ascertain the scale and scope of their local activities. This was presented and analyzed in *The Economic Impact of the Japanese Business Community in New York* (1978). Our findings disclosed that, with fewer than ten thousand Japanese nationals, the Japanese enterprises in the city provided about 57,500 local jobs, a strong and convincing answer to the senator's gloomy assessment.

Some months later, the Japanese embassy in Washington asked me to drop by: They had a related project that they wanted to explore. They inquired whether we would be willing to undertake a survey of the nature and scale of direct Japanese investments in the United States. My conditional answer was yes, subject to their identifying and introducing us to the key companies. Charles Brecher and Vladimir Pucik carried out the field work for this assignment and the interesting finding was that, as late as 1979, we were able to come up with only a very small total—about $3.4 billion—of such investments in the United States. Even allowing for a sizable undercount, it is still a strikingly small figure in light of the developments of the late 1980s, when the total approximated over $53 billion in direct investments alone.

Business Week has a special Japanese advertising section once a year in connection with which it publishes a special editorial. I was invited to write this editorial for 21 July 1980 issue. One of the go-betweens in the preparation of this section told me that the principal sponsors in Tokyo had asked *Business Week* to invite me to write the editorial because they were so pleased with our two reports. The go-between also gave me to understand that if I were interested in maintaining and expanding the relationship, all that I needed to do was to be open to periodic suggestions. I thanked him for his offer but indicated that Japan was really not an area of my interest or competence.

No one who reads the newspapers can fail to have an opinion, or opinions, about the merger, acquisitions, and leveraged buyouts that have dominated the U.S. corporate scene in the 1980s and that recently is being imitated abroad. Once again, I do not pretend to be an expert in "corporations and trusts," as the subject used to be called in the economics department's listings in an earlier era, but I have a few views about what has been going on and its likely outcomes. If the increase in takeover prices makes sense, it reflects adversely on the prior management's capacity to manage and if it does not make sense, it suggests that the new management is likely to face a spill. The substitution of high-yield junk bonds for equity may yield high profits for the issuers and the sellers of the bonds, but it is hard to see how the substitution can help the former bondholders or the current stockholders.

The devotees of the market insist that whatever happens is, by definition, for the best, but that is not my view. Markets are driven by the amounts of money and credit that are floating around and by the speculative moods of buyers and sellers. When each reinforces the other, prices rise, often steeply. But the reinforcement mechanism works only for a time, and then it shifts into reverse. One need not conclude that all corporate transactions of recent years were misconceived to retain a healthy skepticism about whether most of them were for the good of the U.S. economy. Thorstein Veblen, perhaps the nation's most astute social critic, recognized at the turn of this century that one must distinguish between the pecuniary and the productive levels of activity—a reminder that we may yet pay dearly to relearn.

What have I learned, after six decades of continuing, if not intimate, exposure to the operations of U.S. corporations, supplemented by occasional interactions with such major foreign companies as Shell, Marks and Spencer, Phillips, Fiat, Sony, and still others? First and foremost, that it is difficult to conceive how the advanced national economies of Western Europe, the United States, and Japan could have developed in the absence of large manufacturing and service companies. The specialists continue to disagree among themselves over whether the striking success of the Japanese and German economies in recent decades is grounded in subtle and largely hidden relations between the dominant business interests and their respective governments. Even if this explanation were confirmed, it would, in my opinion, detract very little, if at all, from the skill with which many foreign corporations plan, manage, and operate. There is no reason to conclude that the corporate-governmental relations that exist in the United States are or should be the only acceptable contemporary model.

A second observation: With the advantage of a lengthened perspective, it is clear that even the most successful large corporations encounter great difficulties in remaining in the lead, often even in surviving, in the face of continuing rapid technological and market changes. The energy, flexibility, and responsiveness to new opportunities that were the basis for their original growth and profitability are difficult to maintain once scale, bureaucracy, and playing it safe come to dominate their environment.

But the structure of the future corporation in an increasingly global economy remains to be revealed. Many pluses as well as minuses are associated with scale and scope. Some of the largest international oil companies have an impressive track record, spanning most of this century. But they are the exception.

A reasonable forecast is to assume that the large multinational corporation of the late twentieth century will be transformed into a new and not-yet-discernible global corporation of the twenty-first century, and that most of these global corporations will go through a life cycle of growth, domination, and decline. But the corporate entity, even if greatly transformed, is almost certain to survive.

17

Foundations

It has long been claimed that the charitable foundation is uniquely a New World, and specifically a U.S., institution. There is evidence to substantiate this claim, though a number of similar foundations exist in Western Europe and Japan. I am somewhat in a bind when it comes to discussing foundations critically because I have been a beneficiary of their largesse ever since I received my first external grant from the Rockefeller Foundation in 1941 and had benefited even as early as 1939 and 1940 from Rockefeller's pass-through of research funds to the Columbia University Council for Research in the Social Sciences.

Over the intervening half-century my research group has received support from fifteen or more foundations, several continuing their support for a decade or even longer. Reference to selected long-sustained foundation support provides a good jumping-off place to ask whether it is possible to identify how foundations pick the areas for which they provide support and whether such support is for short, medium or longer periods of time. But before we explore these and related policy considerations we need to define the type of foundation that will be appraised in this chapter.

There are a great number of "private" foundations that enjoy certain privileges under federal and/or state law that enable the sponsors to make charitable gifts while sheltering the owners from various tax liabilities. At the opposite extreme, there are corporate foundations that receive their funds from their corporate sponsors. These funds are usually spent in support of eleemosynary causes in communities where the corporation has a plant or other business linkages.

Our focus, however, is on the independent foundation, with a self-perpetuating board of trustees whose grant-making may or may not be heavily influenced by the initial specifications of the donor. In most instances, the original specifications were broad enough to provide the trustees with sufficient freedom to design and redesign their grant-making, but occasionally a board petitions the court for more degrees of freedom in light of changing circumstances.

A few additional introductory observations: Foundations are the beneficiaries of special tax advantages on the ground that their aim and purpose is to contribute to the "public good," not to make money nor to lobby. The "public good" is an elastic concept and spans a wide range of activities, from providing monetary or other forms of assistance to needy people to financing long-term educational and/or research programs.

The sources of philanthropic giving for "good" purposes have always been relatively limited: donations by individuals; earnings on endowments (that is, dividends and interest on gifts made in the past); grants by private and community foundations; and corporate giving (including corporate foundation giving). To illustrate: The major Ivy League colleges and universities in the East owe a great deal to the gifts received over many generations, many from grateful alumni, others from wealthy individuals who sought personal recognition and/or who were genuinely interested in contributing to a specific program or to the university as a whole.

On the other hand, most of the distinguished educational institutions in the Midwest and the West were the creation of state legislatures (with an assist from the federal government, which made available sizable land grants) that appropriated sizable amounts of taxpayers' money to establish and expand universities open to all qualified young people in the state, without reference to their family origin or economic circumstances.

From many vantages, the heyday of the philanthropic foundation was the first three-and-a-half decades of the twentieth century, from 1900 to 1935. The latter year marks the entrance of the federal government into social welfare legislation over an extended front, the first and lasting consequences of which have been to provide large amounts of public support for the categorical poor and elderly, societal tasks that had previously been primarily addressed by philanthropy. The worst depression in the nation's history forced the federal government to act, since private resources were grossly inadequate to cope with the exploding need by growing numbers of the poor for assistance.

The second major turning point in the relations of philanthropy, particularly public foundations, and government, primarily the federal government, dates from the immediate post-World War II period when, based on science's contributions to the Allies' victory, the president and Congress decided that henceforth the federal government would become a major source of financing for basic and applied research, initially focused on the natural and biological sciences but, slowly and modestly, for the social sciences as well.

A few more stage-setting notations: The largest private foundations, such as Ford, Pew, MacArthur, and Robert Wood Johnson, have in recent years been appropriating between $100 and $200 million annually; there are a somewhat larger number of foundations whose annual grant-making is in the $25 to $100 million range; and a considerably larger number with annual grants of between $1 million and $25 million. The combined grant-making of all private foundations for the year 1987 was estimated to be in the range of $5 billion; compare this sum to the total social welfare outlays by all three levels of government in that same year, about $900 billion, and to the federal government's total R&D expenditure, $68 billion.

Even the Howard Hughes Medical Institute (technically not a foundation), with more than $5 billion in assets, is a relatively small player in the world of biomedical R&D, a field where government, primarily the federal government, currently spends over $11 billion annually.

In the heyday of the public foundation, that is, during the first third of this century, Rockefeller, Carnegie, and Rosenwald were able to make and leave their mark on critical sectors of American experience—medicine, public health, education, race relations, and other important areas of our national life. With government a minor player in these arenas, well-heeled foundations were able to make a difference, in fact a big difference, when they picked their targets with care and were able to carry through a path-finding inquiry, such as Abraham Flexner's 1910 report on American medical schools or Gunnar Myrdal's *An American Dilemma* (in the early 1940s), both of which Carnegie underwrote. With the advent of the New Deal, and more particularly after World War II, government became the dominant player in opening up new domains for social experimentation and action: public housing; the GI Bill; large-scale support for science; funding for the expansion of community hospitals; and steady broadening and deepening of income transfer programs for the poor and the elderly.

Except for an occasional congressional inquiry, or an occasional book written more often in glorification than in critical appraisal, foundations have not attracted much attention from either the scholarly community or the media. This chapter draws selectively on my half-century of interactions with foundations, in the belief that my observations may illuminate facets of this unique American institution, today relatively less potent than in days gone by, but still a potential and on many occasions a real force for the good. Because the changing external environment has such a strong influence on foundation goals and behavior, I will follow a more or less chronological approach.

My first exposure to the foundation world came when my cousin, Sol Ginsburg, M.D., invited me to accompany him to Chicago in the mid-1930s to attend the ceremonies that marked the end of the Rosenwald Fund, which had done so much to assist talented blacks to make their mark as well as to assist many black institutions, primarily in the South, to function and grow in the face of oppressive poverty and repressive segregation. (It is worth remembering that up to World War II, Tuskegee Institute published yearly the number of blacks who had been lynched during the preceding twelve months.)

Julius Rosenwald had stipulated that his fund was to spend all of its assets and close shop by the mid-1930s. He was convinced that it was unwise for a donor to specify narrowly the uses to which his money was to be put and that "under no circumstances should funds be held in perpetuity—I have confidence in future generations and in their ability to meet their own needs wisely and generously."

It was not until the mid-1980s that I had a second direct encounter with a similarly structured foundation, the Markey Charitable Trust, whose donor, Mrs. Lucille P. Markey, of Calumet Farms fame, specified that the $300 to $500 million dollars left in her will for biomedical research had to be expended by 1997, a period of a little more than a decade. I was invited by Dr. Robert Glaser, the medical director of Markey, to attend a meeting with the trustees, the staff, and a distinguished panel of biomedical researchers to explore the alternative approaches that the trust might pursue to optimize its expenditures over the constrained time period available to it. The chairman of the board, Louis Hector, before closing the day's interesting discussion, gave each of us an opportunity to make a few final remarks. When my turn came, I pointed out that, while Markey had an impressive amount of money to disperse, it was important to put its potential grant-making in context, and that compared to the annual budgets of the National Institutes of

Health, its total assets represented a relatively small sum. Accordingly, I suggested that somewhere along the line Markey could make a contribution to public policy by looking at the total sums available for biomedical research to point up the additional public and private policies required to assure the continuing viability of the national effort. In 1989, funded by a two-year grant from Markey, my associate Anna Dutka and I published a volume that addressed this issue.

To return to my first exposures to foundations: I recently recalled that my father, a renowned scholar of Judaica, was frequently asked by Henry Allen Moe, the long-term secretary of the Guggenheim Foundation, to assess proposals for grants by applicants in his areas of expertise. He always made time to review the proposals that Moe forwarded and to indicate without equivocation whether he considered the applicant to be a good bet. Almost without exception Moe followed my father's advice, I presume because he appreciated both my father's judgment and integrity. It is questionable whether foundation executives, in dealing with applications from individuals, can do better than follow Moe's principle: Find competent assessors and follow their advice.

That was the basis, as reported earlier, on which I got my first external grant from the Rockefeller Foundation in 1941. Joseph Willits, the head of the Social Science Division, had asked his predecessor as dean of the Wharton School, Roswell McCrea (who at the time was my dean and mentor at Columbia's Business School), to recommend a junior faculty member engaged in research that warranted support. McCrea submitted my name and a short proposal as to what I planned to do in opening up the complex arena of occupational decision-making, which was all that Willits wanted or needed. Willits made us a second grant the following year, presumably because he was satisfied with the progress that we had made.

In my periodic meetings with Willits, most or all of which I initiated because I enjoyed talking with him, I had the opportunity to stress the critical role of early foundation support for young scholars who had not yet had time to develop a reputation. Willits agreed, but at war's end, when I returned to Columbia, I found that for "administrative reasons" Willits had abandoned his earlier initiative. It created too much administrative hassle at the foundation and he returned to making an annual lump-sum grant to the Social Science Council at Columbia and gave it the task of doling out the funds.

The other prewar foundation executive with whom I became acquainted was Alan Gregg, vice-president for medical affairs of the Rockefeller Foundation. Gregg's contributions to medical education do not require detailing. He was a long-term worker in the vineyard and accomplished a great deal, including establishing a strong base for psychiatry in many of the nation's leading medical schools. What has always impressed me was Gregg's perception of the time that change needs. He recognized that it would require about a decade of sustained effort to bring about one or another significant change in medical education, and he did not shy away from such a lengthy commitment. Clearly he must have had the confidence and support of his president and the foundation's trustees to pursue such long-range plans. But pursue them he did, and with impressive results.

We are now able to return and examine the two important questions that we identified at the beginning of this chapter: How do foundations determine what areas they will support and the time period of such support? Foundations compete with each other for prestige, influence, and results, and therefore trustees look to the president and his or her staff to be one or more steps ahead of other foundations operating in the same general area.

But even the largest foundations, those that are able to dispense around $200 million annually—and there are only one or two such organizations—face serious difficulties in realizing their self-selected goals of social significance and public impact. One of the outstanding success stories of recent decades was the green revolution spearheaded by Rockefeller and expanded by Ford, which, through advances in the laboratory and later at demonstration sites, set the stage for improving the agricultural productivity of many nations in Asia, Africa, and Latin America to a point where, to take India as an example, the new nation was transformed within a single decade from one suffering periodic famines to one that exported food. But such outstanding successes are the exception, not the rule.

Following a long-established practice of high-yield results, many larger and smaller foundations have continued to invest in promising young scientists and scholars, particularly those just getting started in their careers after having acquired their doctorates. In the biomedical arena one thinks of Markey, Hughes, and Markle, each with an impressive track record. But these records notwithstanding, the scope for continuing foundation initiatives in fellowship support has been narrowed by virtue of the large-scale competition offered by vastly expanded financing by the federal government for R&D, which has made it possible for ever larger numbers of pre- and postdoctoral students to work in the laboratories of senior investigators.

In the pre-World War II era, large foundations often made capital grants to universities, research centers, hospitals, and related institutions, but in recent decades they have increasingly eschewed such grants, among other reasons because of the adverse impact that such grants have on their future ability to give. Foundation leaders want to be relevant, which means that they must protect their future cash flow. But relevance is easier to stipulate than to achieve.

Just what can foundations, even those with the largest annual budgets, possibly achieve in the short and middle term to moderate, if not eliminate, the major ills affecting American society, beset as it is with the major problems of poverty, crime, drugs, broken families, teen-age pregnancy, alcoholism, racism, urban decay, homelessness, and many other types of individual and group malfunctioning?

One could argue that this litany of past societal failures and future threats provide foundations with a large number of opportunities for significant societal experiments. But selecting a subject to receive foundation support is only the first step in the launching and carrying through of a foundation program leading to amelioration. The best that foundations can hope to accomplish with their sizable, but still limited, available funds is to stimulate research, finance demonstrations, and organize public informational efforts, usually through the creation of prestigious commissions, to help mobilize public attention and effort so that a hitherto neglected problem is placed on the public's agenda for future action.

In the late 1940s and early 1950s, the IRS exerted pressure on the Ford Foundation to reorganize and to start spending much larger amounts of its substantial and steadily accumulating assets. As reported earlier, H. Rowan Gaither, president of the Ford Foundation between 1953 and 1956 and chair of the board of trustees until 1958, who had the assignment to get things moving and to step up grant-making, looked favorably on making a substantial grant to the Conservation of Human Resources Project (my research group) until Anna Rosenberg (and possibly other advisors) persuaded him that the foundation could get more mileage (in the form of political leverage, policy influence, and publicity) from a grant to a National Manpower Council whose members would be leading citizens appointed by General Eisenhower. With Columbia staff support, the Council's work could be focused on assessing critical problems facing the nation, including compulsory military service, shortages of scientific and engineering personnel, skilled manpower, womanpower, and similar issues.

Since foundations want to be relevant and constructive, and to make contributions to the public weal, it is not easy, even for a major beneficiary, to fault the Ford Foundation for moving away from long-term support of basic research in human resources in favor of the prospective council, which would provide policy guidance on manpower issues. The fact that Eisenhower was in the White House throughout most of the years of the council's existence and that I became a senior advisor to U.S. Secretary of Labor James P. Mitchell surely made it easier for the council's reports to get close attention in the Washington policy arena. And the reports were based on research substantial in both breadth and depth. A fair judgment would be that the Ford Foundation lost little, and perhaps gained, in shifting from its original goal of supporting research to a policy orientation.

Among the major foundations, the Carnegie Corporation in recent years has concentrated on appointing commissions supported by staff to study and advise on a wide array of problem areas, from reducing the threat of nuclear conflict to a comprehensive assessment of how the United States can improve its policies to strengthen its technological base. There are inherent difficulties that attach to such an approach, including the number of years that the commission members require to gain mastery of their subject and the risk that, by the time the commission is ready to report, the external environment may have changed substantially.

At least as important is the question of the audiences that must respond to give life to a commission's recommendations. Congress and state legislatures pay relatively little attention to advisory bodies that they establish even when leading legislators are members; that is, legislative bodies tend not to focus much attention on the advice proffered by others. And the attention of the media, even the serious press, seldom extends much beyond the release date of the commission's report. At best, a prestigious commission can make a contribution to the complex of forces that are struggling to shape and give direction to an emerging public policy. More frequently, it is difficult to trace any positive effects of its work.

As noted earlier, my first contact with the Carnegie Corporation dates from the early 1960s when John Gardner, the president of Carnegie, asked me to come down to talk about the subject of human resources. Gardner was surely one of the most impressive "philanthropoids" that it was my good fortune to get to know. He had one foot firmly planted in the world of knowledge, the other in the world of affairs, and he drew on each to enrich the other. Carnegie made a liberal grant to our Conservation Project that enabled us to undertake a longitudinal study of all the graduate students at Columbia in the 1945–1950 quinquennium who had been awarded university fellowships.

Early in our investigation we recognized that the life-styles of talented women differed in major regards from the life-styles of educated men, and we decided to focus our initial investigation exclusively on men, leaving for a later date the study of talented women. But Carnegie decided not to sponsor the second study. It asked an outside consultant to assess our study of talented men, and his report was, if not negative, restrained and unenthusiastic.

I report this incident not to argue with the consultant's appraisal but to emphasize the limitations and uncertainties that are built into the decision-making process of even well-led foundations. I had incorrectly assumed, since we had carried out the first study satisfactorily, Carnegie would be willing to finance the parallel study of *The Life-Styles of Educated Women*. However, I had little difficulty in getting the study on talented women financed by the Rockefeller Brothers Fund, where my contact was Nancy Hanks, a person of charm and talent who later became the chair of the National Endowment of the Arts, but whose life was cut short by cancer. Although I had ongoing relations with the fund over a number of years, I never had any contact with its president, William S. Dietel, although I had the opportunity to interact with Laurance Rockefeller, one of the key trustees.

In the mid-1970s one of the fund's staffers began to explore what the fund might do to get a better fix on the problems of New York City, in the hope of designing some useful new approaches. Marilyn W. Levy talked with Louis Winnick of the Ford Foundation and was steered in our direction. As a result of exploratory discussions, a research project was designed with a strong advisory committee headed by the then president of Landauer Associates, John R. White. As noted in the previous chapter, we demonstrated for the first time that despite the sizable out-migration of corporate headquarters, the city's economy was being transformed into the major center of advanced business services—from financial to communications—which continued to serve the relocated companies and many other national and multinational firms. The results of the inquiry foreshadowed the remarkable period of growth in the New York City economy between 1977 and 1989.

There is a considerable amount of informal and formal consultation among foundation staffs in the hope and expectation that expert knowledge can be transformed into effective grant-making more soundly and more quickly. There are at least two major competing forces at work that govern this interchange. The one supports the sharing of information. In fact it goes further: increasingly, it has led to collaboration that calls for the sharing of funding support. In an effort to extend their reach and depth, even some of the nation's largest grant-makers seek to interest other foundations in contributing funds to projects that they have designed and are about to launch. In addition to the desire noted above of extending their research reach, the lead foundation sees another advantage: The willingness of one or more parties to join, especially in funding large projects, can help reassure the lead staff that their plan is sound and can also help the staff "sell" the proposal to their trustees by noting that one or more cosponsors wait in the wings.

So much for the forces contributing to cooperation. We must not, however, minimize the intense competition that exists among foundation staffs in their efforts to be the first to identify an important new area or an important new approach in an area where progress up to this point has been slow and inauspicious. Foundation staffs are under continuing pressure to demonstrate their creativity to be the first to design new approaches.

The preceding discussion brings us face to face with some of the more complex issues of foundation policy that derive from the specificity of the benefactor's initial instructions, the selection of trustees, the appointment of the president, the quality of the senior staff, and, not least important, the orientation, perceptions, and goals of the research community, whose members comprise a significant proportion of grant applicants.

The following illustrate some if not all of the potential issues identified above. Recall that Henry Ford II felt constrained to leave the board of the Ford Foundation in 1976 because of differences with his fellow trustees about the direction in which the foundation was heading and his inability to force a change in direction.

A quite different situation is reflected in the structure and experience of the Robert Wood Johnson Foundation (RWJF), the basic endowment of which was provided for under the will of General Robert Johnson, the long-term head of Johnson and Johnson. I had some casual contacts with General Johnson when he served in the Quartermaster Corps during World War II, and they sufficed to impress me with his assurance, self-confidence, and determination to get his way. In establishing the RWJF, he stipulated that the executive power be vested in the chairman of the board. The first and long-term chairman was Gus Leinhard, a former CEO of Johnson and Johnson. He served as CEO of the Foundation with Dr. David Rogers, the former dean of Johns Hopkins Medical School, who became the foundation's president having primary responsibility for staff recruitment and program development.

There was nothing easy or compatible about this two-headed arrangement, particularly because the dominant trustees were largely ex-Johnson and Johnson senior executives, who wanted the foundation to undertake useful projects in health care delivery, while Rogers and his senior staff, particularly Margaret Mahoney, Robert Blendon, and advisor Walsh McDermott, had a broader vision and sought to make some "risky" investments in the belief that such investments were the raison d'être for foundation activities.

As a long-term grantee of the RWJF I had the opportunity to interact frequently not only with the senior staff but also with Gus Leinhard who considered me to be a sensible fellow because my academic base was in the Graduate School of Business at Columbia University. On one occasion David Rogers decided that I might help the senior staff communicate with the trustees and had me participate in an extended meeting of the board. As far as I was able to judge, the most interesting member other than the chairman was McChesney Martin, the former chairman of the Federal Reserve System.

A few more points about RWJF: I was impressed that Rogers avoided building up a large in-house staff and opted instead for committees of outside consultants to oversee the principal demonstration projects to which most of the large annual appropriations, currently in excess of $100 million, were directed. I was also impressed with the commitment made by the foundation to evaluation, though from the one evaluation effort in which the Conservation Project was involved, the Municipal Health Services Program, the effort appeared to be overambitious in terms of resources expended for returns received. Also, once the trustees determined that the foundation would limit itself, for the most part, to supporting national demonstrations aimed at improving the delivery of health care services for those facing barriers to access, the staff found it difficult to design and implement a sufficient number of such demonstrations to absorb all of the expanding foundation budget. Moreover, the replication of successful demonstration projects never received adequate attention or follow-up.

Fortunately the difficulty of spending all available funds on realistic demonstration projects enabled Rogers and his staff to undertake a number of imaginative, constructive programs that absorbed relatively small amounts of money but that turned out to have long-time leverage. The Clinical Scholars Program was one such effort, in which competitively selected medical schools were provided funds to encourage young clinicians to obtain basic and advanced training in one or another of the social sciences so that they could play a larger role in the health-policy arena.

The foundation had a significant interest in supporting minority medical education. Assistance was provided for the training of minority physicians and the enlargement of the pool of potential minority faculty. For fifteen years substantial support was provided to the Meharry Medical College School of Medicine. This long-term effort points up the inherent difficulties in reaching a balanced judgment on various foundations' efforts. Clearly the expansion of minority members as practitioners and faculty was a worthwhile objective. Clearly RWJF stayed with this effort for a long period of time. Clearly its special support for Meharry, the second-largest black institution training minority physicians was an appropriate effort within its larger goal. And yet, two decades later, the total effort has relatively little to show by way of significant results, not because the foundation failed but because the difficulties of finding qualified candidates were so great.

RWJF has been in a transition phase during the five years from Leinhard's retirement in early 1986 for reasons of health and age and the

Rogers's resignation and the subsequent senior staff relocations until the recent appointments of a new chairman (June 1989) and a new president, Steven Schroeder (July 1990).

While RWJF devotes itself exclusively to the health arena in the United States, the nation's largest foundation, Ford, has a much broader scope, both as to programs and geographic coverage. Its primary thrusts involve urban poverty, rural development, refugees and immigrants, education and public policy, and the arts. Its programs seek to be responsive not only to the problems of the United States but also to those in the developing world, particularly Latin America, Africa, and Asia.

The Ford Foundation was substantially restructured during the presidency of McGeorge Bundy (1966 to 1979) who pursued an activist program of socioeconomic change both in the United States and abroad. Mitchell Sviridoff, a close personal friend and Martha's Vineyard neighbor, was appointed vice-president of national affairs in 1967 and remained until shortly after Bundy's retirement. Sviridoff built up a strong in-house staff, had an excellent sense for evaluating people, and understood, much more than most foundation executives, that philanthropic funds should be viewed as venture capital and that the best way to leverage them was to assist small organizations that showed promise to help them find allies. Nowhere was this successful strategy better demonstrated than by Sviridoff's persuading three major federal departments—Labor, HEW, and Justice—to join with Ford in the early 1970s in creating the Manpower Demonstration Research Corporation (MDRC), to serve, as its name suggests, as a demonstration-research organization capable of "testing" the effectiveness of social interventions before launching large-scale reform efforts.

When Sviridoff left Ford, he became the head of the Local Initiatives Support Corporation (LISC), in which he used a substantial initial Ford grant to leverage large amounts of corporate money to encourage local community organizations to take the lead in refurbishing and rebuilding their eroding neighborhoods. A decade or so later, it is clear that LISC must be judged a substantial success in a development arena where so many who try fail.

This is neither the time nor place, nor do I have sufficient knowledge, to venture even a superficial evaluation of Ford's current grant-making. But I can report selected observations based on personal experience. From the late 1960s to the early 1970s I learned first hand in Pakistan and India about the substantial contribution that Ford, as well as Rocke-feller, made in speeding the green revolution that laid the basis for India's achieving self-sufficiency in food within the brief period of one decade, a period during which its population continued to increase rapidly.

It was not easy, however, for a major U.S. foundation such as Ford to continue to operate successfully in India in a political climate in which no ambitious politician could afford to be publicly associated with an American power center such as Ford. On the return from my second visit to India in 1971, I recommended to the senior executives at Ford that they reduce their visibility in New Delhi because of the increasingly strained political climate.

As the first chairman of MDRC and as a continuing member of its board, I have been in a good position to observe how the Ford staff (and trustees) have provided encouragement and resources, first to help the organization get established and grow, and next to help it restructure itself and survive after it lost most of its federal funding base in the Reagan era. I have been impressed by the ways in which Ford combined endow-ment support, matching grants, specific grant support, and all sorts of useful advice and counsel without preempting the MDRC's decision making. Only a sophisticated foundation, with sophisticated staff, could do this successfully not just for a few years, but for the better part of two decades.

In consonance with its worldwide programmatic efforts, Ford had the good sense early on to add several trustees from other countries to inform its decision making. Ford has consistently been more concerned than most U.S. foundations with the urgency of improving the lot of American minorities, particularly blacks and Hispanics. In 1979, after Bundy's retirement, Franklin Thomas, the long-term head of the Bedford-Stuyvesant Restoration Corporation, was appointed the new president, which underscored the trustees' determination not only not to shift focus away from racial issues, but to intensify their focus on them. After a somewhat stormy reorganization that led to the dismissal of large num-bers of staff, the Thomas regime merged its total programmatic efforts, domestic and foreign, under Susan Berresford, a former member of Sviridoff's staff.

Some concluding observations about Ford: First, the trustees see Ford-supported programs in action. They are not limited to judging important projects solely on the basis of paper documentation. Second, the trustees are involved in "big" policy discussions and decisions defining program areas and adjusting or changing them and allocating funds accordingly. Thereafter, the monies are suballocated through the senior staff to program officers with Berresford playing a key directorial and oversight role. There may be other, even better, ways to dispose of about $250–300 million annually, but the present structure and operations appear to be working effectively. If Ford faces a problem, it is how to communicate the scale and scope of its efforts and the significance of its successes to the larger interested public.

Through Lloyd Garrison, the late distinguished member of the New York bar and a trustee of the National Urban League, I was introduced in the early 1950s to Audrey and Stephen Currier, a young couple who were in the process of organizing a foundation, the funding of which stemmed from money left by Audrey's grandfather, Andrew W. Mellon. Over the next decade and more, until their untimely death in the Caribbean in early 1967, I saw a lot of the Curriers and their conscientious effort to put a foundation in place that would be responsive to their values and goals. Very early on, they decided to single out the plight of black Americans as their primary field of interest.

At one point I had the interesting assignment of identifying a limited number of consultants who would meet with the Curriers and the other board members, who included Garrison and the family's psychologist, Edith Entenman, to discuss both programming and administration. I persuaded Harold Lasswell of Yale, Harlan Cleveland of Syracuse, Robert MacIver of Columbia, and Jean Gottmann of Oxford and Paris to spend a Friday and Saturday listening and reacting to the problems that the Curriers faced in putting an effective foundation in place.

To make sure that no valuable ideas would be lost, I arranged for a stenotypist to record the discussion. When we were ready after dinner on Friday to resume our discussions, the stenotypist was nowhere to be found. We were later informed that she could not expose herself, a second time, to the problem before the group: How the Curriers should spend their money! More important than the stenotypist's escape was the unanimous recommendation of the five consultants: each of us recommended that the Curriers play the dominant role in giving their money away and that they avoid building up and relying on an extended staff.

Without the tragic accident that prematurely took their lives, almost $1 billion of current assets of the Andrew W. Mellon Foundation would have come through Audrey's mother, Ailsa Mellon Bruce, to Taconic, the Curriers' Foundation. It is difficult to know how effectively Audrey and Stephen would have used their money to further their goals. But it would have been an important experiment, since they had been inclined to follow their consultants' advice and play a dominant role in their grant-making. One thing I can attest to: They both made sizable taxable dollar contributions to furthering voter registration projects in the South. Theirs was a deep commitment and investment.

Another highly personal perspective of foundations involves the Revson Foundation, created under the will of Charles Revson, the founder of the Revlon cosmetics empire, who left a sizable estate with three principal goals: support for cancer research, Israel, and the improvement of New York City.

In 1978, Eli Evans, the president of the foundation and a former member of the Carnegie Corporation staff, got in touch with President McGill of Columbia with a tempting offer, subject to my agreeing to direct the program. He wanted Columbia to sponsor a Revson Fellows Program for the Future of the City of New York, providing mid-career opportunities for urban activists to return to the university for a year's study, research, and career reappraisal and consolidation, similar to the Nieman program for journalists at Harvard.

The program is currently in its thirteenth year. Midway through the decade the foundation renegotiated its agreement with Columbia, which enabled it to cut its annual cost for ten fellows from about $350,000 to $225,000; but otherwise, except for programmatic improvements, it has followed the principles worked out early on: no formal educational or other requirements other than the selection committee's judgment that the applicant can make good use of the university's resources; as much freedom as possible for the individual to design his or her own program, subject only to attending the Tuesday-evening dinner seminars for discussions with outside urban specialists; access to all the facilities and research institutions of the university; a laissez-faire attitude toward the pursuit of credits or degrees.

Although almost without exception the fellows report that their year (actually eight months) at Columbia has been extremely valuable and rewarding to them, I have observed on occasion that I am probably the major beneficiary, since I have had to interact with a highly intelligent, deeply committed group of activists. These men and women find many serious deficiencies in the life both of the city and of the nation, for which they insist remedial programs must be designed so that the waste of human potential can be reduced, even if it cannot be eliminated.

An interesting sidelight on foundations: When the Revson Foundation in mid-stream sought to lighten its annual financial commitment to Columbia, I approached a great many other foundations and many large corporations located in New York City to encourage their participation. But with one single exception, the effort failed. Admittedly the prospective participants had other options available to them to underwrite fellowships at Columbia, but I came away with the definite impression that they didn't want to share "glory" with Revson, even though we assured them that they could attach their own name to whatever fellows they were willing to subsidize.

In 1980 the Commonwealth Fund broke the gender barrier and appointed a woman, Margaret Mahoney, at the time a vice-president of RWJF, as president. Many years had to pass before the second woman was appointed to a top foundation post—Adele Simmons became the president of the John D. and Catherine T. MacArthur Foundation in 1989. Reference was made earlier to the key role that Susan Berresford has come to play at Ford, and note should be taken of the new staff structure at the Pew Charitable Trusts, where the senior vice-president for programs is Rebecca W. Rimel. After a long delay, women have finally breeched the barriers to reach the top of the foundation world.

The above reference to Pew invites elaboration. It is only very recently that the several Pew charitable trusts have been amalgamated into a single institution, which today ranks close to the top of public foundations with annual expenditures in the $140 million range. While still sensitive to the needs of the poor and the disadvantaged, as well as the arts, in the Philadelphia area, Pew has over the last few years become much more national in its grant-making, with primary emphasis on health and human services and with a continuing interest in education, cultural affairs, religion, public policy, health and human services, and conservation.

Over the years, I have also been closely connected with the Commonwealth Fund, both as grantee and as a consultant and advisor. Based on these exposures and experiences I have been impressed with its record. A foundation with relatively small total assets, about $250 million and with an annual grant-making budget in the late 1980s of $15 million, it has, through strong leadership (Margaret Mahoney) and superior staff work (Thomas Moloney was for a long time the senior vice-president), extended the scope of its influence far beyond the dollars in its own budget by encouraging the building of funding consortia, by providing direction for community-based foundations, by managing related philanthropic funds (Picker), by influencing other foundations (through Mahoney's membership on the board of MacArthur), and by leveraging its well-deserved reputation as a leading constructive force in the field of medical education and health care.

Despite these considerable strengths, the Commonwealth Fund, similar to other well-run foundations, has encountered difficulties in taking the lead in such complex arenas as the future of academic health centers, the hospital nurse shortage, and the problems of the elderly. I have been involved in all three. Matters of timing, the presence of strongly entrenched interest groups, shifts in government policy, and a host of other powerful external forces make it difficult for any foundation to identify an emerging critical problem area, to probe it in depth, and to have its recommendations available for public review and action at the right time. The most that a foundation can hope for is a .350 to .400 batting average.

Over the years I have had the opportunity to interact with a considerable number of other foundations in addition to those identified above, and, what is more, I have benefited from the support of some, if not all, of them for our research for shorter or longer periods of time. Except for the few that have strong ideological commitments that strictly define the limits within which they make grants and the inevitable differences in terms of structure and staffing between small foundations—those at the $10 million annual level—and those fifteen to twenty times larger, I have been impressed more by the similarities than the differences between public foundations.

As an outsider looking in, it seems to me that the trustees, for the most part important members of the establishment, want to be sure in the first instance that their foundation does not become the target of public criticism and that public foundations do not run afoul of Congress that might constrict their activities or, worse, endanger their special tax status. Once these important defensive goals have been assured, the trustees face more difficult choices. Most boards would welcome the opportunity to make grants that would lead to important social gains. On the other hand, they recognize the danger that in pursuing such ambitious goals they may at the end have little to show for their money, since failure is the more likely outcome of a high-risk investment. Accordingly, the conservative businessmen and professionals who dominate foundation boards are much more likely to pursue a low-risk rather than a high-risk strategy in their grant-making. Although they like to think of themselves as venture capitalists, they do not act in that vein where one successful effort more than justifies five failures. With foundation money scarce and the nation's policy agenda very crowded, trustees do their level best not to "waste" their scarce revenues. They find it easier to live with a small success than a large failure.

Most trustees look to their president to show them the way—both to keep the foundation out of trouble and to assure that its annual report reflects a menu of sound grants. Presidents in turn have their work cut out for them. Their first and overriding task is to be sure that no trustee is surprised at the foundation's quarterly or annual meeting, because a surprised trustee can precipitate far-reaching discussions among the members of the board, which might take the initiative away from the president and his or her staff. But a president who concentrates on relations with the trustees will not have the time or the energy to be deeply involved in program development, which then becomes the responsibility of senior staff. The number of creative, informed, and energetic staff members is seriously limited because of the talents required and because of the relatively small number of persons who have had experience working in a foundation environment. And without such experience, even a highly talented person is likely to be only modestly effective.

In light of these structural, organizational, and staffing problems, it is easy to appreciate that what might at first appear to be a relatively simple task—giving other people's money away—turns out to be an activity of considerable difficulty.

It is fitting that I close this chapter with a brief reference to the recent history of the Rockefeller Foundation, the prototypical U.S. foundation, from which we received support first in the 1940s and again in the early 1980s. After the sudden and unexpected death of its dynamic president, Dr. John Knowles, in 1979, the Rockefeller Foundation, at least to me as an outsider, appeared to flounder. The trustees did not appear to have a clear-cut vision as to where the foundation should be heading; the office of the president, both in terms of temporary and permanent incumbents, was not able to provide the required leadership, and the staff was without adequate direction. The foundation floundered for the better part of a decade, but after Peter Goldmark was appointed president in 1988, progress occurred on each of the foregoing fronts, progress that continues. The Rockefeller Foundation can never hope to recapture the unique role that it had played during the first third of this century, but it can surely look forward to becoming once again an important player in using its considerable grant-making potential and its great prestige for the public good.

The thrust of this chapter has been centered on how foundations are structured and how they function, with special attention to their scale, board members, president, and staff. But it would be an oversight not to remind the reader that what foundations are able to accomplish depends in considerable measure on the imagination, energy, and brains of the applicants who seek foundation grants. As far as academics are concerned, and they represent a significant proportion of all applicants for foundation grants, their narrow discipline orientation is a deterrent to the submission of exciting proposals. And in the absence of exciting proposals, the results of foundation grants are likely to be mundane.

There is no easy out for foundations from this heavy dependency on a professoriat that has its own career objectives and goals. But as we have noted most experienced foundations have long appreciated that they must allocate a share of their budget to the training of able young people, who, in the final analysis, will determine the quality of foundation performance in the next generation.

Retrospective

I have been busy for sixty of my eighty years studying the changing contours of the economic and social structures of the United States, with a primary focus on its human resources, with some considerable time and effort also directed to parallel explorations of other countries, more and less developed, particularly in Europe and Asia. A second overriding activity has been my engagement full-time during World War II and part-time thereafter in consulting with the federal government, pursuing a number of policy goals involving the improved development and utilization of the nation's human resources.

What I have not done up to this point, because of a lack of interest, has been to devote much time or effort to introspection, that is, to figuring out the reasons that I have pursued these patterns of work and life; even less have I kept score of my successes and failures. But now at the end of this extended autobiographical account I owe the reader—and possibly even myself—to make at least an effort at a trial balance sheet of a person who has spent his life seeking to develop and pursue a policy agenda focused on human resources.

A few boundary facts: The United States was only 122 years old when I was born and as of 1991 it has just passed its 200th birthday. That means that my life has been coterminous with 40 percent of the nation's history. That should provide me some reasonable perspective in length, if not necessarily in depth. I remember talking with my wife's grandmother, a native of Charleston, South Carolina, who clearly remembered the day the news arrived that Lincoln had been assassinated. And when the students of the Graduate Department of Economics at Columbia in 1932 hosted an eighty-fifth birthday party for John Bates Clark, the distinguished economist, and the father of another distinguished economist, our teacher J. M. Clark, I established a direct link with an individual who had been born in 1847, who in turn had many links to individuals who were alive when the nation was first formed in 1789.

Taft was president when I was born in 1911. Since then, the country has had thirteen presidents in the White House. In 1911, the population of the United States totaled 92 million; in 1991 it exceeds 250 million. In 1911 Arizona was still to be admitted as the forty-eighth state.

I noted early on the principal formative influences that helped to shape my life and work: a father who excelled in his discipline and whose life was largely bounded by his library; a non-bookish mother who was deeply involved and concerned about making this a better world; unbreakable ties with New York City and Columbia University; a knowledge of and a pride in my ancestry and the fact that I carried, as a collateral descendant, the name Elijah, the Gaon of Vilna.

One more biographical detail: I married late, not by accident but by intent. I wanted to get my career well started without having to balance it with the needs and demands of family and, if truth be told, I enjoyed my decade and a half of bachelorhood. There are more and less appropriate times to engage in certain behaviors, and it seemed to me at the time, and since that entering into and withdrawing from close relationships was more fitting in one's twenties than in one's forties.

I have often told my students that if they picked their parents right, made an appropriate career decision, and chose an agreeable mate, they had it made. I was fortunate with respect to all three. My wife of forty-six years, Ruth, the mother of our three children, has been a delight to live with, having as she does two life-sustaining qualities: humor and self-reliance. To add to my good fortune, her father bought enough of the right stocks at the right times so that the money that I did not want to devote my time pursuing was there in sufficient amount.

The foregoing, while relevant, is not particularly illuminating about the ways in which I shaped my work and life. At the deeper levels of personality analysis, I am reasonably sure that, had I ever undergone a period of psychoanalysis, I would recognize even more clearly than I do the positive-negative effects of my relations with my father, from whose disciplinary interests I could not have distanced myself further but from whom I absorbed a great many attitudes and values toward work and life and with whom I have probably been competing in terms of scholarly output these many decades.

Again, without pushing psychoanalytic theory very far, I suspect that I owe my policy orientation—which has dominated my work—to my mother, who always sought to make the world a little better.

With at least some of the formative factors identified above, what directions have I been following these last six decades? I will remind the reader that my basic approach to economics first took shape in the tumultuous early 1930s when the Great Depression was undermining the American economy to an extent that even the Marxists had not anticipated. I have written elsewhere about the teaching of economics at

Columbia in those unsettling years (see "Economics at Columbia: Rec-ollections of the Early 1930s," *The American Economist* 34, no. 2 [1990]: 14-19). Neoclassical economics, with its optimistic view that market forces will lead to an optimal outcome for all buyers and sellers, made no sense to me when I saw the devastation that was being brought on millions of industrious, hard-working Americans who, through no fault of their own, lost their jobs, their life savings, their homes. The gap between the presumed virtues of the competitive model and the economy in disarray galloping toward disintegration was one that left its mark.

I had a second, more intellectual, reason to reject the dominant theory. Classical and neoclassical economics are predicated on the rationality principle: People's behavior is determined by their continuing efforts to maximize their monetary income or, more sophisticatedly formulated, their utility. I was willing to accept the view that the pursuit of money is a potent factor in human behavior, but I was unwilling to rule out all other motivations as being of little or no importance. I had read enough of Freud and had learned enough from Karen Horney's lectures to reject the simplistic psychological postulates of economics. Even more important, I had read and studied enough history, anthropology, political science, and sociology to recognize that the maximizing principle, wrong in conception, would inevitably lead to wrong policy conclusions.

Since I could not find direction and reinforcement by escaping into economic theory, I faced the challenge of finding other means and approaches to strengthen my knowledge and understanding of how the economy *really* works. I decided that I wanted and needed to come into direct contact with corporate America, its executives, managers, and workers. Hence my desire, and success, in spending my first postdoctor-ate year (1933-34) in the field.

I started out to explore the experiences of a group of leading U.S. corporations that had experimented with the "stabilization of seasonal employment" in the late 1920s, corporations that included Kodak, Proc-tor and Gamble, and General Electric. Shortly after I began my field visits, I realized that the severe depression of 1930-1933 had wrecked havoc with these experiments, and as a result I shifted tack.

In the place of "seasonal stabilization," I began to ask why the leaders of American business had adopted the view that the U.S. economy in the period 1922-1929 had entered a New Era, an era that was supposed to be free of cyclical downturns. Furthermore, I paid close attention to whether large corporations responded the same or differently to the Great Depression that they had not anticipated.

An ancillary piece of learning from that critical episode: I had the opportunity to meet and explore my questions with a wide array of senior and middle managers, a few of whom were brilliant, many of whom were smart, and some of whom were dull, if not stupid. In short, the distribution of talent among businessmen was not all that different from the distribution of talent among professors and, I suspected other occupational groups, some of which I would later become exposed to in depth, as for instance, the armed services, the federal bureaucracy, the diplomatic corps. If economists see their task as figuring out what is happening in the production and distribution of goods and services, I cannot imagine why they spend almost all of their time reading, criticizing, and extending the work of their colleagues rather than directing more effort to becoming better acquainted with the decision-making processes of the world of business.

With the advantage of hindsight, I can identify a number of related character traits and behavior patterns that I had when I earned my doctorate in 1934 that foreshadowed much of my later work. To mention a few of the more important: I ended my fellowship year with a wealth of undigested, or at best partially digested, materials. Hence I responded enthusiastically to the suggestion of one of my mentors that I apply for a grant to the Columbia University Council for Research in the Social Sciences, which would enable me to synthesize what I had learned and to write it up. It took me not one year but close to four to complete *The Illusion of Economic Stability*, but I found great satisfaction in completing that difficult task. Ever since that effort, I have found it essential to achieve closure, and the only way that I know what I really believe is to commit my ideas to paper and to publish them. At that point, I am able to close the account and start on something new.

In 1934 I also made the first of three crucial career decisions that reveal the drummer to whom I was responding. Professor Mitchell offered to recommend me for an assistant professorship at Wisconsin, a recommendation that probably would have resulted in a definitive offer. I had no job, nor any prospect of a job, at Columbia, which I had come to believe would at least in theory provide me with an ideal working environment. I saw the University of Wisconsin, and more particularly living in a small town such as Madison, as unduly constrictive—too far from where the action was (Washington and New York)—and as too uni-cultured an environment, with professors and students the dominant population. I decided that accepting the offer would probably be less rewarding in the long run than having no job at present or any immediate prospect of getting one.

In the summer of 1942, when I was ready to change my governmental assignment from consultant to full-time work, I had a tempting offer from the research group of the War Production Board (Robert Nathan), but I opted instead for a position in the Office of the Commanding General, Services of Supply, at a much lower salary, in the belief that I could be more useful and effective if I were in an environment with fewer economists and closer to where the key military decisions were being made. Although I stumbled badly during the early weeks of my assignment in the Pentagon, I was able to catch on in time about the ways of the military, which later fully justified the gamble I had taken.

As noted earlier, when the war came to an end I had to decide about one challenging offer and one lucrative offer, either of which would have prevented my returning to Columbia University; but after some reflection I decided to put both aside. I had come to recognize that I needed an environment—and Columbia offered it—where I could simultaneously or sequentially pursue four highly charged interests. I enjoyed teaching and knew that I looked forward to continuing teaching. In fact, I had missed teaching to such an extent during the war years that I arranged for at least one staff meeting a month, during which I briefed my staff about what we had to do next, in what time frame, and with what performance standards. And I always looked forward to the ensuing discussion.

Next, I knew that research was a stimulating and highly rewarding activity for me, and I wanted the opportunity to continue to set my research agendas and proceed to explore and answer the questions that engaged me. I had no question about the strength of this pull.

Third, my four years in Washington had left their mark. I realized that I was able to function effectively in the federal government, both in the executive department and in hearings before congressional committees. I not only had a large number of exciting and rewarding assignments, but I enjoyed being part of the federal decision-making process. While I was not willing to become a full-time member of the bureaucracy, I was determined if at all possible to maintain an ongoing consulting relationship with the federal government, not only with the Pentagon, but also with one or another civilian agency, such as Labor or HEW, whose missions overlapped my academic and research interests.

Finally, it became clear to me that all matters affecting Jews, particularly the Holocaust survivors and the struggling community in Palestine, were matters of deep and continuing concern to which I wanted to contribute what I could, not for a brief period, but on an ongoing basis. Despite this pull, I did not contemplate seriously at any time emigrating to Palestine or, later, to Israel.

I realized at the time that the foregoing agenda was both broad and deep, and that it would not be easy for me to find the time and energy to work and contribute over such a broad terrain. But I also recognized that I would be able to lead a more exciting and rewarding life if I could pursue these four goals, not necessarily simultaneously, but at least in varying combinations.

I did not find it easy to restructure my research program and research staff when I returned to Columbia in 1946. I had to find mature colleagues, sketch out a research agenda, and obtain the required funding. I had early recognized that if I were going to continue to work in the interstices between economics and psychology I needed strong colleagues. Graduate students would not fill the bill. I had no option but to become an academic entrepreneur both in designing my research agenda and in finding the funding to carry it out.

Two strokes of good fortune solved what could otherwise have become a grueling obligation that could have deprived my research career of much of its challenge and satisfaction. In 1948 General Eisenhower became president of Columbia University and, with his personal physician, Major General Howard McCrum Snyder, Medical Corps, acting as intermediary, Eisenhower took the initiative to establish the Conservation of Human Resources Project and, further, played a key role in assuring its initial financial support.

From the early 1960s, when the U.S. Department of Labor received congressional authorization and funds to support external manpower research, the Conservation Project had a reliable source of major funding. For most of the three decades 1950 to 1980, critical decades in my research career, fundraising was a minor chore that required little of my time or energy. Not many scholars have been that fortunate. But I like to believe that my colleagues and I did our best to take advantage of our good fortune and to put in place and execute a research program in human resources that was responsive to major policy issues by pointing directions where new and strengthened governmental and nongovernmental policies held promise of improving the development and employment prospects particularly of disadvantaged individuals and groups—women, blacks, the poor, youth, immigrants, the elderly.

My principal mentors in economics, Wesley Clair Mitchell and John Maurice Clark, each provided me with a powerful model. To overstate the case only slightly, Mitchell had devoted his entire career to rewriting his opus *Business Cycles*, which he had first published in 1913. Clark had a much more diversified bibliography that covered a great many discrete parts of contemporary economics, from railroad rate-making to the *Social Control of Business* and *Alternative to Serfdom*. But a close reading of his books reveals that Clark was engaged in a lifelong effort to refine and deepen his understanding of the role and limits of competitive markets in a society that had concerns and interests that went beyond efficiency. What I learned from my two great teachers, a lesson that I absorbed without consciousness or effort, was that a productive research career required a long-term commitment. In light of my aforementioned need for closure, I found that Clark's style of breaking his research products into manageable pieces, that is, into publishable studies, was the model that I found more congenial.

A few observations about the three correlative goals that I had identified for myself at the end of World War II: health policy, government consulting, and Jews, especially the efforts of the immigrants to Palestine to establish a viable state. How did these interests and concerns relate to my dominant focus on human resources research?

I came to recognize that the unusual exposures and experiences that I had had in overseeing the medical logistics of the U.S. Army during the war opened all sorts of opportunities in the arena of health policy, including lucrative opportunities to consult with hospitals, medical centers, and health care associations. Although I accepted a request by Governor Thomas Dewey to undertake a major assessment of its hospitals for the State of New York (which resulted in *A Pattern for Hospital Care* [1949]), I deliberately withdrew from the health care arena until the early 1960s, when the imminent passage of Medicare convinced me that my wartime experience would be apposite for dealing with a host of critical policy issues that were just beyond the horizon, a judgment in which time proved me right.

From the war's end until December 1981 when President Reagan asked for the resignation of all the members of the National Commission for Employment Policy, government consulting had engaged an important and ongoing part of my time and energies. My activities were divided primarily among the White House (under Eisenhower), and the Departments of State, Defense, Labor, HEW, and GAO. Moreover, I testified several times a year before congressional committees and subcommittees.

Some might view this considerable investment in Washington as a deflection from my research, but I early came to appreciate that my consulting activities had a stimulating and deepening effect on my research. After all, our concerns at the Conservation Project were with policy issues affecting the improved development and utilization of the nation's human resources. My government consulting activities enabled me to move back and forth easily between our research work at Columbia and the design and implementation of employment and training policies in Washington, both in the civilian and military spheres.

In 1953, the State Department, responding to a request from the Israelis, asked me to spend two months helping the young state put a manpower planning mechanism in place, a request that I was pleased to accept. In the succeeding two decades I undertook a great number of overseas assignments for the Department of State, as well as for other organizations, and soon discovered that these study missions also sharpened my perceptions of the U.S. economy and its human resources infrastructure. Contrast and distance provide important perspectives. Much that I had long taken for granted about our patterns of human resources development and utilization at home had to be looked at anew in terms of the new insights and understanding that I developed from my work abroad.

And this new learning took place not only as a result of my study missions to the advanced nations—the United Kingdom, France, Germany, Sweden, Italy, and Japan—but also from my contact with such underdeveloped and developing nations as Ethiopia, Egypt, Nigeria, India, and Indonesia. And my fifteen study missions to Israel, with its complex human resources, economy, and political structure, have forced me to confront problems formerly beyond my awareness, the analysis of which has deepened my research equipment and my understanding of the dynamics of economic change.

But the foregoing is a pro forma, not a substantive, answer. The critical question that needs to be asked and answered is, How, with the benefit of hindsight, do I evaluate these many decades of research that my colleagues and I devoted to the policy arena, both in deepening analysis and in formulating plans for reform?

To start at the end: The outcomes comprise a mixed bag with a few successes, some contributions, and many efforts that resulted in few if any positive results. Another way of reaching at least some tentative judgments about our efforts in the areas of policy research is to contrast our style of work to that of mainline academics in the social sciences. The latter operate within the structure of an academic discipline: professors start with the extant theory and write articles and books aimed at advancing it. They spend considerable time with their graduate students, particularly in directing and supervising their dissertations. They help to place the best of their students at leading institutions. Their work is largely contained within a self-sufficient environment consisting of their teachers, colleagues, and students, in which the criteria for performance are profession-determined, career opportunities are increasingly allocated by competition among the talented, and the larger world outside is more often than not ignored. And most important, each of the social sciences cultivates its own domain, with its own methodologies, little interested in or concerned about whether the scope of its theories and approaches are adequate to explain the behavior of people and institutions in the larger society.

We have proceeded differently. To begin with, our point of departure has been to identify and analyze major social problems—unemployment, military manpower, the wastes of discrimination, the life-styles of educated women, the shift of the economy to services, work and welfare, the political economy of health care, and a great many other societal issues of current and emerging importance in the hope of focusing attention and pointing directions for remedial interventions. With these ambitious goals inherent in our policy research, it should come as no surprise that the researcher's influence is difficult to trace and policy successes are at best likely to be few and far between.

A few illustrations may help to clarify why influence and impact are so difficult to assess in policy research. In 1991 the dominant view among the leaders of most advanced nations is that we have entered the era of global competition, the victors of which will be the nations with the most sophisticated labor forces. When we chose the name "Conservation of Human Resources" for our research in the late 1940s, most well-educated persons had no idea of what the term "human resources" meant. We used to get telephone calls at Columbia University asking whether we sold artificial limbs! I like to believe that our long-term research helped to speed the recognition of the critical role of talent and skill in the operation of modern economies.

In 1958 the chief economist of the Prime Minister's Office in Japan, Suburo Okita, visited me at Columbia to talk about Japan and its prospects. I told him that I had visited Japan only once—immediately after the end of World War II—and had not followed except superficially its recent development. However, I offered the opinion that as far as I could judge, Japan was not well positioned to carve out a significant role for itself in the world economy. Okita wanted to know the reason for my pessimistic appraisal, and I told him that no country where the majority of its future labor force had only two years of high school education could hope to become a leader. We talked some more about human resources, and before he left Okita indicated that he would like to translate my *Human Resources: The Wealth of a Nation*, which had just been published and which was based on a set of lectures that I had delivered at the University of California, Berkeley. By the early 1960s the Japanese government had moved to introduce major reforms in its educational system.

In the 1950s our work called attention to the large-scale wastes resulting from discrimination against blacks in the labor market; and further called attention to the fact that, with discriminatory job practices being reduced, advances in the jobs and incomes for blacks would depend increasingly on whether they acquired more and better schooling.

At about the same time, the National Manpower Council, a parallel activity at Columbia with joint leadership and staff with the Conservation Project, published a definitive volume on *Womanpower*, pointing out the major gains that American society could secure if it lowered and removed the major barriers based on gender. Almost forty years later, these issues of race and gender discrimination remain on the nation's agenda—despite considerable progress in the interim. The Conservation's pioneering investigations on both of these fronts made and left their mark, the more so because of subsequent Conservation studies that strengthened and reinforced the original findings and recommendations.

But not all or even most of our policy efforts can be assessed as successful. Three critical undertakings reflect this fact. Between 1962 and 1981 I served as the chair of the federal oversight committee and commissions on employment and training programs. During these nineteen years, Congress appropriated a cumulative total of $85 billion for skill training and related programs aimed at the employment of the unemployed. Although Congress, the press, and the public became increasingly disenchanted with these programs on the ground that they were riddled with fraud and corruption, I never bought into this negative view. The employment program monies went overwhelmingly to the poor and the disadvantaged as Congress had intended. But CETA must be judged to have been, if not a failure, also not a success because except for a small minority it did not accomplish its primary objective of helping the unemployed gain permanent jobs in the private sector.

Even with President Eisenhower's interest and support our carefully crafted research effort on *The Ineffective Soldier: Lessons for Management and the Nation*, as well as related efforts in military manpower research, never made much of a mark on the Pentagon.

On a quite different front: The federal government had just entered upon its 1963 expansion of the physician supply when I warned in *The New England Journal of Medicine* and through subsequent publications about the danger of pursuing a too-aggressive policy, which I feared would cost the nation dear by increasing total expenditures without improving the access of underserved populations to essential medical care. Almost a third of a century later, and despite a growing number of prominent allies within the medical profession, the issues involved in a rapidly expanding supply of physicians continue to be largely ignored. Opening new medical schools proved to be much more attractive than cutting back on class size and merging or closing medical schools.

There is no point in developing an even-more-detailed trial balance sheet. The conclusion that I have arrived at and must live with is that policy research, like discipline-focused research, is subject to many vicissitudes in formulation, implementation, and obsolescence. And the odds are against the survivability and significance of most research, discipline-based or policy-oriented.

With the collapse of Communism, the influence of Karl Marx will surely rapidly diminish. Only Adam Smith among the economists is likely to survive as a preeminent contributor into the twenty-first century with his reputation secure. But young economists earn their doctorates these days without ever having read a single page in *The Wealth of Nations.*

And now the finale: I early understood that every choice both broadens and constricts. It was not possible for me to pursue a career in interdisciplinary research in human resources without creating a distance, which widened with the years, from my disciplinary origins—economics. Most academics need intellectual companionship, which is one principal reason that the folkways and institutions of their discipline exercise such potent influences on how they think and what they do. But I early came to accept and live with the widening gulf between my fellow economists and myself. I did not find Keynesian theory intellectually exciting nor particularly policy-relevant. And when after World War II economics became heavily mathematical, I found myself increasingly alienated, to the point that I could no longer understand the titles, much less the content, of most journal articles. This widening estrangement was cushioned by the fact that my faculty appointment, though in economics, was in the Graduate School of Business, where I had little difficulty in establishing congenial relationships with many colleagues trained in different disciplines. Moreover, a number of them became members of the Conservation staff for periods of time, and this established the basis for ongoing intellectual companionships.

With ties to a great number of different professions and different centers of policy action, including psychology, psychiatry, guidance and counseling, history, religion, Judaica, women's studies, minorities, and medicine, and with the opportunity to interact on an ongoing basis with the federal government, foreign governments, selected corporations, foundations, trade unions, the National Institutes of Health, the Industrial College of the Armed Forces, and many more, I never had time to regret that I seldom attended the annual meetings of the American Economics Association and did not participate in any of its committee work.

It would be not only foolish but misleading to suggest that all or even most of the connections as well as lack of connections identified above were part and parcel of a carefully designed plan. Clearly that was not so. Some of the sequencing was carefully planned and implemented, such as my decision to pursue an academic career with a strong propulsion to empirical research directed to human resources. Much was fortuitous, such as the opportunities that I confronted during World War II that enabled me to develop sophistication in health services research.

My desire to remain an active consultant to the federal government in the years after 1946 was high on my priorities and in that sense was planned. But there was very little planning on my part connected with the stroke of good fortune that brought Eisenhower to the presidency of Columbia University, where he decided to take a leading role in the establishment and initial financing of the Conservation of Human Resources Project. It is not often that an academic researcher is sponsored by a national hero who within a few years enters the White House.

So much for the relation of planning to good fortune. Neither one alone would have led to a satisfactory outcome. And whether the outcome is satisfactory in an objective sense of the term remains for others to judge. What I must still do is to provide the interested reader with a purely subjective assessment as to the reasons that I have found my life full of stimulation and satisfaction.

First and, probably most important, is the place that work came to occupy in my life, not recently but since the late 1930s, when my research began to command the bulk of my time and energies. The last extended vacation that I took, that is, a vacation without pads to write on, was in the summer of 1938 when I met my cousin, Herzl Rome, in Bergen, Norway, to spend a month mountain climbing, and we then spent a second month in Paris where he had an atelier.

My wife says that I am addicted to work, and she may be right. What I do know, and readily admit, is that I like to work. In fact I cannot really conceive of living without working, for each is but a mirror image of the other. In my youth I was a devoted Yankee fan, but I follow none of the sports—not baseball, football, basketball, or tennis—and have not done so for more than half a century. I don't care much for bridge and not at all for gambling. My private avocations are reading, swimming, walking, and sleeping. I am a good sleeper, and I prefer nine hours of sleep, which I try to get most nights because the quality of my work is directly linked to my sleep. I have never done any serious work after dinner, among other reasons because I usually retire early.

I know from my reading and also from my research that a good many people get little or no pleasure from their work. While I "know" this fact in some cognitive sense, I really have no appreciation of what it really means. As I noted above and here reemphasize, work is a source of continuing and deep satisfaction for me. Of course I encounter blocks, but not often enough to be seriously unsettled. I have a good instinct about the goals that I set myself and I try to avoid having them far outdistance my capacities—the major source, I suspect, of most people's work frustrations.

Much of the credit for establishing and maintaining a conducive environment for my working constantly and my continuing gratification from work has been my wife's understanding and support. She has made most of the adjustments at what I hope has been a sustainable cost to her. She carried almost all of the responsibility for raising our three children, Abigail, Jeremy, and Rachel, and they were out of the house before I realized that my preoccupation with my work had shortchanged them and me and had put an unwarranted burden on my wife. But learning after the event does not give one a second chance, neither parent nor children.

Although it is decades since I left my "psychoanalytic period" behind me, it would be a travesty to conclude this chapter and this book without reporting on the picture I have of my father's working in his crowded library from early morning until dinner time, all the days and years of his life, except on the Sabbath and other religious holidays when work was forbidden or when poor health in his last years robbed him of the energy required to add to his prodigious output of extraordinary quality. Only an estranged son, which I am not, would have been uninfluenced by such an example.

Index

A

Abortion, 204
Abrahamson, Albert, 162
Abramovitz, Moses, 4, 216
Abt, Clark, 74
Acheson, Dean, 145
Adams, Sherman, 1990
Adenauer, Konrad, 217
Adolescents, at-risk, 89–90
Advisory Committee on Labor Markets, Research Center Berlin (WZB), 112–113
Advisory Committee to the National Institutes of Mental Health (NIMH), 81–83
Affirmative action, 276–278
Afghanistan, 237, 248–250
African-Americans; in corporations, 276–279; Ford Foundation and, 300; as military recruits, 148, 151; in New York, 8; resettlement in Africa of, 243–244; studies of, 66, 68
AIDS, 92
Air Corps, 132, 134
American Economic Association, 80–81
Anderson, James K., 54
Anderson, Martin, 179
Anderson, Robert B., 149, 153, 191
Anderson, Ron, 88
Andrew W. Mellon Foundation, 301–302
Anti-Semitism, 112
Arbeitslosen von Marienthal (Lazarsfeld & Yahoda), 48
Armstrong, George, 140
Army, U.S.. *See also* Pentagon; Ginzberg during World War II in, 123–141; Medical Department during World War II, 83; studies of, 64–66
Army Service Forces (ASF), 123–125, 127, 128, 133
Arrow, Kenneth, 30

Asian students, 10
Atomic bomb, 139
AT&T, 275
Axelrad, Sidney, 48

B

Bailey, Thomas, 54, 59, 72–73
Balinsky, Warren, 87
Banking industry, 284
Baruch, Bernard, 35
Basu, Jyoti, 260
Beard, Charles A., 35
Bearse, Peter, 70–71
Belgrade, Yugoslavia, 231
Belgrade Lakes, Maine, 115
Bellisario, Marissa, 219
Berg, Ivar, 53
Berger, Sam, 261
Bergson, Abram, 38
Berresford, Susan, 300, 301, 303
Bertrand, Olivier, 73
Beth Israel Hospital, 7
Bevan, Aneurin, 220
Biomedical research, 90
Blacks. *See* African-Americans
Blendon, Robert, 297
Bliss, Raymond, 128–129, 132, 134, 135, 138, 140, 141, 144
Boaz, Franz, 29
Bower, Marvin, 273
Bowles, Chester, 256
Brandeis, Louis, 269
Bray, Douglas, 54
Breakdown and Recovery, 65
Brecher, Charles, 54, 69, 71, 85, 284
Brennan, William, 162
Bridge, Lee Du, 15
Brown, Courtney C., 33, 39, 53, 97, 274
Brown, Douglas, 163
Bruce, Ailsa Mellon, 302
Bucharest, Romania, 231
Budapest, Hungary, 231, 232